Editorial project:
2018 © booq Publishing, S.L.
c/ Domènech, 7-9, 2º 1ª
08012 Barcelona, Spain
T: +34 93 268 80 88
www.booqpublishing.com

ISBN 978-84-9936-139-0 (EN)
ISBN 978-84-948616-0-4 (ES)

2018 © Éditions du Layeur

ISBN 978-2-915126-53-2 (FR)

Editorial coordinator:
Claudia Martínez Alonso

Art director:
Mireia Casanovas Soley

Editor:
Cayetano Cardelús

Layout:
Cristina Simó Perales

Translation:
Thinking Abroad

Printing in Spain

In 1972, the science fiction film Silent running (1972) portrayed a future (2008) in which plant life had disappeared from the face of the Earth and its last remaining vestiges orbited Saturn in three botanical spaceships. The film, through a markedly eco-friendly message, reflected the rise, in the second half of the 20th century, of society's awareness of environmental issues.

More than forty years later, the international community's awareness regarding the need to respect and protect nature and its resources seems practically irreversible. Movements and initiatives based on the concept of sustainability have permeated all spheres of society and are being incorporated into public body regulations. Due to its responsibility for creating environments working in harmony with the planet, the application of these sustainable precepts is especially important in the field of architecture.

The projects presented in this book are excellent examples of how the many facets of sustainability can be applied in the field of architecture. By using the term "green" to cover them we have attempted to highlight not only the most quantifiable factors, such as optimal energy efficiency values, but also other less tangible ones, such as architecture's respectful and harmonious integration with the natural environment and social sustainability, present to a greater or lesser degree in all the projects included here and closely linked to environmental sustainability.

From 23 countries, the selection of projects of the 30 studios taking part in this book includes the most diverse range of types and scales, each of which reflects a special sensitivity towards its environment and shows that sustainability in architecture represents a global and ever-growing movement.

1972 entwarf der Science Fiction-Film „Lautlos im Weltall" ein Zukunftsszenario für 2008, in dem die Pflanzen vollständig von der Erdoberfläche verschwunden waren und ihre letzten Überlebenden in drei botanischen Raumschiffen den Saturn umkreisten. Mit seiner äußerst umweltfreundlichen Botschaft zeigte der Film das steigende Umweltbewusstsein unserer Gesellschaft in der zweiten Hälfte des 20. Jahrhunderts.

Mehr als vierzig Jahre später ist das weltweite Bedürfnis, die Natur und ihre Ressourcen zu schützen und zu respektieren, praktisch unumkehrbar geworden. Bewegungen und Initiativen für mehr Nachhaltigkeit sind in allen gesellschaftlichen Bereichen präsent und werden stets bei der Gesetzgebung berücksichtigt. Diesen Vorgaben wird auch in der Architektur eine besondere Bedeutung zugemessen, denn hier kommt es darauf an, Bereiche zu schaffen, die in Einklang mit ihrer Umwelt stehen.

Die in diesem Buch vorgestellten Projekte sind hervorragende Beispiele für die Einbindung der vielfältigen Fassetten der Nachhaltigkeit in die Architektur. Der, diesen Projekten zugedachte, Begriff „grün" beinhaltet nicht nur die messbaren Größen wie optimale Energieeffizienz, sondern auch andere, weniger materielle Aspekte wie die harmonische und respektvolle Einbindung der Architektur in ihre natürliche Umgebung und die in allen hier vorgestellten Projekten mehr oder weniger präsente und eng mit der umweltlichen Komponente verbundene soziale Nachhaltigkeit.

Die in diesem Buch vorgestellten Projekte von unterschiedlicher Art und Größe, von 30 Architekturstudios aus 23 Ländern, entstanden alle in einem ganz besonderen Bewusstsein für ihre Umgebung und zeigen, dass die nachhaltige Architektur ein weltweiter und stets an Bedeutung gewinnender Trend ist.

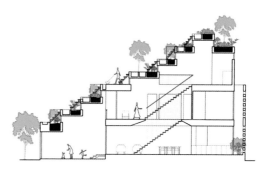

En 1972, le film de science fiction intitulé « *Silent running* » (1972) donnait à voir un futur (2008) dans lequel la flore avait disparu de la surface de la Terre et ses derniers vestiges étaient en orbite autour de Saturne dans trois vaisseaux spatiaux botaniques. Ce film, avec son message expressément écologique, était le reflet de l'essor, dans la deuxième moitié du 20e siècle, de la prise de conscience des questions environnementales.

Plus de quarante ans plus tard, cette prise de conscience dans la communauté internationale du besoin de respecter et de protéger la nature et ses ressources semble pratiquement immuable. Les mouvements et initiatives basés sur le concept de durabilité ont pénétré toutes les sphères de la société et sont incorporés aux règlements des organes publics. De par sa responsabilité dans la création d'environnements en accord avec la planète, l'application de ces préceptes durables revêt une importance particulière dans le domaine de l'architecture.

Les projets contenus dans ce livre sont d'excellents exemples de la façon dont les multiples facettes du développement durable peuvent être appliquées dans le domaine architectural. En utilisant le terme « écologique » pour les désigner, nous avons cherché à souligner non seulement les facteurs les plus quantifiables, comme les valeurs d'efficacité énergétique optimales, mais aussi d'autres, moins tangibles, comme l'intégration respectueuse et harmonieuse dans leur environnement naturel et la durabilité sociale, présents à un degré plus ou moins important dans tous les projets présentés et intimement liés à l'écologie.

Représentant 23 pays différents, la sélection de projets des 30 studios inclus dans ce livre comporte des propositions de divers types et d'échelles variées, chacune reflétant une certaine sensibilité à l'égard de son environnement et démontrant que la durabilité en architecture représente un mouvement international et en constante expansion.

En 1972, la película de ciencia ficción *Silent running* planteaba un «futuro» (el año 2008) en el que la vida vegetal había desaparecido de la faz de la Tierra y sus últimos vestigios orbitaban alrededor de Saturno en tres naves espaciales botánicas. La película, a través de su marcado mensaje ecologista, reflejaba el auge de la sensibilización de la sociedad hacia los temas medioambientales que se produjo a partir de la segunda mitad del siglo XX.

Más de cuarenta años después, la toma de conciencia de la comunidad internacional con respecto a la necesidad de respetar y salvaguardar la naturaleza y sus recursos parece ya irreversible. Los movimientos e iniciativas basadas en el concepto de sostenibilidad se han instalado en todos los ámbitos de la sociedad y están siendo incorporados en las regulaciones de los estamentos públicos. Por su responsabilidad en la creación de entornos que convivan en armonía con el planeta, la aplicación de estos preceptos sostenibles se hace especialmente importante en el campo de la arquitectura.

Los proyectos presentados en este libro son excelentes ejemplos de las múltiples facetas con las que la sostenibilidad puede ser aplicada en el ámbito arquitectónico. Con la denominación «*green*» empleada para reunirlos se ha pretendido dar relevancia no solo a los factores más cuantificables, como pueden ser unos valores óptimos de eficiencia energética, sino también a otros valores menos tangibles, como son la integración respetuosa y armónica de la arquitectura en el entorno natural y la sostenibilidad social, presente en mayor o menor grado en todos los proyectos presentados e íntimamente ligada a la sostenibilidad medioambiental.

Procedentes de veintitrés países, la selección de proyectos de los treinta estudios participantes en este libro incluye las más diversas tipologías y escalas, cada una de las cuales refleja una sensibilidad especial hacia su entorno y demuestra que la sostenibilidad en la arquitectura representa un movimiento global y al alza.

ACTUAL / OFFICE

WWW.ASLASHO.COM

actual . . . pertaining to action, not merely potential
/ (slash) . . . can punctuate separation (black/white), or simultaneity (blue/green)
office . . . a post to which certain responsibility are attached; an assigned or assumed task

In a name, actual / office frames an attitude toward the practice of architecture. The freedom to actualize hidden potentials, bringing the previously unimagined into focus, is alternately separated from, and simultaneous to, the weight of responsibility and authority. a/o takes on a wide variety of work including residential, exhibit design, furniture design, and research projects. Adam Dayem is the principal of a/o. He received a Bachelor of Arts in architecture from the University of California Berkeley and a Master of Architecture from Columbia University. Dayem is currently a Lecturer at Rensselaer Polytechnic Institute where he teaches architectural design studios and representation classes.

actual . . . mot anglais se rapportant à l'action, et non pas à son simple potentiel
/ (barre oblique) . . . peut marquer la séparation (noir/blanc), ou la simultanéité (bleu/vert)
office . . . mot anglais désignant un poste auquel est attachée une certaine responsabilité ; une tâche attribuée ou assumée

De par son nom même, actual / office définit une attitude à l'égard de la pratique de l'architecture. La liberté de réaliser des potentiels cachés, de mettre en perspective ce qu'on n'imaginait pas auparavant, est alternativement séparée, et inséparable, du poids des responsabilités et de l'autorité. a/o s'applique à différents types de travaux tels que l'architecture résidentielle, la conception d'expositions, la conception de meubles, et des projets de recherche. Adam Dayem est le directeur de a/o. Il a passé son diplôme d'architecture à l'Université de Berkeley et un Master en architecture à l'Université Columbia. Il est actuellement chargé de cours au Rensselaer Polytechnic Institute où il enseigne la conception architecturale et la représentation.

Derzeit . . . Teil der Maßnahme, nicht nur potentiell
/(slash) . . . Kann mit Punkten getrennt werden (schwarz/weiß), oder gleichzeitig (blau/grün)
Büro . . . Eine Stelle mit bestimmten Zuständigkeiten, eine zugewiesene oder übernommene Aufgabe

Aktueller Büroname / zeigt den Rahmen der Architekturarbeit. Die Freiheit, verstecktes Potential wieder ans Licht zu bringen und das zuvor Unvorstellbare in den Fokus zu setzen, ist eine Alternative und verläuft gleichzeitig simultan zu Verantwortung und Autorität. a/o übernimmt eine Vielzahl von Projekten, darunter Wohnungsbau, Gestaltung von Ausstellungen, Möbeldesign und Forschungsprojekte. Adam Dayem ist der Chef von a/o. Er verfügt über einen Bachelor of Arts in Architektur der University of California Berkeley und einen Master in Architektur der Columbia University.
Derzeit arbeitet Dayem als Dozent am polytechnischen Institut, wo er architektonische Gestaltung und bildliche Darstellung unterrichtet.

actual . . . palabra inglesa que implica acción no mero potencial
/ (barra diagonal) . . . signo de puntuación que puede indicar separación (blanco/negro) o simultaneidad (azul/verde)
office . . . palabra anglosajona que designa un lugar sobre el que se tiene cierta responsabilidad; una tarea asignada o asumida

En su propio nombre, actual / office establece los parámetros en relación a la práctica arquitectónica. La libertad de materializar un potencial oculto, poniendo el centro de atención en algo inimaginable previamente, es alternativamente separado de –o simultáneo a– el peso de la responsabilidad y la autoridad. a/o asume una amplia variedad de proyectos, incluyendo residenciales, diseño de exposición, diseño de mobiliario y proyectos de investigación. Adam Dayem es el director de a/o. Tiene una licenciatura en arquitectura de la Universidad de California Berkeley y un máster en arquitectura por la Universidad de Columbia. Actualmente Dayem es profesor en el instituto politécnico Rensselaer donde imparte clases de diseño arquitectónico y representación.

[SLEEVE HOUSE]

SLEEVE HOUSE

This House, facing the mountains surrounding it, can be perceived as two elongated blocks: an internal one, containing private areas on a more intimate scale, sheathed by the external one. In the spaces between them the larger scale shared areas are to be found. The project is characterised by the image projected by its outer cladding of carbonised wood using the traditional Japanese *Shou-sugi-ban* technique, making the finish sustainable, durable and low-maintenance. The pure image of the two blocks and their cladding evokes the simplicity of the traditional barns and silos to be found in the region. The dwelling's design implements various energy efficiency measures, such as solar panels, heat recuperators, triple glazing, its own water supply, and the use of native plants in the garden.

Dieses Haus blickt auf die umliegenden Berge und besteht aus zwei langgestreckten Blöcken: dabei wird der innere mit seinen eher intim gehaltenen Privatbereichen vom äußeren umschlossen. Zwischen den beiden Blöcken befinden sich die größer gehaltenen öffentlichen Bereiche. Wichtige Merkmale des Projekts sind die Außenverkleidung aus verkohltem Holz in der typisch japanischen *Shou-sugi-ban*-Technik, wodurch die Oberfläche nachhaltig und widerstandsfähig wird und kaum Instandhaltungsarbeiten bedarf. Das reine Bild der beiden Blöcke und ihrer Fassaden lässt an die Einfachheit der traditionellen Scheunen und Silos der Ursprungs-Region denken. Die Wohnungen enthalten verschiedene Vorrichtungen für mehr Energieeffizienz wie Solarzellen, Wärmerückgewinnung, Dreifachverglasung, eine eigene Wasserversorgung und heimische Pflanzen im Garten.

Cette maison, face aux montagnes environnantes, peut être perçue comme deux modules allongés : un interne contenant les espaces privés à une échelle plus intime, enchâssé dans la partie externe. Dans les espaces les séparant se trouvent des zones partagées, plus larges. Ce projet se caractérise par l'image projetée par son bardage extérieur en bois carbonisé utilisant la technique japonaise traditionnelle appelée *Shou-sugi-ban*, qui rend la finition écologique, durable et facile d'entretien. L'image pure de ces deux modules et de leur habillage de bois évoque la simplicité des étables et des silos traditionnels qu'on peut trouver dans la région. Le design de ces habitations met en application diverses mesures d'économie d'énergie comme des panneaux solaires, des récupérateurs de chaleur, du triple vitrage, leur propre source d'approvisionnement en eau, et l'utilisation de plantes indigènes dans le jardin.

Esta casa, orientada hacia las montañas que la rodean, se percibe como un juego de dos volúmenes alargados: uno interior, que contiene las zonas privadas y de escala más íntima, enfundado dentro de otro exterior. En los espacios situados entre ambos se sitúan las zonas comunes, dotadas de una mayor escala. El proyecto se caracteriza por la imagen de su envolvente exterior, de madera carbonizada según la técnica tradicional japonesa del *shou sugi ban*, que supone un acabado sostenible, muy resistente y de bajo mantenimiento. La imagen pura de los dos volúmenes y su envolvente evoca la simplicidad de los graneros y silos históricos de la región. El diseño de la vivienda desarrolla diversas medidas de eficiencia energética, como paneles solares, recuperadores de calor, triple acristalamiento, autoabastecimiento de agua o el uso de plantas autóctonas en la jardinería.

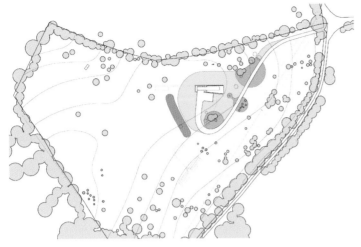

Site plan

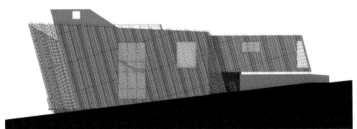

West elevation

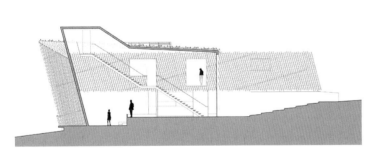

Longitudinal section

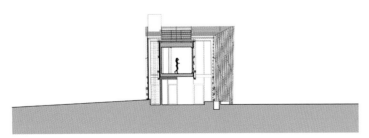

Cross section

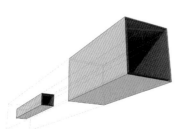

Sleeve diagrams

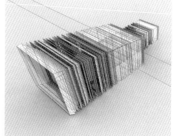

Skin diagrams

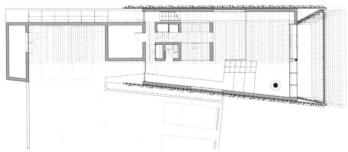

First level plan

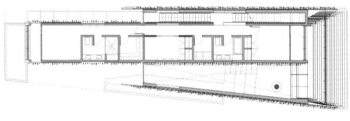

Second level plan

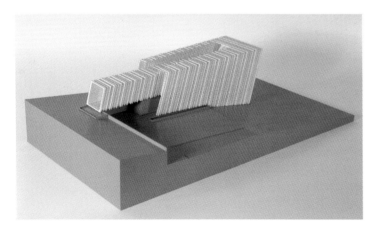

Model view from southeast

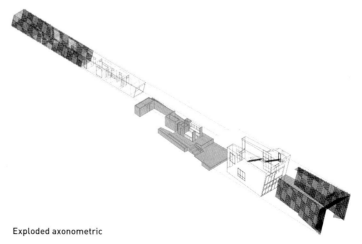

Exploded axonometric

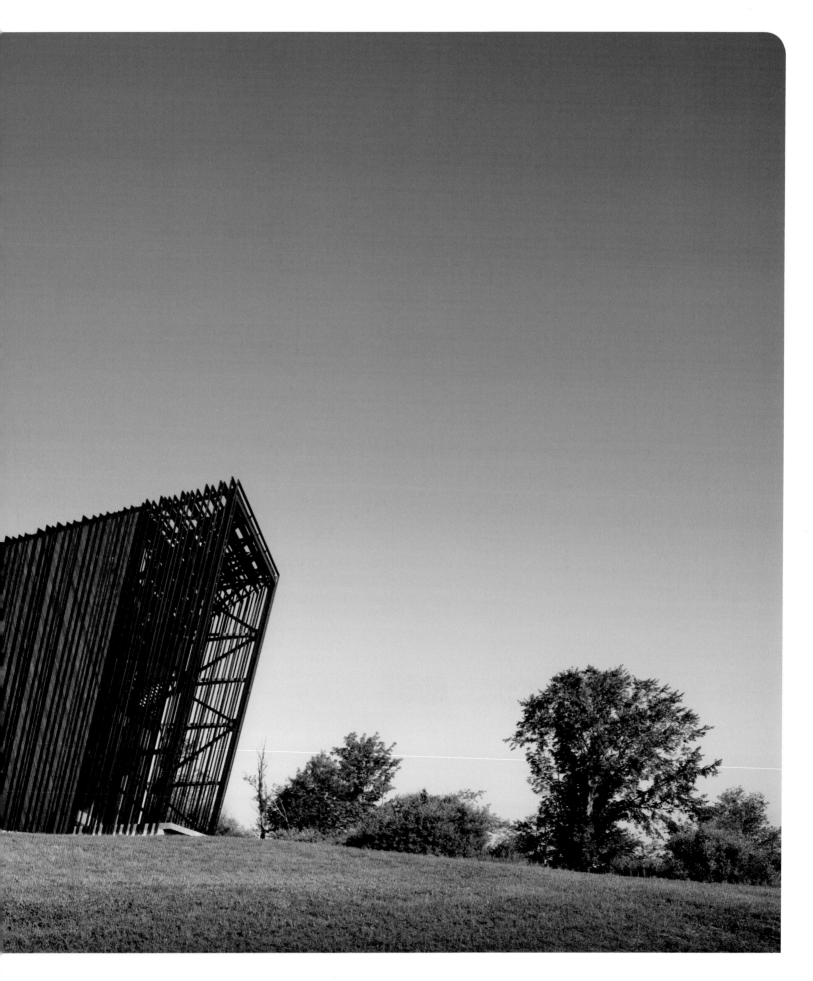

ALAIN CARLE

WWW.ALAINCARLE.CA

Alain Carle has worked in Montreal in the field of architecture since 1998. Based on an educational approach developed as a lecturer and researcher in the School of Architecture at the University of Montreal, his achievements derive from a critical approach to representation in the design process. Carrying out a modest and reflective practice, his projects are based on using perception as a theoretical model. This conceptual approach proposes that the perceptual experience of any location is an essential piece of knowledge, at a time when images represent the new architect's expertise.

From 2000 onwards, the firm has developed architecture and urban design projects for public and private organisations and practices internationally, having received commissions in both the United Kingdom and United States. The firm's achievements have appeared in various publications and have been recognised by the architectural community with several awards.

Alain Carle travaille à Montréal dans le domaine de l'architecture depuis 1998. Fondées sur une démarche pédagogique développée à titre de chercheur et d'enseignant à l'École d'architecture de l'Université de Montréal, ses réalisations s'appuient sur une approche critique de la représentation dans le processus de conception. Engagés dans une pratique modeste et réflective, ses projets partent de l'usage de la perception comme modèle théorique. Selon cette approche conceptuelle, l'expérience perceptive de tout lieu est un élément de savoir essentiel, à une époque dans laquelle les images deviennent le nouveau savoir-faire de l'architecte.

Depuis 2000, ce cabinet a développé des projets d'architecture et de design urbain pour des organismes et sociétés publics et privés au niveau international, ayant été commissionné à la fois par les États-Unis et le Royaume-Uni. Ses accomplissements ont fait l'objet de diverses publications et sont reconnus dans le milieu architectural, ayant obtenu de nombreux prix.

Alain Carle arbeitet seit 1998 als Architekt in Montreal. Durch seine Erfahrung als Dozent und Forscher an der School of Architecture der University of Montreal geht er den Architekturprozess von einem eher kritischen Standpunkt aus an. Er arbeitet bescheidend und reflektierend und legt all seinen Projekten einen theoretischen Ansatz zu Grunde. In einer Zeit, in der ein Architekt vor allem visuell wahrgenommen wird, verdeutlicht sein Ansatz der Wahrnehmung eines Ortes diesen Wissensstand.

Seit 2000 übernimmt das Unternehmen international Architektur- und Städteplanungsprojekte für öffentliche und private Einrichtungen, wofür es sowohl in Großbritannien als auch in den USA Auszeichnungen erhielt. Zudem wird es in zahlreichen Veröffentlichungen gewürdigt und erlangte durch verschiedene Auszeichnungen Anerkennung in der Architekturbranche.

Alain Carle trabaja en el campo de la arquitectura en Montreal desde 1998. Basados en un enfoque educativo desarrollado como docente e investigador en la Escuela de Arquitectura de la Universidad de Montreal, sus logros se basan en un enfoque crítico de la representación en el proceso de diseño. Ejerciendo una práctica modesta y reflexiva, sus proyectos están anclados en la percepción como un modelo teórico. Este enfoque conceptual propone la experiencia perceptiva de cualquier lugar como un conocimiento esencial, en un momento en las imágenes representan el nuevo know-how del arquitecto.

Desde 2000, la firma desarrolla proyectos de arquitectura y diseño urbano para organizaciones públicas y privadas y ejerce su práctica internacionalmente, con encargos en el Reino Unido y Estados Unidos. Los logros de la firma han aparecido en diversas publicaciones y han sido reconocidos con varios premios por la comunidad arquitectónica.

[LA HÉRONNIÈRE]

LA HÉRONNIÈRE

The project was born from the client's willingness to build a dwelling harmoniously occupying the natural environment and developed to strict environmental requirements. Situated on a hillside, the dwelling is organised on the basis of a horizontal plane extending beyond its perimeter, creating terraces on the top floor, where the bedrooms are located, with the sheltered areas below, containing the shared spaces. The upper floor's appearance of lightness contrasts with the rocks and the exposed concrete on the lower floor. A small greenhouse and planting areas confirm the dwelling's inclination towards self-sufficiency. In terms of energy, the building is self-supplying through biomass and photovoltaic panels which produce a surplus in summer. The concepts of recycling and reuse were reflected in different aspects of the design, in collaboration with the users.

Projektgrundlage war der Wunsch des Kunden nach einem sich harmonisch in seine Umgebung einfügenden Wohnhaus nach den strengsten Energievorgaben. Das Haus liegt an einem Hang und streckt sich auf einer horizontalen Ebene über dessen Grenzen hinaus. Hierdurch entstehen im oberen Stockwerk - in dem sich auch die Schlafzimmer befinden - Terrassen, unter denen sich geschützt liegend die Gemeinschaftsbereiche befinden. Das helle Obergeschoss steht im Kontrast zu Felsen und Sichtbeton im unteren Stockwerk. Ein kleines Gewächshaus mit Pflanzgärten verdeutlicht das energieautarke Konzept des Hauses. Dank Biomasse und einer Photovoltaikanlage erzeugt das Gebäude seinen kompletten Energiebedarf selbst und erzielt im Sommer sogar einen Überschuss. Recycling und Widerverwertung zeigen sich in verschiedenen Aspekten des Designs, in das der Kunde stets miteingebunden war.

Ce projet est né de la volonté du client de construire une habitation qui occuperait harmonieusement l'environnement naturel et a été développé selon de stricts critères environnementaux. Situé sur une colline, cette maison est organisée sur la base d'une plan horizontal qui s'étend au-delà de son périmètre, créant des terrasses à l'étage supérieur, où sont situées les chambres, les espaces couverts au-dessous contenant les espaces communs. L'aspect léger de l'étage supérieur contraste avec les rochers et le béton apparent de l'étage inférieur. Une petite serre et des zones de plantation confirment le penchant de la maison pour l'auto-suffisance. En matière d'énergie, ce bâtiment est auto-suffisant de par la biomasse et les panneaux photovoltaïques qui produisent un surplus en été. Le concept du recyclage et de la réutilisation est incarné par différents aspects du design, en collaboration avec les usagers.

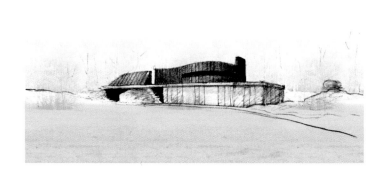

El proyecto nació de la voluntad del cliente de edificar una casa que ocupase el entorno natural de forma armoniosa y desarrollase unos estrictos requisitos medioambientales. La vivienda se sitúa en una ladera y se organiza en base a un plano horizontal que se extiende más allá del perímetro construido, generando terrazas en la planta superior y zonas resguardadas en la inferior. La ligera imagen de la parte superior, que alberga los dormitorios, contrasta con las rocas y el hormigón visto de la inferior, que contiene las zonas comunes. Un pequeño invernadero y zonas de siembra refrendan la vocación auto-suficiente de la casa; en términos energéticos, el edificio se autoabastece mediante el uso de biomasa y de paneles fotovoltaicos. Los conceptos de reciclaje y reutilización se plasmaron en diferentes aspectos del diseño, en estrecha colaboración con los usuarios.

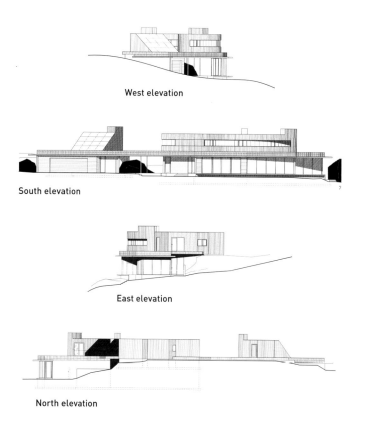

West elevation

South elevation

East elevation

North elevation

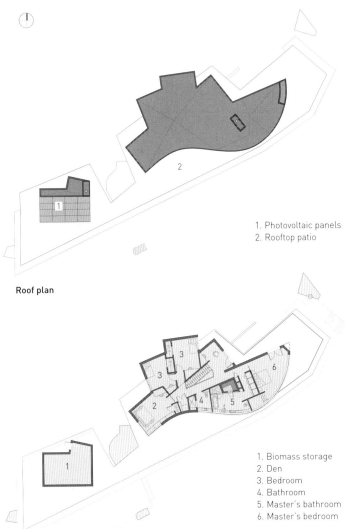

Roof plan

1. Photovoltaic panels
2. Rooftop patio

Second floor plan

1. Biomass storage
2. Den
3. Bedroom
4. Bathroom
5. Master's bathroom
6. Master's bedroom

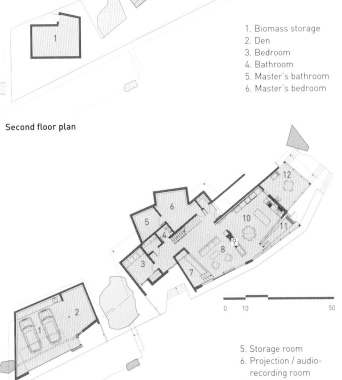

First floor plan

0   10   50

1. Garage
2. Combustion
   equipment room /
   electric accumulator
3. Mudroom
4. WC
5. Storage room
6. Projection / audio-
   recording room
7. Office
8. Living room
9. Fireplace
10. Kitchen & dining area
11. Green house
12. Screen parch

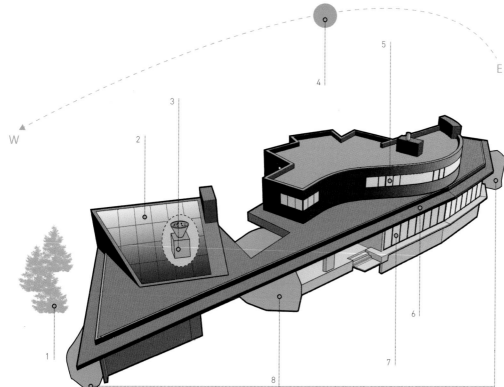

1. **Pines in the west**
   Wind protection

2. Solar passive:
   4,32kW Photovoltaic panels
   16 batteries totaling 39,8 kWh to ensure
   electric autonomy

   Inverter: electric surplus sold
   Hydro-Québec ← Export

3. **Biomass central heating** by granules of
   recycled residues from softwood lumber.
   Supplies the radiant floors, the propelled-
   air furnace and domestic hot water

4. Sun's path:
   The program is placed to optimise the
   natural light reception throughout the day

5. **Summer ventilation:**
   Casement windows to let air enter from
   the west

6. **Structural platform**
   Crossing the site, resting on the rocks.
   Protection against environmental factors
   and sunrays

7. Maximum **south-facing fenestration** to
   accumulate the maximum heat during the
   winter

8. Three existing rocks whose highest points
   are at the same geodesic level

W   E

Site strategies
LEED Gold Certification

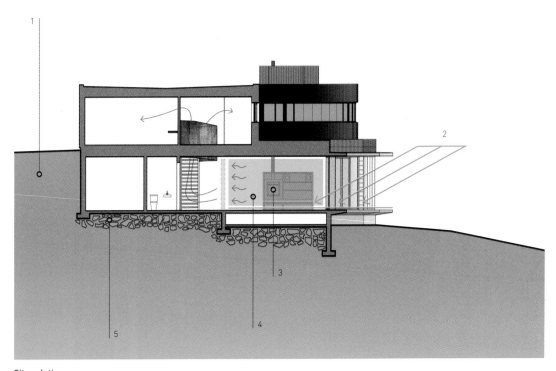

1. Buried ground floor on the north side for **better energy conservation**

2. Maximum south-facing fenestration to accumulate the maximum heat during the winter. The concrete floor also helps to retain the heat

3. Slow combustion fireplace

4. Heat control: Slicing wall to store the heat

5. Recovery of the blasting residus resulting from the excavation work

Other green elements:

-Drain-water heat recovery (DWHR)

-Insulation and sealing complying Novoclimat standards

-Materials without VOC, formaldehyde nor carcinogenic components

Site relations
LEED Gold Certification

ARCHITECTEN
EN BOUWMEESTERS

WWW.ARCHITECTENBOUWMEESTERS.NL

ARCHITECTEN EN BOUWMEESTERS is an all-round Dutch architecture and building management firm.

With a great deal of passion, we develop spatial concepts in which the user is the central focus. Interested in creative design solutions and specialised in energy-neutral building concepts, as an architect we are aware of our social responsibility. By means of smart trade-offs in terms of functionality, manufacturability, the impact on energy and the environment, maintenance and cost elements, we contribute to the creation of sustainable buildings.

We believe that sustainability offers opportunities in terms of comfort, finance and the environment. We create sustainable designs, by making the best choices with regards to the use of materials and energy-efficient construction methods.

In 2017 we received the international BREEAM-Award for the EnergiePLUS offices of Geelen Counterflow.

ARCHITECTEN EN BOUWMEESTERS est un cabinet hollandais d'architecture et de gestion de construction.

Avec une grande passion, nous développons des concepts spatiaux dont l'usager est le centre. Intéressés par des solutions de design créatives et spécialisés dans la conception de bâtiments à énergie neutre, nous sommes conscients de notre responsabilité sociale en tant que cabinet d'architecture. Au moyen de compromis astucieux en matière de fonctionnalité, de fabricabilité, d'impact sur l'énergie et l'environnement, d'éléments d'entretien et de coûts, nous contribuons à la création de bâtiments durables.

Nous croyons que la durabilité offre des opportunités en termes de confort, de finance et d'environnement. Nous créons des designs durables, en faisant les meilleurs choix possibles quant aux matériaux utilisés et aux méthodes de construction écoénergétiques.

En 2017 nous avons obtenu le prix BREEAM pour les bureaux EnergiePLUS de Geelen Counterflow.

ARCHITECTEN EN BOUWMEESTERS ist ein niederländisches Allround-Unternehmen für Architektur und Baumanagement.

Wir entwickeln mit viel Leidenschaft Raumkonzepte, bei denen der Bewohner/Besucher im Mittelpunkt steht. Unser Architekturunternehmen ist an kreativen Designlösungen und energieneutralen Baukonzepten interessiert und ist sich dabei der Verantwortung für die Gesellschaft bewusst. Mit unseren intelligenten Kombinationen aus Funktionalität, Machbarkeit, Einfluss auf Energie und Umwelt, Instandhaltung und Kosten gelingen uns nachhaltige Gebäude.

Wir glauben an die Möglichkeiten der Nachhaltigkeit im Hinblick auf Komfort, Kosten und Umwelt. Unsere wohlüberlegte Auswahl an Materialien und energieeffizienten Bauformen ermöglicht nachhaltige Designlösungen.

2017 erhielten wir den internationalen BREEAM-Award für die EnergiePLUS-Büroräume des Geelen Counterflow.

ARCHITECTEN EN BOUWMEESTERS es una empresa holandesa que engloba estudio de arquitectura y gestión de edificios.

Nos apasiona desarrollar conceptos espaciales en los que el usuario es el punto central del diseño. Somos conscientes de nuestra responsabilidad social como arquitectos, por ello nos interesan las soluciones de diseño creativas y nos especializamos en conceptos constructivos de energía neutra. Por medio de ingeniosos intercambios en temas de funcionalidad, fabricación, el impacto energético y medioambiental, el mantenimiento y coste, contribuimos a la creación de edificios sostenibles.

Creemos que la sostenibilidad ofrece ventajas en términos de comodidad, economía y medioambiente. Para crear diseños sostenibles, elegimos con atención las materias y los métodos de construcción más eficientes en términos de energía.

En 2017, nuestro diseño de las oficinas de EnergiePLUS de Geelen Counterflow fue galardonado con el premio internacional BREEAM.

[ZERO ENERGY HOME SITTARD]

[ENERGY PLUS OFFICE GEELEN COUNTERFLOW]

ZERO ENERGY
HOME SITTARD

This luxurious dwelling was designed and completed as a energy-neutral building, which means that the amount of energy it generates is at least equal to that it consumes. The project adopted a series of architectural and technical approaches aimed at achieving this goal. Following the guidelines set by the client, the dwelling's design focuses on lowering environmental pressure, while obtaining high comfort levels and low energy costs; without concessions to aesthetics. In the interior the architect has developed a smart spatial design for the family with 3 children, that is adapted to everyone's activities in the household. A subtle play between distance and proximity provides surprising spatiality to the design that was mainly developed from a cross-section, by integrating a split level in the house.

Diese luxuriöse Wohnung wurde als energieneutrales Gebäude konzipiert und fertiggestellt, was bedeutet, dass die Energiemenge, die sie erzeugt, mindestens der Menge entspricht, die sie verbraucht. Das Projekt verfolgt eine Reihe von architektonischen und technischen Ansätzen, um dieses Ziel zu erreichen. Nach den Vorgaben des Bauherrn wird bei der Planung der Wohnung darauf geachtet, die Umweltbelastung zu senken und gleichzeitig einen hohen Komfort und niedrige Energiekosten zu erzielen, ohne dabei auf Ästhetik zu verzichten. Im Innenbereich hat der Architekt eine intelligente Raumgestaltung für die Familie mit 3 Kindern entwickelt, die an die Aktivitäten im Haushalt angepasst ist. Ein subtiles Spiel zwischen Distanz und Nähe sorgt für eine überraschende Räumlichkeit des Entwurfs, der hauptsächlich aus einem Querschnitt entwickelt wurde, indem eine geteilte Ebene in das Haus integriert wurde.

Ce luxueux logement a été conçu et réalisé comme un bâtiment neutre sur le plan énergétique, ce qui signifie que la quantité d'énergie qu'il génère est au moins égale à celle qu'il consomme. Le projet a adopté une série d'approches architecturales et techniques visant à atteindre cet objectif. En suivant les directives établies par le client, la conception de l'habitation se concentre sur la réduction de la pression environnementale, tout en obtenant des niveaux de confort élevés et de faibles coûts énergétiques, sans concession à l'esthétique. A l'intérieur, l'architecte a développé une conception spatiale intelligente pour la famille avec 3 enfants, adaptée aux activités de chacun dans la maison. Un jeu subtil entre la distance et la proximité apporte une spatialité surprenante au design qui a été développé principalement à partir d'une section transversale, en intégrant un niveau divisé dans la maison.

Esta lujosa vivienda fue diseñada y acabada como un edificio de energía neutral, lo que significa que la cantidad de energía que genera es al menos igual a la que consume. El proyecto adoptó una serie de enfoques arquitectónicos y técnicos dirigidos a conseguir este objetivo. Siguiendo las directrices marcadas por el cliente, el diseño de la vivienda se focaliza en reducir la presión ambiental, a la vez que obtener altos niveles de confort y costes bajos de energía, sin concesiones a la estética. En el interior el arquitecto ha desarrollado un ingenioso diseño espacial para una familia con tres hijos, que se adapta a las actividades de todos en el hogar. Un juego sutil entre distancia y proximidad proporciona una sorprendente espacialidad al diseño que fue principalmente desarrollado a partir de una sección transversal, integrando un nivel separado en la casa.

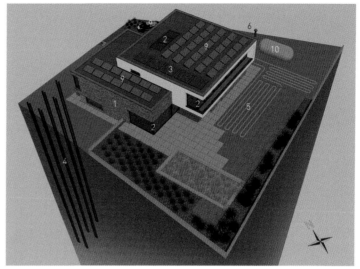

Impression Sustainability

1. **Minimise architectural losses**
   - maximum insulation
   - maximum air tightness
   - no heat bridge
2. **Maximum direct sun radiation**
   - south orientation
   - triple glazing
   - automatic sun blinds
3. **Maximum solar energy produced hot water**
   - 5 x 3m² vacuum heat pipes, directly on the roof
   - 2000 litres 'smart' buffer recipient of 35-90 degrees for tap water, heating and swimming pool
   - heat recycling in shower drain water
4. **Geothermal probes for when the sun does not shine**
   - 5 55 metres-deep probes in the front garden
   - 12 kW heat pump in the technical room
5. **Floor heat switches for the ventilation air**
   - 300 metres duct in the garden, 1.5 metre under the ground
   - pre-heating in winter up to 12-13 degrees, pre-cooling in summer up to 12-13 degrees

6. **Counterflow Heat Recovery system (WTW) ventilation**
   - 2 x 400 m³/h, with 95% energy recovery
   - balanced ventilation system, star-shaped, insulated
   - number of rotations set by CO_2 control per area
7. **Economical electric appliances**
   - LED lighting
   - economical dishwasher, refrigerator, freezer, etc.
8. **Domotics building control**
   - everything on/off at the switch of a single button
   - presence detection and timers etc.
   - weather-dependent control of heating, sun blinds etc.
9. **Solar panels to compensate energy consumption**
   - 48 x 240Wp = 11.520 Wp: +/- 10,000 kWh/year
   - use electric car as buffer
10. **Re-use of rain water**
    - 10,000 litres tank for rain water from the roof
    - separate circuit for toilets, garden and garage

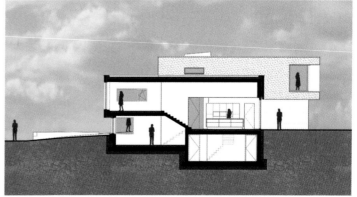

Section

ENERGY PLUS OFFICE
GEELEN COUNTERFLOW

This ambitious office project based on sustainability and Superior energy efficiency obtained a score of 99.94% on the BREEAM certification scale. Its construction is based on a system of prefabricated solid wood components assembled on-site using sustainable materials which, according to "cradle to cradle" principles, can be recycled at the end of their useful life. Multiple design strategies, such as rainwater recycling, solar panels for hot drinking water, the use of geothermal energy or photovoltaic panels which produce 50% more energy than that consumed by the offices, are a sign of the project's environmental commitment. The interior is a pleasant work environment encouraging mutual interaction, spacious, transparent interaction, with plenty of natural light, dominated by a stunning double-height wall of plants.

Grundlage dieses ehrgeizigen Büroprojekts waren Nachhaltigkeit und enorme Energieeffizienz mit einem Wert von 99,94 % auf der BREEAM-Zertifizierungsskala. Die Gebäudekonstruktion besteht aus vorgefertigten Massivholzkomponenten, die vor Ort mit nachhaltigen Materialien, die nach Nutzungsdauer „Credle to credle"-Prinzip recycelt werden können, zusammengebaut wurden. Verschiedene Planungsstrategien wie Regenwasser-Recycling, Sonnenkollektoren für warmes Trinkwasser, die Verwendung von geothermischer Wärme und Photovoltaikanlagen, die 50 % mehr Energie als vom Büro benötigt produzieren, verdeutlichen die umweltbewusste Verpflichtung des Projekts. Das Gebäudeinnere ist eine angenehme und geräumige Arbeitsumgebung mit viel natürlichem Licht, in deren Mittelpunkt eine zweireihige Pflanzenwand steht.

Cet ambitieux projet de bureau basé sur la durabilité et une efficacité énergétique supérieure a obtenu un score de 99,94 % sur l'échelle de certification BREEAM. Sa construction est basée sur un système de composantes en bois massif préfabriquées assemblées sur site en utilisant des matériaux durables qui, selon les principes du « berceau au berceau », peuvent être recyclés à la fin de leur cycle d'utilisation. De multiples stratégies de conception, comme le recyclage de l'eau de pluie, l'usage d'énergie géothermique et de panneaux photovoltaïques qui produisent 50 % d'énergie de plus que la quantité consommée par les bureaux, sont un signe de l'engagement environnemental de ce projet. L'intérieur est un environnement de travail plaisant qui encourage l'interaction mutuelle, spacieuse et transparente, bénéficiant d'une lumière naturelle abondante, et dominé par un impressionnant mur végétal en double hauteur.

Este ambicioso proyecto de oficinas basado en la sostenibilidad y la alta eficiencia energética obtuvo un 99,94% en la escala de certificación BREEAM. Su construcción se basa en un sistema de elementos prefabricados de madera maciza ensamblados en obra, y en el uso materiales sostenibles que, según los principios del "cradle to cradle", puedan ser reciclados al final de su vida útil. Múltiples estrategias de diseño, como el reciclaje de agua de lluvia, los paneles solares para agua caliente sanitaria, el uso de energía geotérmica o los paneles fotovoltaicos que producen un 50% más de la energía que consumen las oficinas, constatan el compromiso medioambiental del proyecto. El interior constituye un agradable entorno de trabajo que fomenta la interacción mutua, espacioso, transparente y con abundante luz natural, presidido por un imponente muro vegetal a doble altura.

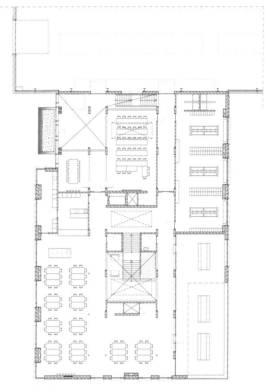

First floor plan

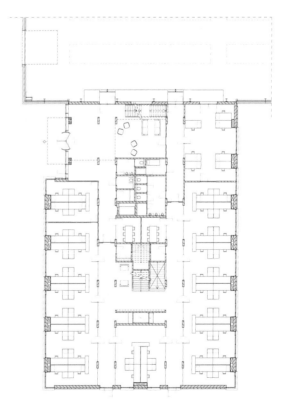

Ground floor plan

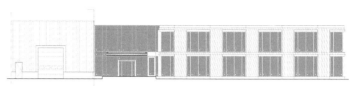

Front facade

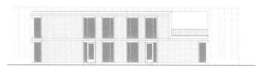

Side facade

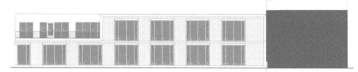

Rear facade

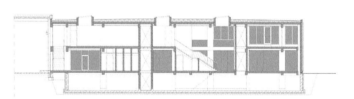

Longitudinal section

Climatic diagram

1. **Passive construction with solid wooden shell**
   - Solid wooden walls, floors and columns; glueless with wooden screwed joints
   - 1,200m^3 spruce wood, CO_2 footprint -/- 2,400 tonnes; PEFC certified
   - Thermal mass 120Wh/Km^2
   - Wall insulation value: Rc= 4.4 m^{2}K/W at 35 cm. wall thickness; roof Rc= 10.8 m^{2}K/W
   - Air permeability blower door test result n50 = 0.46 1/h and thermographic control
   - Heating demand = 14 kWh/m^{2}a
   - Primary energy demand = 63 kWh/m^{2}a

2. **Large window openings and skylights**
   - Reduced power consumption of lighting
   - Passive heating
   - Frames constructed from Accoya FSC sustainable wood with triple glazing Uw = 0.90 W/m^{2}K
   - Automatic sun blinds, regulated via the air conditioning system

3. **Recyclable materials**
   - Vegetal, biodegradable roofing
   - Recyclable carpet, rubber floors, tiles, ceilings and cradle-to-cradle glass

4. **Air conditioning system**
   - Fully load-controlled basad on CO_2, heat and cooling demand per room
   - Bauer Optimising technology creates a draught-free and pleasant indoor climate and ensures optimal energy efficiency
   - Heat wheel to recover heat and moisture
   - 5,200 m^3/h ventilation capacity
   - Fresh air supply based on 450 ppm CO_2 outside and < 800 ppm in the offices
   - Thermal efficiency of 78%

5. **Lighting**
   - LED lighting, via motion and daylight sensors

6. **Greenwall**
   - Converts CO_2 from employees into oxygen

7. **Geothermal heat**
   - 8 x 112 meter deep probes to provide heating and passive cooling
   - 17.3 + 9.6 kW (BOW35) heat pumps to provide heating and active cooling

8. **Solar collectors**
   - 23 m^2 for hot water and heating during spring and autumn

9. **Solar panels**
   - East-west position on the roof
   - 334 panels x 327 Wp; 90,000 kWh per year

10. **Ecological garden**
    - Natural pool for amphibians
    - Bat boxes, insect hotels and bird nest boxes in a natural garden

    Water
    - 10,000 litres of rainwater for rainwater collection to flush toilets and for the green wall
    - Waterless urinals
    - Water measurements with leak detection and presence-regulated zone valves

ARKIS

WWW.ARK.IS

ARKÍS is a progressive design partnership practicing architecture, design, planning and green design consultancy based in Reykjavik, Iceland. ARKÍS was founded in 1997, but from the firm's founding ARKÍS architects have executed projects at various scales and levels of complexity, both in Iceland and internationally, for institutional, private, and civic clients.

ARKÍS architects are driven by the pursuit of quality and the belief that the built environment has the inherent potential to improve the quality of our lives. Moreover, ARKÍS architects are committed to sustainable design practices.

ARKÍS recent works and awards include Holmen Aquatics Center (Building of the Year in Norway 2017), Holmsheidi Prison (Nomination to the Mies van der Rohe award 2016), the Icelandic Institute of Natural History, Snaefellsstofa Visitor Center (Icelandic Concrete Prize, 2016), and University of Reykjavik.

ARKÍS est un partenariat progressif de design pratiquant l'architecture, le design, la planification et la consultance en design écologique basé à Reykjavík, en Islande. ARKÍS a été créé en 1997, mais depuis lors les architectes fondateurs ont exécuté des projets de différentes envergures et de divers niveaux de complexité, en Islande comme à l'international, pour des clients institutionnels, privés, et civils.

Ces architectes sont mus par la recherche de qualité et la conviction que l'environnement bâti a le pouvoir intrinsèque d'améliorer notre qualité de vie. De plus, ils se sont engagés à user de pratiques de design durables.

Parmi leurs travaux et prix récents on trouve le *Holmen Aquatics Center* (bâtiment de l'année en Norvège en 2017), la prison Holmsheidi (Nomination au prix Mies van der Rohe 2016), l'*Icelandic Institute of Natural History*, le *Snaefellsstofa Visitor Center* (Prix *Icelandic Concrete*, 2016), et l'Université de Reykjavík.

ARKÍS ist eine fortschrittliche Designkooperation für Architektur, Planung und Beratung zu Umweltfreundlichem Bauen in Reykjavik, Island. ARKÍS wurde 1997 ins Leben gerufen, die Gründungsarchitekten von ARKÍS realisierten jedoch auch sowohl in Island als auch international bereits Projekte unterschiedlicher Form und Komplexität für Bildungs-, Privat- und Verwaltungsgebäude.

ARKÍS architects ist getrieben vom Streben nach Qualität und dem Glauben daran, dass das Bauumfeld unsere Lebensqualität verbessern kann. Zudem hat sich ARKÍS zu nachhaltigem Design verpflichtet.

Zu den letzten Auszeichnungen und Arbeiten von ARKÍS gehören das Holmen Aquatics Center (Gebäude des Jahres Norwegen 2017), das Holmsheidi Prison (nominiert für den Mies van der Rohe Award 2016), das isländische Institut für Naturgeschichte, das Snaefellsstofa Visitor Center (Icelandic Concrete Prize, 2016) und die Universität Reykjavik.

ARKÍS (Reikiavik, Islandia) es una asociación que trabaja en los campos de la arquitectura, diseño, planificación y consultoría sobre diseños ecológicos. ARKÍS se fundó en 1997, pero desde su nacimiento la empresa ha ejecutado distintos proyectos a varias escalas y con diversos niveles de complejidad, tanto en Islandia como en el extranjero, para clientes institucionales, privados y entidades civiles.

Los principios de ARKÍS son la búsqueda de la calidad y la creencia de que el entorno constructivo tiene un inherente potencial de mejorar la calidad de nuestra vida. Además, ARKÍS architects sigue prácticas de diseño sostenibles.

Los trabajos y galardones más recientes de ARKÍS incluyen el centro Holmen Aquatics (Edificio del año en Noruega en 2017), el centro penitenciario de Holmsheidi (Nominación al premio Mies van der Rohe de 2016), el Instituto islandés de Historia Natural, el centro de visitantes Snaefellsstofa (Premio *Concrete* de Islandia, 2016) y la universidad de Reikiavik.

[SNÆFELLSSTOFA VISITOR CENTER]

[HOLMSHEIDI PRISON]

[HOLMEN AQUATICS CENTER]

SNÆFELLSSTOFA VISITOR CENTER

Inspired by the creative power of glaciers forcing their way through the landscape and carving out new natural wonders on the way, the shape and the spaces of this building attract visitors and fusing the architecture with its surroundings. The building is divided into three parts allowing for different uses depending on the season and is structured using a main educational and expositional axis, which intersects with another dedicated to services forming an X. Its design reflects the natural environment through shapes and colours inspired by the layers of lava, the nearby deep valley and forest, and through the use of local materials such as larch or peat moss roofs. The visitor center was designed following sustainable criteria aimed at transmitting environmental values to the community and is the first building in Iceland with BREEAM certification.

Form und Räume dieses Gebäudes erinnern an die Kraft der Gletscher, die sich ihren Weg durch die Landschaft bahnen und dabei einzigartige Naturwunder erschaffen. Diese Verbindung der Architektur mit ihrer Umgebung macht das Haus zu einem wahren Besuchermagnet. Das Gebäude besteht aus drei Bereichen und erlaubt so eine unterschiedliche Nutzung je nach Saison. Den Mittelpunkt bilden ein Flügel für Bildung und Ausstellungen und einer für den Servicebereich, die ein X aus zwei Achsen bilden. Formen und Farben erinnern an Lavaschichten, das nahe Tal, die Wälder und durch die Verwendung von Lärche und Torf ähnelt auch das Dach dem der benachbarten Gebäude. Für den Bau des Besucherzentrums wurden Nachhaltigkeitskriterien zu Grunde gelegt, um der Öffentlichkeit den Wert unserer Umwelt bewusst zu machen. In Island ist es das erste Gebäude mit BREEAM-Zertifizierung.

Inspirés par la puissance créative des glaciers imposant leur présence dans le paysage tout en sculptant des merveilles naturelles sur leur passage, la forme et les espaces de ce bâtiment attirent les visiteurs et fondent leur architecture dans son environnement. Cette bâtisse est divisée en trois parties, offrant plusieurs utilisations selon la saison et elle est structurée à partir d'un axe principal pédagogique et d'exposition qui en recoupe un autre, dédié aux services, formant un X. Son design évoque la nature environnante par ses formes et ses couleurs inspirées par les couches de roche lavique, la vallée et la forêt profondes voisines, et par l'utilisation de matériaux locaux comme le mélèze ou les toits en mousse de sphaignes. Ce centre d'information a été conçu en fonction de critères durables visant à transmettre des valeurs environnementales à la communauté concernée et c'est le premier bâtiment d'Islande à avoir obtenu une certification BREEAM.

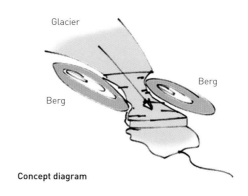

Glacier

Berg

Berg

Concept diagram

Inspirados en la fuerza creadora del glaciar que se abre camino a través del terreno y talla nuevas maravillas naturales en el paisaje, la forma y los espacios de este edificio atraen a los visitantes e integran la arquitectura en el entorno. El edificio se divide en tres partes que permiten diferentes usos en función de la temporada y se estructura mediante un eje principal, educativo y de exposiciones, que se cruza con otro de servicios formando una X. Su diseño refleja el entorno natural a través de formas y colores inspirados en las capas de lava, el profundo valle y el bosque cercanos, y mediante el uso de materiales locales como el alerce o las cubiertas de turba. El centro de visitantes fue diseñado con criterios sostenibles que aspiran a transmitir unos valores medioambientales a la comunidad y constituye el primer edificio con certificación BREEAM de Islandia.

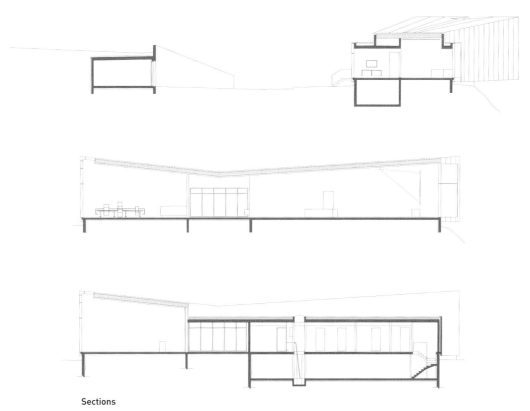

Sections

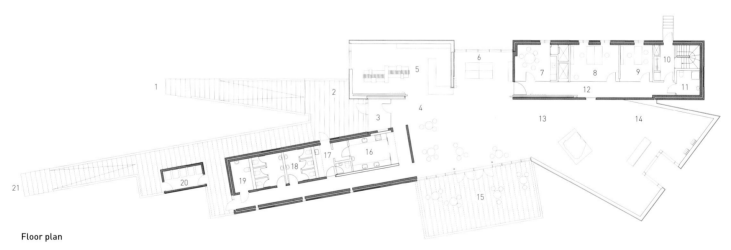

Floor plan

1. Wooden terrace
2. Entrance
3. Foyer
4. Coffee
5. Shop/library
6. Meeting area
7. Staff coffee
8. Office

9. Office
10. Staff entrance
11. Staff lavatory
12. Staff hallway
13. Exhibition computers
14. Exhibition area
15. Wooden terrace
16. Kitchen

17. Hallway
18. Lavatories
19. Handicapped-
    accesible lavatory
20. Storage
21. Wooden terrace

HOLMSHEIDI PRISON

The project design centred on creating an architecturally outstanding prison and one which was sustainable not only in its environmental aspects, but also economic and socially, an institution for improving prisoners. Its composition is characterized by three components: a circular central body, corresponding to the guards' module, which rises above the building channelling the entry of natural light; internal recreation courtyards, a key component of each of the prisons wings, and the protuberance of the cells, providing views and natural light while delimiting the visual field from inside. The palette of materials is clear and simple, aimed at durability and robustness based on an LCC (life cycle cost) analysis. The entire building's design focuses on creating healthy environments to assist the well-being of its users.

Bei der Projektplanung konzentrierte man sich auf ein architektonisch herausragendes, jedoch auch in umweltbewusster, wirtschaftlicher und gesellschaftlicher Sicht nachhaltiges Gefängnisgebäude, in dem sich die Gefangenen noch wohler fühlen sollten. Ein runder Zentralbereich für die Wärter überragt das restliche Gebäude und sorgt für den Einfall natürlichen Lichts. Zu jedem Gefängnistrakt gehören Innenhöfe zur Freizeitgestaltung. Die vorgelagerten Zellen bieten nur wenig Einblick, dafür aber einen guten Ausblick und viel Tageslicht. Bei der Materialauswahl ging es ausschließlich um Langlebigkeit und Robustheit auf Grundlage einer Lebenszykluskosten-Analyse. Das gesamte Gebäudedesign ist auf eine gesunde Umgebung für die Gefangenen ausgerichtet.

La conception de ce projet était axée sur la création d'une prison architecturalement remarquable et qui serait durable non seulement dans ses aspects environnementaux, mais aussi économiquement et socialement, une institution dédiée à l'évolution positive des prisonniers. Sa composition est caractérisée par trois composantes : un corps central circulaire, correspondant au module des gardiens, qui s'élève au-dessus de la bâtisse, canalisant l'entrée de lumière naturelle ; des cours intérieures pour la promenade, composante clé de chaque aile de la prison ; et la protubérance des cellules, avec des vues et de la lumière naturelle tout en délimitant le champ de vision depuis l'intérieur. La palette de matériaux est claire et simple, l'objectif, basé sur une analyse du CCV (coût du cycle de vie), étant la durabilité et la robustesse. Le design de l'intégralité du bâtiment vise à créer des environnements sains pour contribuer au bien-être de ses usagers.

El diseño del proyecto se centró en crear una prisión de gran calidad arquitectónica y que fuese sostenible no sólo en el aspecto medioambiental, sino también en el económico y en el social, como institución para la mejora de los reclusos. Su composición se caracteriza por tres elementos: un cuerpo central redondo, correspondiente al módulo de guardias, que se eleva por encima del edificio y que canaliza la entrada de luz natural; los patios internos de recreo, elementos centrales de cada ala de la prisión, y las extrusiones de las celdas, que proporcionan vistas y luz natural a la vez que acotan las visuales desde el interior. La paleta de materiales, simple y clara, busca durabilidad y robustez basándose en análisis tipo LCC (coste del ciclo de vida). Todo el diseño del edificio se focaliza en crear entornos saludables que ayuden al bienestar de los usuarios.

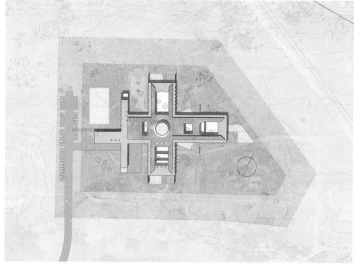

Site plan

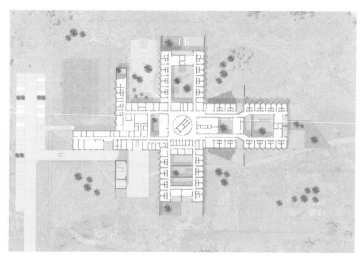

Floor plan

HOLMEN
AQUATICS CENTER

The proposal for this aquatic center focused on enhancing its roof as part and continuation of the neighbouring beach's recreational area. The roof garden replaces the building's carbon footprint and faces southwards offering a panoramic view of the Oslo fjord. The main entrance, reception, changing rooms and pool are located on the main floor, above the lawn. The lower level contains a gymnasium, multifunction room, technical spaces, and staff facilities. The passivhaus approach used for the building comes with a special concern for reusing energy, aimed mainly at heating water. The building is equipped with 650 m² of solar panels and 15 geothermal wells to extract bedrock heat, in summer any excess heat is transferred to the ground.

Der Plan für dieses Wassersportzentrum bestand hauptsächlich in der Verbesserung des Daches und der Erweiterung des benachbarten Freizeitstrandes. Der Dachgarten sorgt für ein kohlenstoffneutrales Gebäude und die Südfassaden bieten einen tollen Ausblick auf den Fjord von Oslo. Haupteingang, Rezeption, Umkleidekabinen und Pool befinden sich im Hauptgeschoss über dem Rasen. Im unteren Bereich befinden sich eine Sporthalle, Mehrzweck-, Technik- und Personalräume. Das Passivhaus-Konzept wurde bei diesem Gebäude hauptsächlich durch Energiewiederverwertung speziell für Warmwasser umgesetzt. Das Gebäude verfügt über 650 m² Sonnenkollektoren und 15 Geothermiebohrungen zur Gewinnung von Erdwärme, wobei überschüssige Wärme im Sommer in den Boden zurückgeleitet wird.

Cette proposition de centre aquatique s'axait sur la mise en avant du toit-terrasse en tant que partie et continuité de l'aire de loisirs de la plage voisine. Ce toit-terrasse végétalisé compense l'empreinte carbone du bâtiment et est orienté vers le sud, offrant une vue panoramique sur le fjord d'Oslo. L'entrée principale, l'accueil, les vestiaires et la piscine sont situés sur le niveau principal, au-dessus de la pelouse. Le niveau inférieur contient une salle de gym, une salle multifonctions, des locaux techniques, et les infrastructures allouées au personnel. L'approche passivhaus appliquée au bâtiment est accompagnée d'un souci particulier pour la réutilisation de l'énergie, visant principalement le chauffage de l'eau. Ce bâtiment est équipé de 650 m² de panneaux solaires et de 15 puits géothermiques pour extraire la chaleur du socle rocheux. En été tout surplus de chaleur extrait est transféré dans le sol.

La propuesta para este centro acuático se centra en potenciar su cubierta como parte y continuación del área recreativa de la playa vecina. La cubierta ajardinada reemplaza la huella ocupada por el edificio y se orienta hacia el sur para ofrecer una vista panorámica sobre el fiordo de Oslo. La entrada principal, recepción, vestuarios y piscina se sitúan en el nivel principal, elevándose por encima del césped. El nivel inferior alberga gimnasio, sala multifunción, espacios técnicos e instalaciones para el personal. La metodología passivhaus utilizada en la construcción se complementa con una especial preocupación por la reutilización de la energía, destinada principalmente al calentamiento de agua. El edificio está dotado de 650m² de paneles solares y quince pozos geotermales que extraen calor del lecho de roca y en verano transfieren el calor sobrante al terreno.

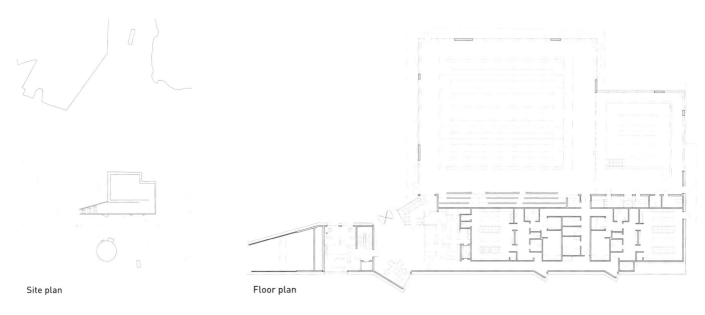

Site plan

Floor plan

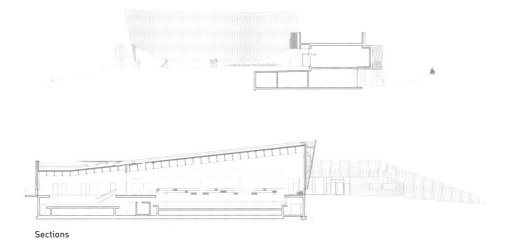

Sections

ASGK DESIGN

WWW.ASGK.CZ

At ASGK, we believe that an architect´s responsibility extends beyond the design of particular building. We strive to create dignified human habitats in ecological, social and economic harmony with their surroundings.

Each project we work on bears the influence of open wide-ranging communication: careful to listen to what the client has to say, respectful of the local community, mindful of the relationship between initial investment in sustainable building and subsequent maintenance costs.

Founded in 2006 as a continuation of the professional accomplishments of its founder, architect Gabriela Kapralova, the studio was quick to garner attention at home and abroad, winning awards for both residential and commercial projects. Its cutting-edge wooden house Zilvar has achieved international renown.

Chez ASGK, nous pensons que la responsabilité d'un architecte dépasse le design d'un bâtiment particulier. Nous cherchons à créer des habitats humains dignes en harmonie écologique, sociale et économique avec leur environnement.

Chaque projet sur lequel nous travaillons porte l'influence d'un vaste effort de communication ouverte : nous sommes soucieux d'être à l'écoute de ce que le client veut dire, respectueux de la communauté locale, attentifs à la relation entre l'investissement initial dans l'habitat durable et les coûts d'entretien qu'il entraînera.

Fondé en 2006 pour continuer les avancées professionnelles de sa fondatrice, l'architecte Gabriela Kapralova, ce studio a rapidement attiré l'attention dans son pays comme à l'étranger, gagnant des prix pour des projets résidentiels comme commerciaux. Zilvar, maison en bois avant-gardiste de sa conception, a atteint une notoriété mondiale.

Wir von ASGK glauben, dass die Verantwortung eines Architekten über die Planung der einzelnen Baudelemente hinausgeht. Wir möchten ansprechende Wohnräume in Harmonie mit den ökologischen, gesellschaftlichen und wirtschaftlichen Gegebenheiten ihres Umfelds schaffen.

Jedes unserer Projekte steht unter dem Einfluss einer offenen und weitreichenden Kommunikation: Wir hören sorgfältig auf das, was uns der Kunde zu sagen hat, respektieren die Gegebenheiten des Ortes und achten auf ein angemessenes Verhältnis zwischen anfänglicher Investition in ein nachhaltiges Gebäude und den späteren Instandhaltungskosten.

Das Studio wurde 2006 als berufliche Weiterentwicklung seiner Gründerin Gabriela Kapralova ins Leben gerufen und erlangte rasch lokal und überregional Aufmerksamkeit, was zu Auszeichnungen für Projekte im Wohn- und Geschäftsbereich gleichermaßen führte. Sein supermodernes Holzhaus Zilvar erlangte internationale Anerkennung.

En ASGK, creemos que la responsabilidad de un arquitecto se extiende más allá del diseño de un edificio en particular. Luchamos para crear hábitats humanos dignos en armonía ecológica, social y económica con su entorno.

Cada proyecto en el que trabajamos está condicionado por una comunicación abierta en muchos ámbitos: escuchamos atentamente las peticiones del cliente, respetamos la comunidad local, somos conscientes de la unión entre la inversión inicial en un edificio sostenible y los costes posteriores de mantenimiento.

Fundada en 2006 como continuación a los logros profesionales de su fundadora, la arquitecta Gabriela Kapralova, el estudio captó rápidamente la atención a nivel nacional e internacional, siendo galardonado tanto por proyectos residenciales como comerciales. La innovadora casa de madera Zilvar ha alcanzado prestigio internacional.

[HOUSE ZILVAR]

HOUSE ZILVAR

Surrounded by fields and forests, this open plan and power saving wooden dwelling represents for its occupants a peaceful haven close to nature. Its shape, suggested by the client's son, is inspired by an arthropod leaning towards the huge oak tree next to it. The dwelling's interior is a unique space, where the ground floor lounge, the kitchen and dining room open on to the upper floor bedrooms and galleries and extend towards the large east-facing porch. The façade, roof and interior are made of larch board. However, the external wood cladding uses a "seared and stained" technique providing durability. The large windows in the main space take advantage of solar power in winter, while wood sliding panels provide protection against solar radiation in summer.

Dieses großräumige und stromsparende Holzwohnhaus liegt inmitten von Feldern und Wäldern und ist für seine Bewohner ein Stück Himmelreich inmitten der Natur. Die Form war ein Vorschlag des Sohnes des Kunden und spiegelt die Vorstellung eines Gliederfüßlers an der großen Eiche neben dem Haus wider. Das Innere besteht aus einem einzigen Raum. Wohnzimmer, Küche und Esszimmer befinden sich im Erdgeschoss, das sowohl zum ersten Stockwerk mit Schlafzimmern und Galerien als auch zur Veranda an der Ostseite hin offen ist. Fassade, Dach und Innenbereich bestehen aus Lärchenbrettern. Für die Langlebigkeit der hölzernen Außenverkleidung bediente man sich der sogenannten „seared and stained"-Technik. Im Winter profitieren die Bewohner durch die großen Fenster im Hauptgebäude von der Kraft der Solarenergie und im Sommer schützen Holzschiebewände vor zu starker Sonneneinstrahlung.

Entourée de champs et de forêts, cette habitation de plain-pied en bois, économe en énergie, représente pour ses occupants un havre de paix proche de la nature. Sa forme, suggérée par le fils du client, est inspirée par un arthropode se penchant vers l'énorme chêne avoisinant. L'intérieur est un espace unique, où le salon du rez-de-chaussée, la cuisine et la salle-à-manger s'ouvrent sur les chambres et les galeries de l'étage supérieur et s'étendent vers le grand porche orienté vers l'est. La façade, le toit et l'intérieur sont faits de planches de mélèze. Cependant, le bardage extérieur de bois est traité selon une méthode de « calcinage-teinture » qui le rend plus résistant. Les grandes fenêtres de l'espace principal bénéficient de l'énergie solaire en hiver, tandis que des panneaux coulissants en bois apportent une protection contre les rayons du soleil en été.

Rodeada de campos y bosques, esta casa de madera de planta abierta y bajo consumo de energía representa para sus ocupantes un tranquilo refugio cercano a la naturaleza. Su forma, sugerida por el hijo del cliente, se inspira en un artrópodo inclinado hacia el enorme roble vecino. El interior de la casa constituye un único espacio, en el que el salón, la cocina y el comedor de la planta baja se abren a las galerías-dormitorio del piso superior y se extienden hacia el gran porche orientado al este. La fachada, el techo y el interior están hechos de tablas de alerce; sin embargo, el revestimiento exterior de madera utiliza una técnica de «quemado y teñido» que aporta durabilidad. Los grandes acristalamientos del espacio principal aprovechan la ganancia solar en invierno, mientras que unos paneles correderos de madera brindan protección contra la radiación del sol en verano.

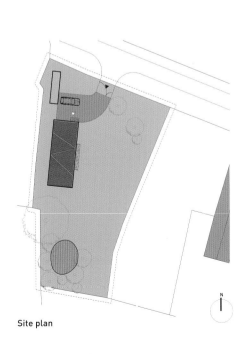

Site plan

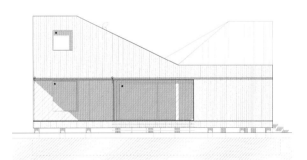

East elevation

North elevation

West elevation

South elevation

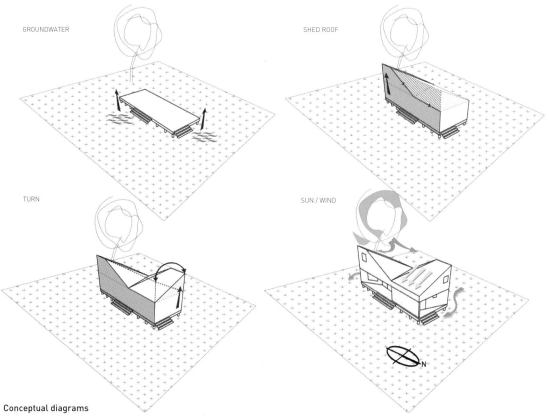

GROUNDWATER

SHED ROOF

TURN

SUN / WIND

Conceptual diagrams

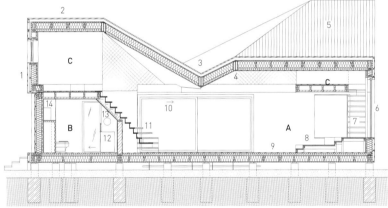

Cross section

A. Lounge, kitchen and dinning area
B. Bathroom
C. Open bedroom galleries

1. 2 by 4 KVH larch timber construction / diffusion - open wall assembly / the facade wood cladding uses a "burn and stain" technique, for longer - lasting life
2. Roof construction - the larch timber - framed structure / hydro insulation is hidden under the roof wood cladding
3. Roof valley heated when necessary
4. Supporting roof structure - ULTRALAM beam
5. The cladding goes all the way to roof level and forms a cover for the roof waterproofing sheet

6. Windows are designed with wood (inside) and aluminium (outside) frames and insulated triple glazing
7. Subtle stain industrial staircase in front of a large window enable view on the close oak tree
8. Podium with storage area
9. Larch timber strip flooring
10. Sliding glass doors with high performance low - E coated glass / windows are designed with wood (inside) and aluminium (outside) frames and insulated triple glazing
11. Plywood boxes staircase with a storage area
12. Storage water heater
13. Recover unit
14. Water treatment
15. Circular monolithic concrete pillars

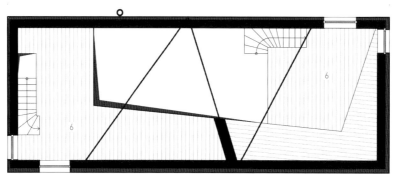

First floor plan

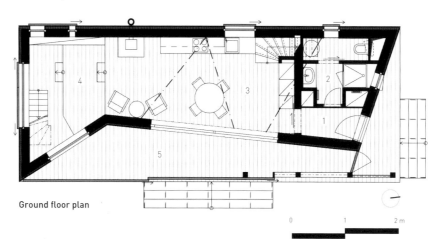

Ground floor plan

1. Entrance hall
2. Bathroom
3. Living space
4. Platform
5. Terrace
6. Gallery / bedroom

0   1   2 m

BAOSOL

WWW.BAOSOL.COM

Andrew Michler, CPHC (Certified Passive House Consultant)

Andrew Michler explores the environment and building through the written word, multi-media including film, has globally lectured on the role of architecture in response to environmental needs and podcasts on Passive House building science and design. In 2015 he released the book [ours] *Hyperlocalization of Architecture* on merging the wisdom of place with the best contemporary worldwide design principles. Baosol Design specializes in passive house and bespoke projects. Andrew has lived off grid in the Colorado Rockies since 1995.

MARTaK Passive House is the first international certified Passive House in Colorado. The project received the project received the Green Builder Magazine 2017 Grand Overall Winner Green Home of the Year Awards.

Andrew Michler, CPHC (zertifizierter Passivhausberater)

Andrew Michler erforscht Umwelt und Gebäude durch das geschriebene Wort und multimediale Möglichkeiten wie Film, referiert weltweit über die Rolle der Architektur bei der Antwort auf Umweltanforderungen und produziert Podcasts zu Wissenschaft und Planung von Passivhäusern. 2015 veröffentlichte er das Buch [ours] Hyperlocalization of Architecture on merging the wisdom of place with the best contemporary worldwide design principles. Baosol Design hat sich auf Passivhäuser und maßgeschneiderte Projekte spezialisiert. Andrew lebte seit 1995 auch ohne Strom in den Colorado Rockies.

MARTaK Passive House ist das erste international zertifizierte Passivhaus in Colorado. Das Projekt erhielt den Green Builder Magazine 2017 Grand Overall Winner Green Home of the Year Awards.

Andrew Michler, CPHC (Consultant certifié pour l'habitat passif)

Andrew Michler explore l'environnement et la construction par le biais du mot écrit, du multimédia y compris des films, a enseigné en université sur le rôle de l'architecture vis-à-vis des besoins environnementaux et produit des podcasts sur la science de la construction et le design de bâtiments passifs. En 2015 il a publié le livre [chez nous] « *Hyperlocalization of Architecture* » sur l'accord entre la sagesse d'un lieu et les meilleurs principes de design contemporain au monde. *Baosol Design* est spécialisé dans les projets d'habitat passif et sur mesure. Il vit coupé du monde dans les Rockies du Colorado depuis 1995.

MARTaK Passive House est la première maison passive certifiée du Colorado. Ce projet a reçu le prix de la maison écologique de l'année, *Grand Overall Winner Green Home of the Year Awards*, du *Green Builder Magazine* en 2017.

Andrew Michler, CPHC (Certified Passive House Consultant)

Usando material multimedia (la palabra escrita, películas), Andrew Michler explora el entorno y la construcción. Ha impartido conferencias en todo el mundo sobre el papel de la arquitectura en respuesta a las necesidades medioambientales y tiene varios podcasts sobre la construcción y el diseño de casas pasivas. En 2015, lanzó el libro [nuestro] *Hyperlocalization of Architecture* sobre la fusión de la sabiduría del lugar con los mejores principios de diseño contemporáneos internacionales. Baosol Design se especializa en casas pasivas y proyectos a medida. Andrew vive sin conexión a la red energética en las Montañas Rocosas de Colorado desde 1995.

MARTaK es la primera casa pasiva de Colorado que recibe un certificado internacional. El proyecto recibió en 2017 el premio *Grand Overall Winner Green Home of the Year* de la revista *Green Builder*.

[MARTaK PASSIVE HOUSE]

[SOL COFFEE]

MARTaK PASSIVE HOUSE

MARTaK investigates how architecture and environmental ambition can work in harmony. Located among pine trees, the shape of this passive, detached dwelling is inspired by the traditional cabins to be found in the local mountains, the hogbacks, and its design is based on small-scale contemporary Japanese residential architecture. Recyclable materials or those that could be "absorbed" by the forest were chosen for its construction, such as wood with FSC certification. Its exterior, formed by walls with insulation cavities using cellulose and mineral wool, covered with steel and cement panels and triple-glazed windows, provides optimum efficiency and protection against the frequent forest fires in the area. The project involves energy consumption three times lower than the level required for *passivhaus* certification, that is 15 kWh/m² per year.

MARTaK sucht nach Möglichkeiten, um Architektur und Umweltschutz in einen harmonischen Einklang zu bringen. Dieses, unter Linden gelegene freistehende, Passivhaus ähnelt in seiner Form den traditionellen Blockhütten (Hogbacks) in den umliegenden Bergen. Sein Design orientiert sich an der modernen japanischen Architektur für begrenzten Wohnraum. Für den Bau wurden recycelbare oder vom Wald aufnehmbare Materialien wie FSC-zertifiziertes Holz verwendet. Die Außenfassade sorgt für optimale Energieeffizienz und Schutz vor Waldbränden. Sie enthält Löcher für mehr Sonneneinstrahlung und besteht aus einer Innenkonstruktion aus Zellstoffen und Mineralwolle, auf der Stahl- und Zementplatten ruhen. Hinzu kommen Fenster mit Dreifachverglasung. Der Energieverbrauch des Gebäudes ist dreimal niedriger als der für das Passivhaus-Zertifikat erforderliche Verbrauch von 15 kWh/m² pro Jahr.

MARTaK étudie la façon dont l'architecture peut fonctionner en harmonie avec une ambition environnementale. Située au milieu de pins, cette maison passive indépendante a une forme qui s'inspire des cabanes traditionnelles qu'on trouve dans les montagnes locales, les « crêts », et son design s'appuie sur l'architecture résidentielle japonaise contemporaine à petite échelle. Les matériaux recyclables ou ceux qui peuvent être « absorbés » par la forêt ont été choisis pour sa construction, comme le bois de certification FSC. L'extérieur, formé par des murs à cavité isolants à base de cellulose et de laine minérale, recouverts de panneaux d'acier et de ciment et percés de fenêtres à triple vitrage, apporte une efficacité et une protection optimales contre les fréquents feux de forêt de la région. Ce projet implique une consommation d'énergie trois fois plus basse que le niveau requis pour la certification *passivhaus*, qui est de 15 kWh/m² par an.

MARTaK investiga cómo arquitectura y ambición ambiental pueden funcionar en armonía. Situada entre pinos, la forma de esta casa pasiva y autónoma se inspira en las cabañas tradicionales y en las montañas locales, las *hogbacks*, y su diseño se basa en la pequeña arquitectura residencial japonesa contemporánea. En la construcción se escogieron materiales que pudiesen ser reciclados o "reabsorbidos" por el bosque, como las maderas con certificación medioambiental FSC. Su envolvente, formada por muros con cavidades de aislamiento de celulosa y lana mineral, cubierta de acero, paneles de cemento y ventanas de triple acristalamiento, proporciona una óptima eficiencia energética y da protección frente a los frecuentes incendios forestales de la zona. El proyecto prevé un consumo energético tres veces inferior al nivel de certificación *passivhaus*, que es de 15 kWh/m² por año.

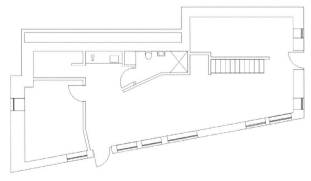

Floor plan

Elevations

SOL COFFEE

Built on the frame of a 1979 Toyota Dolphin Camper Sol Coffee is a mobile espresso bar that can operate autonomously. Utilizing a hybrid espresso machine and 1.4k W solar array the truck provides a clean and quite environment for coffee patrons to enjoy a cup in almost any location. The massing evokes the Rocky Mountains where the truck is located and provides significant angled roof area for the solar array. The skin is composed of polycarbonate panels which are both light weight and illuminate from the interior or exterior to add depth to the volume. The rear opens to allow a congregation of guests and by lowering the main floor patrons are near eye level with the barista. A shelf adjacent to the serving window pulls out for cream, sugar, lids and coffee sleeves. A vertical sandwich board provides access to the propane tanks and storage on the side.

Sol Coffee wurde aus der Rahmenkonstruktion eines Toyota Dolphin-Wohnmobils aus dem Jahr 1979 erbaut und ist eine mobile und selbstständig funktionierende Espresso-Bar. Mit einer Hybrid-Espressomaschine und 1,4 kW Sonnenstrahlung bietet der Wagen eine saubere und ruhige Umgebung, in der Kaffeeliebhaber eine Tasse an jedem beliebigen Ort genießen können. Das Konstrukt passt zu den Rockey Mountains, in denen sich der Wohnwagen befindet, und Dächer im entsprechenden Winkel sorgen für die benötigte Sonneneinstrahlung. Die Wände bestehen aus leichten Polycarbonatpaneelen, die von innen und außen für Licht sorgen, was dem Konstrukt mehr Volumen verleiht. Der offene rückwärtige Teil bietet Platz für Gäste und durch die Absenkung des Bodens können Kaffeeliebhaber auf Augenhöhe mit dem Barista stehen. Neben dem Ausschankfenster befindet sich ein Regal für Milch, Zucker, Deckel und Kaffeebecher. Die vertikale Tafel bietet Zugang zu den Propantanks und seitliche Aufbewahrungsmöglichkeiten.

Construit à partir du châssis d'un camping car Toyota Dophin de 1979, Sol Coffee est un bar à expresso mobile qui peut opérer de façon autonome. Au moyen d'une machine à café hybride et d'un panneau solaire de 1,4kW, ce van offre un environnement propre et silencieux pour que les consommateurs puissent savourer leur expresso dans presque n'importe quel emplacement. Son volume évoque les montagnes Rocheuses où se trouve le camion et procure une zone étendue de toit en angle pour le panneau solaire. L'enveloppe en est composée de panneaux de polycarbonate qui sont légers mais aussi éclairent de l'intérieur ou l'extérieur pour ajouter de la profondeur aux volumes. L'arrière s'ouvre pour permettre d'accueillir plusieurs convives et par le biais de l'abaissement du plan principal permet aux clients d'être presque au même niveau que le barman. Un panneau sandwich vertical permet d'accéder aux bonbonnes de propane et aux rangements latéraux.

Construida sobre el chasis de una caravana Toyota Dolphin Camper del 79, Sol Coffee es una cafetería móvil que puede funcionar de forma autónoma. Con el uso de una máquina expresso híbrida y un panel solar de 1,4 kW, la caravana proporciona un ambiente limpio y tranquilo para que los clientes puedan disfrutar de una taza de café en casi cualquier lugar. El volumen recuerda a las Montañas Rocosas, donde se ubica la caravana, y posee un área de techo angular suficiente para los paneles solares. La envolvente se compone de paneles de policarbonato ligeros que se pueden iluminar desde el interior o el exterior, añadiendo profundidad al volumen. La parte trasera se abre para acoger a varios clientes y bajando la planta principal, los clientes están al mismo nivel que el camarero. Una estantería junto a la ventana mostrador ofrece leche, azúcar, tapas y fundas aislantes para el café. Un panel sándwich vertical da acceso a los tanques de propano y almacenamiento en el lateral.

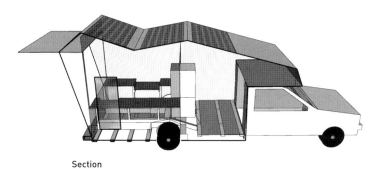

Section

BCHO ARCHITECTS

WWW.BCHOARCHITECTS.COM

Since Byoungsoo Cho has opened his office in 1994, he has been actively practicing with themes such as "experience and perception: existing, existed", "— shaped house", "¬ shaped house", "contemporary vernacular" or "organic vs. abstract". He has taught at Harvard University, Universitat Kaiserslautern, Montana State university and at Aarhus School of Architecture, Denmark as a Chair Professor in 2014. He has received KIA National Award, several AIA Honor Awards in Montana Chapter and in North West Pacific Regional.

BCHO Architects believe that buildings, furniture and art are made, not created. Each architectural project, encompassing various scales and programs, explores the phenomenon of light and space, fabrication and construction methods, recycling and reusing, and a broad sense of sustainability (social/cultural/physical) which uses collective creative energy to reduce the demand for grid energy.

Depuis que Byoungsoo Cho a ouvert son cabinet en 1994, il pratique activement autour de thèmes tels que « l'expérience et la perception : exister, avoir existé », « maison en — », « maison en ¬ », « contemporain vernaculaire » ou « organique versus abstrait ». Il a enseigné à l'Université Harvard, à celle de Kaiserslautern, à celle de l'État du Montana et à l'école d'architecture de Aarhus, au Danemark, en tant que professeur titulaire en 2014. Il a reçu le Prix national KIA, plusieurs prix d'honneur de l'AIA section Montana et dans la région Pacifique nord-ouest.

Selon BCHO Architects, les bâtiments, le mobilier et l'art sont fabriqués, et non pas créés. Chaque projet architectural, dans une grande diversité d'échelles et de programmes, explore le phénomène de la lumière et de l'espace, des méthodes de fabrication et de construction, le recyclage et la réutilisation, et un sens aigu de la durabilité (sociale/culturelle/physique) qui puise dans l'énergie créative collective pour réduire la demande d'énergie de réseau.

Seit Byoungsoo Cho 1994 sein Unternehmen gründete, beschäftigt er sich intensiv mit Projekten wie "experience and perception: existing, existed" "—shaped house", „¬ shaped house", „contemporary vernacular" or „organic vs. abstract". Er unterrichtete bereits an der Harvard University, der Universität Kaiserslautern, der Montana State University und 2014 als Lehrstuhlinhaber an der dänischen Architektenschule Aarhus School of Architecture. Er erhielt die Auszeichnung KIA National Award und mehrere AIA-Ehrenauszeichnungen durch Montana Chapter und North West Pacific Regional.

BCHO Architects glaubt, dass Gebäude, Möbel und Kunst gemacht und nicht geschaffen werden. Jedes Architekturprojekt beinhaltet verschiedene Phasen und Programme und untersucht das Phänomen von Licht und Raum, Fertigungs- und Baumethoden, Recycling und Wiederverwertung und verschiedenste Aspekte der Nachhaltigkeit (sozial/kulturell/physikalisch), wobei es kollektiver kreativer Energie bedarf, um den Bedarf an leitungsgebundener Energie zu reduzieren.

Desde la inauguración de su estudio en 1994, Byoungsoo Cho ha practicado activamente con temas como «la experiencia y percepción: existe, existió», «casa en forma de —», «casa en forma de ¬», «contemporáneo local» o «orgánico vs. abstracto». Ha sido profesor en la Universidad de Harvard, en la de Kaiserslautern y en la universidad estatal de Montana. En 2014 fue profesor principal de la Escuela de arquitectura de Aarhus, en Dinamarca. Ha recibido el premio nacional KIA así como varios premios AIA de honor en el apartado Montana y región del noroeste-pacífico.

En su estudio, BCHO Architects, consideran que los edificios, el mobiliario y el arte se hacen, no se crean. Cada proyecto arquitectónico, que incluye varias escalas y programas, explora el fenómeno de la luz y el espacio; los métodos de fabricación y construcción; el reciclaje, la reutilización y la sostenibilidad en un sentido muy amplio (social, cultural y física) que usa la energía creativa colectiva para reducir la demanda de energía eléctrica.

[TILT ROOF HOUSE]

[JEDONG RANCH MEDITATION SPACE]

TILT ROOF HOUSE

The concept of this semi-subterranean dwelling is an attempt at respecting the flow of natural energy from the peaceful mountains where it is located. A celebration of the primordial relationship between nature and building. Taking advantage of the steep slope, the dwelling melds with the topography and finds itself partially embedded in the ground, thus minimising any excavation. The sloping roof, following the slope of the hill until it disappears into the terrain, becomes a terrace characterised by three square boxes, two of them, partially recessed, play the part of outdoor furniture and delimit areas in the interior. The third box becomes a patio allowing natural light to enter in addition to cross ventilating the interior. The in-situ concrete and black dyed pine wood used for the exterior finishes, contrasts with the warmth of the birch use for those of the interior.

Dieses halb-unterkellerte Wohngebäude entstand in dem Wunsch, den Fluss der natürlichen Energie von den friedlichen Bergen zu respektieren. Das Gebäude in den Bergen ist eine Hommage an das ursprüngliche Verhältnis zwischen Gebäuden und Natur. Dank des steilen Hanges verschmilzt das Wohngebäude vollständig mit der Topografie und ist somit schon teilweise in den Boden eingelassen, was kaum Grabungsarbeiten erforderlich machte. Die Dachschräge ist der Neigung des Hanges nachempfunden und mündet in die Terrasse. Diese besteht aus drei quadratischen Einheiten, von denen zwei teilversenkt sind, was einen Außensitzbereich schafft und Innenbereiche abgrenzt. Die dritte Einheit ist ein Innenhof, der für die Querlüftung sorgt und natürliches Licht in das Gebäudeinnere dringen lässt. Die Außenverkleidung aus Beton und schwarz eingefärbtem Kiefernholz steht in Kontrast zu der Wärme der Birke im Inneren.

Ce concept d'habitation semi-souterraine cherche à honorer le flot d'énergie naturelle provenant des montagnes paisibles où elle est implantée, en une célébration de la relation primordiale entre la nature et ce bâtiment. Profitant de la pente abrupte, cette habitation se fond dans la topographie et se trouve partiellement encastrée dans le sol, minimisant ainsi tout travail d'excavation. Le toit incliné, qui suit la pente de la colline jusqu'à disparaître dans le terrain, devient une terrasse caractérisée par trois cubes ; deux d'entre eux, partiellement encastrés, font office de mobilier d'extérieur et délimitent des zones intérieures. Le troisième cube devient un patio qui laisse entrer la lumière naturelle tout en opérant une aération transversale à l'intérieur. Le béton coulé sur place et le pin teint en noir utilisés pour les finitions extérieures contrastent avec la chaleur du bouleau utilisé pour celles de l'intérieur.

El concepto de esta vivienda semienterrada trata de respetar el flujo de energía natural de las tranquilas montañas donde se ubica, celebrando la relación primordial entre naturaleza y edificio. Aprovechando la fuerte pendiente, la casa se mezcla con la topografía y se incrusta parcialmente en el terreno, minimizando así la excavación. La cubierta inclinada, que sigue la pendiente de la colina hasta desaparecer en el terreno, se convierte en una terraza caracterizada por tres cajas cuadradas; dos de ellas, parcialmente empotradas, actúan de mobiliario exterior y diferencian zonas en el interior. La tercera caja se convierte en un patio que permite la entrada de luz natural y la ventilación cruzada del interior. El hormigón *in situ* y la madera de pino teñida de negro de los acabados exteriores contrastan con la calidez de los revestimientos de abedul del interior.

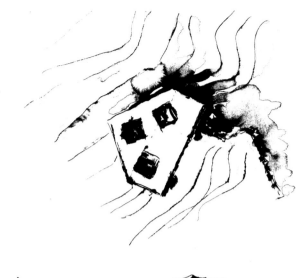

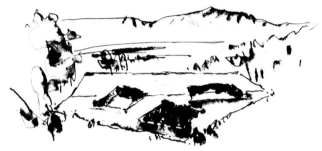

Sketches

Attic plan

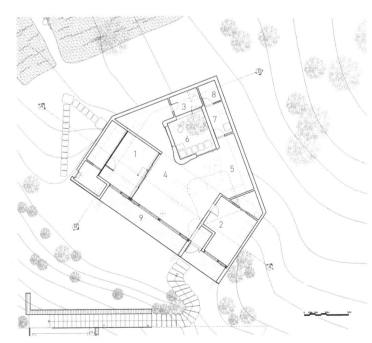

Ground floor plan

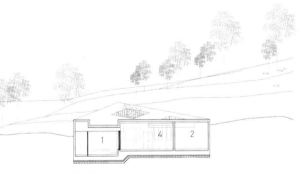

Section A

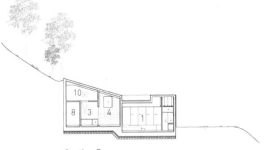

Section B

1. Master bedroom
2. Guest bedroom
3. Tea room
4. Living room
5. Kitchen
6. Courtyard
7. Laundry
8. Storage
9. Terrace
10. Attic

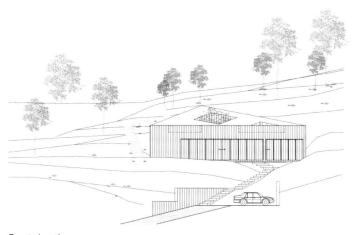

Front elevation

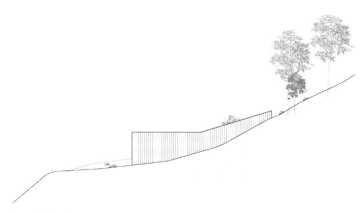

Lateral elevation

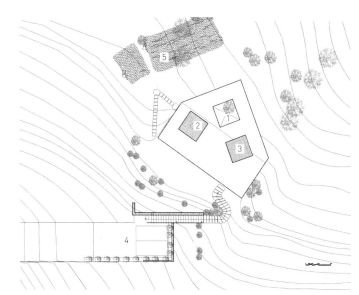

Site plan

1. Courtyard
2. Lowered roof area (barbecue)
3. Lowered roof area (reading)
4. Parking
5. Vegetable garden

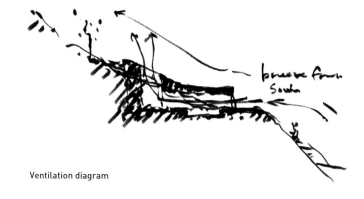

Ventilation diagram

JEDONG RANCH
MEDITATION SPACE

The project is part of a group of buildings that includes a dining pavilion and a guest house. In contrast to those, the meditation space sinks into the ground to be at one with nature. Access to it is deliberately extended via a long staircase gradually revealing an exposed concrete wall, becoming a metaphor for the user immersing themselves in the space. At the end of the staircase, there is a simple patio opening the building out towards the sky. Facing a canopy of trees, the meditation space celebrates the interaction between man and nature creating a true dialogue. The austere interior finishes create a real sense of place for the individual. Sliding wood doors and the prolongation of the flooring towards the trees gives the user intimacy and isolation, within a context of unspoiled nature.

Das Projekt ist Teil einer Gruppierung von Gebäuden, zu der auch ein Speisepavillon und ein Gästehaus gehört. Als Kontrast dazu ist der Meditationsraum in den Boden eingelassen, um so eins mit der Natur zu werden. Der Zugang erfolgt absichtlich über eine lange Treppe, sodass beim Hinabsteigen nach und nach eine nackte Betonwand sichtbar wird, was das Eintauchen des Besuchers in den Raum symbolisieren soll. Am Ende der Treppe öffnet sich das Gebäude zu einem Hof mit Blick in den Himmel. Unter einem Baldachin aus Bäumen können die Besucher des Meditationsraums in einen wahren Dialog zwischen Mensch und Natur eintreten. Die karge Innenausstattung soll Platz für das Individuelle lassen. Holzschiebetüren und eine Ausdehnung des Bodenbelags bis unter die Bäume erlauben dem Besucher Intimität und Isolation inmitten unberührter Natur.

Ce projet fait partie d'un groupe de bâtiments qui comporte un pavillon de restauration et une maison d'hôtes. En contraste avec ceux-ci, l'espace de méditation s'enfonce dans le sol pour ne faire qu'un avec la nature. L'accès y est délibérément étendu via un long escalier révélant progressivement un mur de béton apparent, métaphore pour l'usager qui se fond dans l'espace. Au bout de cet escalier se trouve un simple patio qui ouvre le bâtiment sur le ciel. Face à une voûte d'arbres, l'espace de méditation célèbre l'interaction entre l'homme et la nature en créant un véritable dialogue. Les finitions austères de l'intérieur créent un vrai sentiment d'identité pour l'individu. Des portes coulissantes et la prolongation du sol vers les arbres procurent intimité et isolement pour l'usager, dans le contexte d'une nature préservée.

El proyecto forma parte de un conjunto que incluye un pabellón comedor y una casa de huéspedes. En contraste con estos, el espacio de meditación se hunde en el terreno para unirse con la naturaleza. Su acceso se prolonga deliberadamente mediante una larga escalera que revela de forma gradual un muro de hormigón visto y que se convierte en una metáfora de como el usuario se sumerge en el lugar. Al final de la escalera, un sencillo patio abre el edificio hacia el cielo. Orientado hacia un dosel de árboles, el espacio de meditación celebra la interacción del hombre con la naturaleza creando un cierto diálogo. Sus austeros acabados interiores crean un verdadero sentido de lugar para el individuo. Las puertas correderas de madera y la prolongación del plano del suelo hacia los árboles otorgan intimidad y aislamiento al usuario, dentro de un contexto de naturaleza virgen.

'folded concrete wall'
provides a sense of...

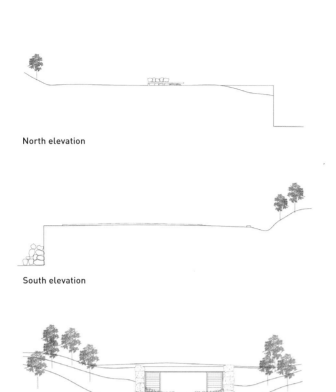

North elevation

South elevation

East elevation

West elevation

0   5m

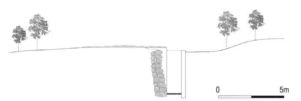

Roof plan

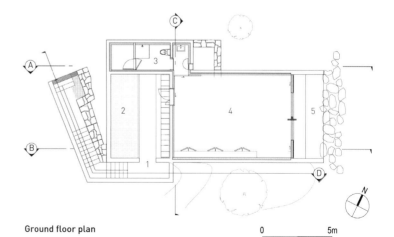

Ground floor plan

0   5m

1. Entryway
2. Water garden
3. Bathroom
4. Meditation room
5. Exterior deck

N

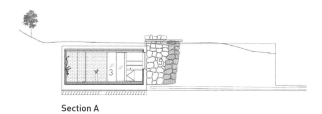

Section A

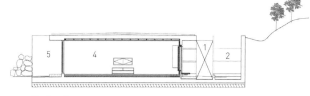

Section B

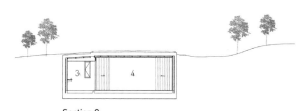

Section C

Section D

1. Entryway   4. Meditation room
2. Water garden   5. Exterior deck
3. Bathroom

C.F. MØLLER

WWW.CFMOLLER.COM

Simplicity, clarity and unpretentiousness, the ideals that have guided our work since 1924, are continually re-interpreted to suit individual projects, always site-specific and combined with sustainable, innovative and socially responsible design solutions.

Over the years, we have won a large number of national and international competitions and major architectural awards. Our work has been on show at architectural exhibitions all over the world as well as published in books and leading professional journals.

With our integrated design approach which seamlessly blends urban design, landscape, building design and building component design, C.F. Møller has received much acclaim for international projects of reference like the University Campus in Aarhus, the Darwin Centre at the Museum of Natural History in London, the Akershus University Hospital in Oslo or the 2012 Olympics' Athletes Village in London.

La simplicité, la clarté et l'humilité, ces idéaux qui guident notre travail depuis 1924, sont continuellement réinterprétés pour s'adapter à des projets individuels, toujours spécifiques aux sites correspondants et associés à des solutions de design durables, innovantes et socialement responsables.

Au fil des années, nous avons gagné un grand nombre de concours nationaux et internationaux et des prix d'architecture majeurs. Notre travail a été exhibé pour des expositions d'architecture dans le monde entier mais aussi publié dans des livres et les principales revues professionnelles.

Notre approche conceptuelle intégrée qui mêle de manière fluide l'architecture urbaine, de paysage, la construction et le design de composantes de construction, ont valu à C.F. Møller d'être salué pour des projets internationaux de référence tels que le campus de l'Université de Aarhus, le Darwin Centre du Musée d'histoire naturelle de Londres, l'hôpital de l'Université Akershus à Oslo ou le village olympique de Londres 2012.

Schlichtheit, Klarheit und Bescheidenheit sind die Ideale, die seit 1924 unsere Arbeit prägen und die wir für jedes einzelne Projekt unter Berücksichtigung des Standorts stets neu interpretieren und mit nachhaltigen, innovativen und sozialverantwortlichen Designlösungen kombinieren.

Im Laufe der Jahre gewannen wir eine Vielzahl an nationalen und internationalen Wettbewerben und Architekturauszeichnungen. Wir zeigten unsere Arbeit auf den weltweiten Architekturmessen sowie in Büchern und führenden Fachzeitschriften.

Unser gesamtheitliches Design ist eine nahtlose Mischung aus Städteplanung, Landschaft, Planung von Gebäuden und Gebäudebestandteilen. C.F. Møller erhielt viel Anerkennung für wichtige internationale Projekte wie den Universitätscampus in Aarhus, das Darwin Centre im Museum of Natural History (Museum für Naturgeschichte) in London, die Akershus-Universitätsklinik in Oslo oder das Olympische Dorf der Sommerspiele 2012 in London.

Simplicidad, claridad y sencillez: estos son los ideales que guían nuestro trabajo desde 1924 y que se reinterpretan constantemente para adaptarlos a proyectos individuales, siempre creados teniendo en cuenta su ubicación y combinados con soluciones de diseño sostenibles, innovadoras y socialmente responsables.

A lo largo de los años, hemos ganado un gran número de concursos nacionales e internacionales y grandes premios arquitectónicos. Nuestro trabajo se ha expuesto en exposiciones arquitectónicas en todo el mundo y también se ha publicado en libros y en las principales revistas profesionales.

En C.F. Møller seguimos una estrategia de diseño integral, que une sin fisuras el diseño de la ciudad, el paisaje y el edificio. Gracias a este enfoque holístico, proyectos internacionales de referencia, como el campus universitario de Aarhus, el centro Darwin en el Museo de Historia Natural de Londres, el hospital universitario Akerhus en Oslo o la villa olímpica para atletas en los Juegos Olímpicos de Londres en 2012, han recibido una gran acogida en el mundo.

[COPENHAGEN INTERNATIONAL SCHOOL NORDHAVN]

[MAERSK TOWER]

COPENHAGEN INTERNATIONAL SCHOOL NORDHAVN

Located in the privileged setting of the new district of Nordhavn, this school has become the largest in Copenhagen. The building is divided into four small "towers" five to seven storeys high, each adapted to the different stages of children's development, brought together by a ground floor dedicated to more outward-looking and shared activities. The covering of this lower floor becomes a terrace which is used as a playground for the entire school representing a safe environment away from the coast. The unique design of the façade contains 12,000 solar panels covering a surface area of 6,048 m² placed at different angles creating a sequin-like effect. In addition to providing more than half of the school's annual electricity requirements, the solar panels form part of its syllabus.

Diese Schule ist im neuen Stadtviertel Nordhang besonders günstig gelegen und in Kopenhagen die größte ihrer Art. Das Gebäude ist in vier kleine „Türme" mit bis zu sieben Stockwerken für die unterschiedlichen Entwicklungsphasen der Kinder aufgeteilt, die durch einen Erdgeschossbereich für offene und gemeinschaftliche Aktivitäten verbunden sind. Auf dem Dach des einstöckigen Bereichs befindet sich ein Terrassenspielplatz für die gesamte Schule in sicherer und beruhigter Umgebung. Die einzigartig gestaltete Fassade enthält 12.000 Sonnenkollektoren auf einer Fläche von 6.048 m², deren Anbringung in unterschiedlichen Winkeln für einen Pailletten-Effekt sorgt. Die Sonnenkollektoren liefern nicht nur die Hälfte des jährlich von der Schule benötigten Stroms, sondern sind auch Teil des Lehrplans.

Située dans l'emplacement privilégié du nouveau quartier de Nordhavn, cette école est devenue la plus grande de Copenhague. Ce bâtiment est divisé en quatre petites « tours » de cinq à sept étages, chacune adaptée aux différents stades de développement de l'enfant, reliées entre elles par un rez-de-chaussée dédié aux activités partagées, plus tournées vers l'extérieur. Le revêtement de ce niveau inférieur devient une terrasse qui sert de cour de récréation pour l'école entière, ce qui en fait un environnement sûr loin de la côte. Le design unique de cette façade contient 12 000 panneaux solaires couvrant une surface de 6 048 m² placés à différents angles, créant un effet rappelant des paillettes. En plus de couvrir plus de la moitié des besoins annuels de l'école en électricité, les panneaux solaires sont inscrits dans son programme.

Situada en un emplazamiento privilegiado del nuevo distrito de Nordhavn, esta escuela se ha convertido en la más grande de Copenhague. El edificio se divide en cuatro pequeñas «torres» de cinco a siete plantas de altura, cada una adaptada a las diferentes etapas del desarrollo de los niños, unidas por una base en planta baja donde se realizan las actividades compartidas y abiertas. La cubierta de esta base se convierte en una terraza que funciona como patio de recreo para toda la escuela y que representa un entorno seguro y alejado de la costa. El diseño único de la fachada contiene 12.000 paneles solares que cubren un área de 6.048 m² y cuya colocación en diferentes ángulos crea un efecto a modo de lentejuelas. Además de suministrar más de la mitad del consumo anual de electricidad de la escuela, los paneles solares se han integrado en su plan de estudios.

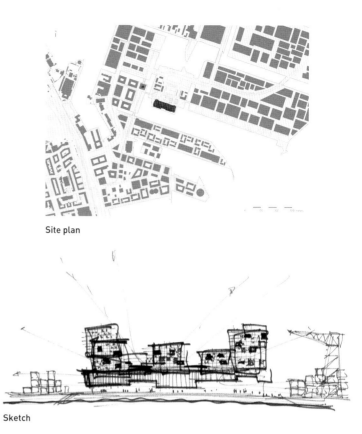

Site plan

Sketch

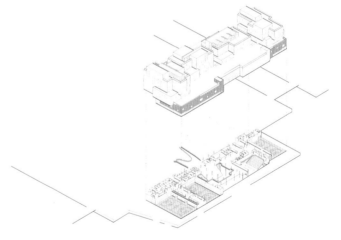

Isometric drawing

Perspective section hall

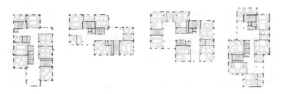

Third floor plan

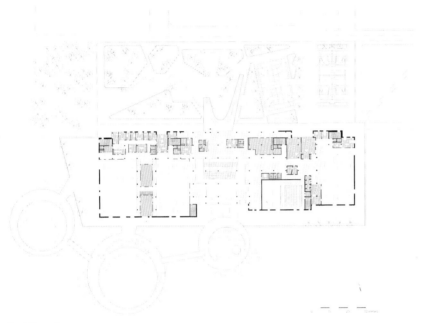

First floor plan

Ground floor plan

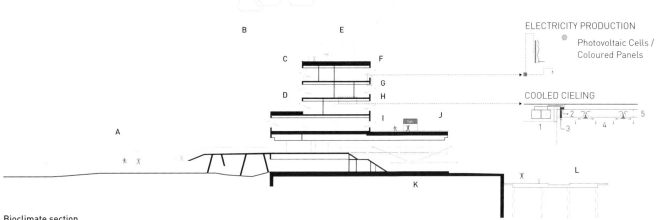

ELECTRICITY PRODUCTION

Photovoltaic Cells /
Coloured Panels

COOLED CIELING

Bioclimate section

A. Active and green playground landscape between building and city

B. Rainwater retention in connection with green roofs

C. The building's geometry encourages natural activity and play as part of daily movement

D. All floor finishes are timber flooring

E. Pupils can grow vegetables, berries and herbs in the roof gardens

F. Solar panels on the facade contribute to the school's energy consumption and can be actively used for teaching purposes

G. Classrooms strategically placed towards building's corners to optimise daylight from two facades

H. Natural ventilation in classrooms through openable windows in facade

I. Views from classrooms towards green external areas

J. Active roofscapes with space for ball games and other sports

K. Strong visual connections between the cantine and surrounding functions

L. Active edge areas and functions towards the harbour

1. Hallway
2. Fresh air
3. Used air
4. Classroom
5. Minimal height

MAERSK TOWER

This extension of the Faculty of Medicine of the University of Copenhagen is home to research areas and a conference centre. The building takes the form of a high block housing laboratories, placed on a clear glass base open to the public containing public areas. This approach frees up space for the campus park, through which a "floating road" brings pedestrians and cyclists towards the building. The interior is unified horizontally and vertically by an open atrium, where a sculptural spiral staircase physically and visually connects 15 floors. A copper-coated grid gives relief to the façade and reduces the tower's scale. It includes a system of blinds controlling the entry of sunlight. These energy-saving measures make the Maersk Tower laboratories the front-runner in terms of energy efficiency in the country.

Diese Erweiterung der medizinischen Fakultät der Universität Kopenhagen beherbergt Forschungsbereiche und ein Konferenzzentrum. Das Gebäude besteht aus einem hohen Block mit Laborräumen, der auf einem öffentlich zugänglichen und zum Großteil aus Fensterglas bestehenden Gebäudekomplex ruht. Diese Bauweise schafft Platz für den Campus-Park, von dem aus Fußgänger und Radfahrer über eine „schwimmende Straße" das Gebäude erreichen können. Der offene Innenhof macht das Gebäude vertikal und horizontal zu einer zusammenhängenden Einheit, wobei die formgebende Wendeltreppe 15 Stockwerke physikalisch und optisch verbindet. Die Fassade wird durch ein mit Kupfer überzogenes Gitter geschützt, das die Fläche des Turms verringert. Hier ist auch das Jalousien-System angebracht, über welches der Einfall von Sonnenlicht reguliert wird. Diese Energiesparmaßnahmen machen die Labore im Maersk Tower landesweit zum Vorreiter in Sachen Energieeffizienz.

Cette extension de la Faculté de médecine de l'Université de Copenhague accueille des espaces de recherche et un centre de conférences. Ce bâtiment prend la forme d'un immeuble élevé contenant des laboratoires, placé sur une base de verre transparent ouverte aux visiteurs englobant des zones publiques. Cette approche libère de l'espace pour le parc du campus traversé par une « route flottante » qui amène piétons et cyclistes jusqu'au bâtiment. L'intérieur est unifié horizontalement et verticalement par un atrium ouvert, où un escalier sculptural en colimaçon relie physiquement et visuellement les 15 étages. Une grille recouverte de cuivre donne du relief à la façade et réduit l'échelle de la tour. Elle comporte un système de stores qui contrôlent l'afflux de la lumière du soleil. Ces mesures écoénergétiques font des laboratoires de la Maersk Tower des précurseurs en matière d'efficacité énergétique dans le pays.

Esta extensión de la Facultad de Medicina de la Universidad de Copenhague alberga áreas de investigación y un centro de conferencias. El edificio se plantea como un volumen en altura que aloja los laboratorios, situado sobre una base de vidrio transparente abierta al público que contiene las zonas comunes. Este enfoque libera espacio para el parque del campus, en el que un «camino flotante» acerca a peatones y ciclistas al edificio. El interior está unido de forma horizontal y vertical por un atrio abierto, donde una escultórica escalera de caracol conecta física y visualmente los quince pisos. Una retícula recubierta de cobre da relieve a la fachada, reduce la escala de la torre e integra un sistema de persianas que controla la entrada de luz solar. Sus medidas de ahorro de energía convierten a la Torre Maersk en los laboratorios de mayor eficiencia energética del país.

Site plan

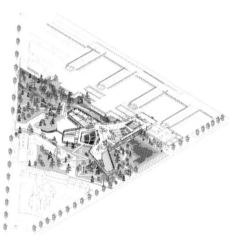

Isometric drawing base level

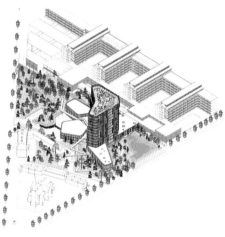

Isometric drawing tower level

00 level plan

01 level plan

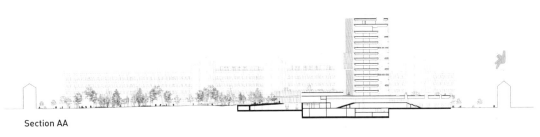

Section AA

Elevation AA

Elevation BB

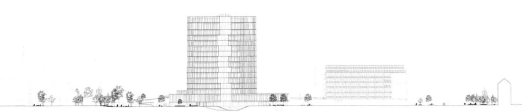

CONG SINH
ARCHITECTS

WWW.CONGSINH.COM

Cong Sinh Architects is a Vietnamese company founded in 2010 by project management architects, engineers, and professionals, directed by Vo Quang Thi, it specialises in planning, architecture, and interior design. It has offices in Hue and Ho Chi Minh City. Cong Sinh Architects offers its clients calm and tranquil spaces in which to live, work or relax. Its aim is to protect the physical and mental health of users through creative, modern, and special solutions. It promotes a vision of sustainability-based Vietnamese architecture. Its works emerge as a response to functional requirements, the project's search for the optimal use of natural light and wind and adaptation to the cultural and social environment. In 2017, the Vegetable Trellis project received an award at the World Architecture Festival Awards (WAF).

Cong Sinh Architects est une société vietnamienne fondée en 2010 par des architectes gestionnaires de projet, des ingénieurs, et des professionnels. Sous la direction de Vo Quang Thi, elle se spécialise dans la planification, l'architecture, et le design d'intérieur. Ses bureaux se trouvent à Hue et à Hô-Chi-Minh-Ville. Cong Sinh Architects propose à ses clients des espaces calmes et tranquilles pour vivre, travailler ou se détendre. Son but est de protéger la santé physique et mentale des usagers par le biais de solutions créatives, modernes, et singulières. Elle promeut une certaine vision de l'architecture vietnamienne basée sur les principes du développement durable. Son travail apparaît comme une réaction aux besoins fonctionnels, le projet recherchant l'utilisation optimale de la lumière et de l'air naturels et l'adaptation à un environnement culturel et social. En 2017, le projet Vegetable Trellis a obtenu un prix aux World Architecture Festival Awards (WAF).

Das vietnamesische Unternehmen Cong Sinh Architects wurde 2010 durch projektleitende Architekten, Ingenieure und Experten unter der Leitung von Vo Quang Thi gegründet und hat sich auf Planung, Architektur und Innendesign spezialisiert. Es verfügt über Niederlassungen in Hue und Ho Chi Minh City. Cong Sinh Architects bietet seinen Kunden ruhige und entspannte Räume zum Wohnen, Arbeiten oder Relaxen. Das Unternehmen möchte durch kreative, moderne und besondere Lösungen die physische und geistige Gesundheit der Kunden schützen. Seine Vision ist nachhaltige vietnamesische Architektur. Seine Arbeiten erfüllen die funktionalen Anforderungen und bei den Projekten wird stets versucht, natürliches Licht und Wind optimal zu nutzen und den Bau in die kulturelle und gesellschaftliche Umgebung einzubinden. 2017 wurde das Projekt Vegetable Trellis bei den World Architecture Festival Awards (WAF) ausgezeichnet.

Cong Sinh Architects es una empresa vietnamita fundada en 2010 por arquitectos, ingenieros y profesionales en la gestión de proyectos y dirigida por Vo Quang Thi, especializada en planeamiento, arquitectura e interiorismo y con oficinas en Hue y Ho Chi Minh City. Cong Sinh Architects ofrece a sus clientes espacios tranquilos y apacibles para vivir, trabajar o relajarse. Sus objetivos son la protección de la salud física y mental de los usuarios a través de soluciones creativas, modernas y especiales y la promoción de una visión de la arquitectura vietnamita basada en la sostenibilidad. Sus obras surgen como respuesta a los requerimientos funcionales, a la búsqueda del uso óptimo de la luz natural y del viento en el proyecto y a la adaptación al entorno cultural y social. En 2017, el proyecto *Vegetable Trellis* fue galardonado en el World Architecture Festival Awards (WAF).

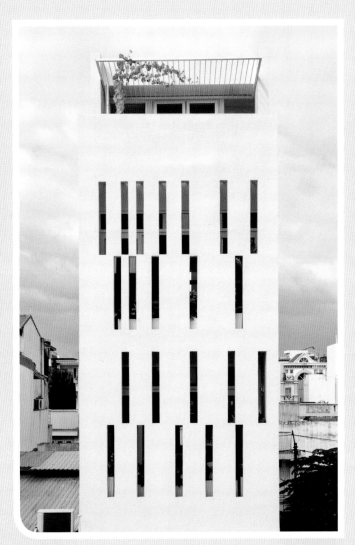

[THE GILLS]

[VEGETABLE TRELLIS]

THE GILLS

Vietnam's tropical climate determined the design of this dwelling, based on controlling sunlight and ventilation. The project proposes a system of perforated walls and aluminium metal grilles structuring the different inner spaces, allowing natural light to reach every corner of the house at the appropriate intensity for each season of the year and favouring cross-ventilation. Natural light penetrates the interior indirectly, filtered by components such as plaster plates located under the skylight, the vertical perforations of the façade and even the abundant vegetation over the building's cladding. The design of the external envelope solves the security problem generated by opening windows for ventilation at night and prevents heavy tropical rains from directly affecting the building.

Das tropische Klima Vietnams lieferte die Vorgaben für das Design dieses Hauses, das eine Möglichkeit zur Kontrolle von Belüftung und Sonnenlicht bieten sollte. Ein System aus Lochwänden und Aluminiummetallgittern bestimmt die Innenaufteilung des Gebäudes, sorgt für Querlüftung und lässt in jeder Jahreszeit genau die richtige Menge an natürlichem Licht in alle Winkel des Hauses dringen. Das natürliche Licht wird durch Gipsplatten unterhalb der Dachfenster, die Lochfassade und die Vielzahl an Pflanzen an der Gebäudeverkleidung gefiltert und gelangt dann auf indirekte Weise in das Gebäudeinnere. Die Gebäudehülle löst das Sicherheitsproblem nachts zum Lüften geöffneter Fenster und schützt das Gebäude vor tropischem Regen.

Le climat tropical du Vietnam a déterminé le design de cette habitation, basé sur la régulation de la lumière du soleil et de l'aération. Ce projet propose un système de murs perforés et de grilles d'aluminium structurant les différents espaces intérieurs, laissant la lumière naturelle éclairer chaque recoin de la maison avec l'intensité adaptée selon la saison et favorisant l'aération transversale. La lumière naturelle s'introduit indirectement à l'intérieur, filtrée par des composantes comme les plaques de plâtre situées sous la fenêtre de toit, les perforations verticales de la façade et même la végétation abondante tapissant le bardage du bâtiment. La conception de cette enveloppe extérieure résout le problème de sécurité généré par l'ouverture des fenêtres pour aérer la nuit et empêche les torrentielles pluies tropicales d'affecter directement le bâtiment.

El clima tropical de Vietnam condicionó el diseño de esta casa, basado el control de la luz solar y de la ventilación. El proyecto propone un sistema de muros perforados y enrejados metálicos de aluminio que estructura los diferentes espacios interiores, permite la entrada de luz natural a todos los rincones de la casa con una intensidad adecuada para cada estación del año y favorece la ventilación cruzada. La luz natural penetra de forma indirecta en el interior, tamizada por elementos tales como las placas de yeso situadas bajo la claraboya, las perforaciones verticales de la fachada e incluso la abundante vegetación integrada en la envolvente del edificio. El diseño de los cerramientos exteriores resuelve el problema de seguridad generado por la apertura de las ventanas para ventilar por la noche y evita la incidencia directa de las fuertes lluvias tropicales.

Roof plan

Fifth floor plan

Fourth floor plan

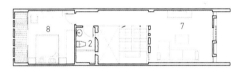

Third floor plan

Second floor plan

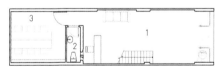

First floor plan

1. Lobby
2. Toilet
3. Office
4. Meeting room
5. Kitchen
6. Pond
7. Family room
8. Bedroom
9. Library room
10. Terrace
11. Bedroom for guest
12. Drying yard

20 MARCH - 23 SEPTEMBER

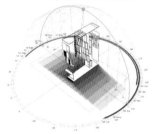

21 JUNE

21 DECEMBER

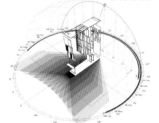

Solar diagram

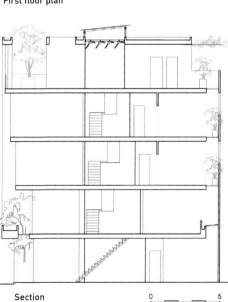

Section   0   5

VEGETABLE TRELLIS

Food problems generated by the effects of climate change in Vietnam led architects to investigate practical solutions to address them. This community space, built with eco-friendly materials, plays host to plantations of different kinds of vegetables that are consumed on-site and can be admired by visitors. A vegetable lattice covers the entire space, filtering air impurities and creating a fresh microclimate, an image with which the Vietnamese are very familiar. Good natural ventilation and the almost exclusive use of solar light means further energy savings. The pavement, consisting of numerous pieces of concrete, helps rainwater penetrate the ground and prevents flooding. The open design of the ground floor connects indoor and outdoor spaces and can be used flexibly and multi-functionally.

Architekten entwickelten praktische Lösungen für die durch den Klimawandel bedingten Nahrungsmittelprobleme in Vietnam. In diesem Gemeinschaftsobjekt aus umweltfreundlichem Material wird verschiedenes Gemüse angebaut, das vor Ort verwertet wird und von Besuchern bestaunt werden kann. Die gesamte Fläche ist mit einem Gemüsegitter abgedeckt, welches Unreinheiten aus der Luft filtert und für ein frisches Mikroklima sorgt; etwas, womit die Vietnamesen sehr vertraut sind. Weitere Energie wird durch die gute natürliche Belüftung und die fast ausschließliche Verwendung von Sonnenlicht eingespart. Der Gehweg aus vielen kleinen Betonteilen lässt das Regenwasser im Boden versickern und schützt so vor Überflutung. Das offene Design schafft eine Verbindung zwischen Innen- und Außenbereich und macht das Konzept flexibel und vielfältig einsetzbar.

Les problèmes d'approvisionnement en nourriture générés par les effets du changement climatique au Vietnam ont poussé les architectes à rechercher des solutions pratiques pour y répondre. Cet espace communautaire, construit avec des matériaux écologiques, héberge des plantations de différents légumes qui sont consommés sur site et peuvent être admirés par les visiteurs. Image très familière chez les vietnamiens, une treille végétale couvre l'intégralité de l'espace, filtrant les impuretés de l'air et créant un microclimat frais. Une bonne aération naturelle et l'usage quasi exclusif de la lumière du soleil entraînent des économies d'énergie supplémentaires. Le trottoir, composé de nombreux blocs de béton, permet à l'eau de pluie de pénétrer dans le sol et prévient les inondations. Le design ouvert du rez-de-chaussée relie les espaces intérieur et extérieur et peut être utilisé de façon modulable et multi-fonctionnelle.

Los problemas alimentarios generados en Vietnam por los efectos del cambio climático llevaron a los arquitectos a investigar soluciones prácticas para hacerles frente. Este espacio comunitario, construido con materiales ecológicos, alberga plantaciones de diferentes tipos de verduras que son consumidas *in situ* y pueden ser admiradas por los visitantes. Un enrejado vegetal cubre todo el espacio, filtra las impurezas del aire y crea un microclima fresco, componiendo una imagen familiar para los vietnamitas. Una buena ventilación natural y el uso casi exclusivo de luz solar fomentan el ahorro energético. El pavimento, formado por numerosas piezas de hormigón, facilita la penetración del agua de lluvia en el suelo y evita inundaciones. El diseño abierto de la planta baja conecta espacios interiores y exteriores, que pueden ser usados de forma flexible y multifuncional.

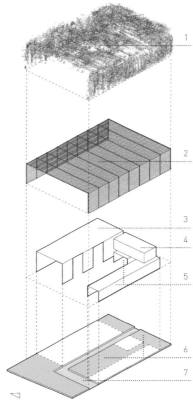

Axonometric exploded

1. Vegetable plants
2. Steel trellis
3. Car care area
4. Multifunctional room
5. Porch
6. Vegetable garden
7. Fish pond

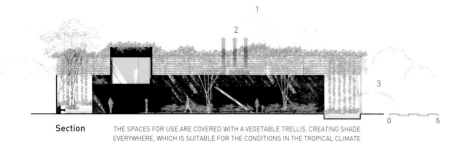

Section THE SPACES FOR USE ARE COVERED WITH A VEGETABLE TRELLIS, CREATING SHADE
EVERYWHERE, WHICH IS SUITABLE FOR THE CONDITIONS IN THE TROPICAL CLIMATE

0   5

1. Sun
2. Hot air
3. Cool air

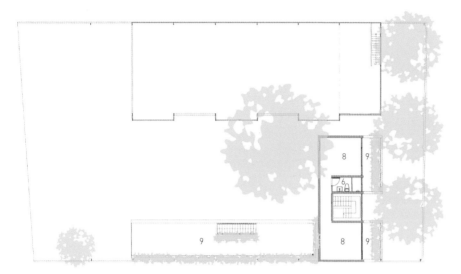

First floor plan

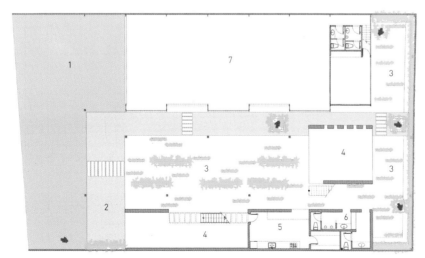

Ground floor plan

1. Front yard
2. Fish pond
3. Vegetable garden
4. Porch
5. Kitchen
6. Toilet
7. Car care area
8. Multifunctional room
9. Terrace
10. Vegetable plants

EDRA
ARQUITECTURA KM0

WWW.ARQUITECTURA.EDRACULTURAYNATURA.COM

EDRA Arquitectura km0 is an architectural studio based in the Aragonese Pyrenees. Part of the EDRA *cultura y natura* project, developing creative sustainability from architecture and agriculture. EDRA are artisans designing vernacular architecture for the 21st century, efficient, healthy, and committed to their natural and social environment. Its work is based on environmental sustainability, respect for tradition and research and experimentation which must always precede action.

Its founder, Àngels Castellarnau Visús, has a degree in architecture from the Universidad Politécnica de Cataluña (UPC), specialising in sustainable building, low environmental impact architecture and building with earth. He also has a PhD from the UPC in Natural Energy in Architecture. His Tapia house located in Ayerbe has been recognised with the Terra Award 2016, the International Prize for Contemporary Earthen Architecture, and the Castilla y León 2015-2016 Prize for Sustainable Construction.

EDRA Arquitectura km0 est un cabinet d'architecture basé dans les Pyrénéens aragonaises. Associé au projet de EDRA *cultura y natura*, il développe la durabilité créative de l'architecture et de l'agriculture. EDRA regroupe des artisans qui conçoivent une architecture vernaculaire pour le 21e siècle, efficaces, sains, et engagés envers leur environnement naturel et social. Son travail réside dans la durabilité de l'environnement, le respect de la tradition et la recherche et l'expérimentation qui doivent toujours précéder l'action.

Son fondateur, Àngels Castellarnau Visús, est diplômé de l'Université Polytechnique de Catalogne (UPC), spécialisé dans l'habitat durable, l'architecture à faible impact environnemental et la construction en terre. Il est également titulaire d'un doctorat de l'UPC en Énergie naturelle dans l'architecture. Sa maison Tapia située à Ayerbe a été reconnue par le Terra Award 2016, prix international de l'architecture contemporaine en terre crue, et le prix Castilla y León pour la construction durable 2015-2016.

EDRA Arquitectura km0 ist ein Architekturstudio in den Pyrenäen von Aragon. Im Rahmen des Projekts EDRA *cultura y natura* entwickelt es nachhaltige Konzepte für Architektur und Landwirtschaft. Die Architekten von EDRA sind Künstler, die effiziente und gesunde Architektur für das 21. Jahrhundert im Einklang mit ihrer gesellschaftlichen und natürlichen Umgebung erschaffen. Im Mittelpunkt ihrer Arbeit stehen ökologische Nachhaltigkeit, Respekt gegenüber Tradition sowie Forschung und Experimenten, denen stets auch Handlungen folgen.

Gründer Àngels Castellarnau Visús verfügt über einen Abschluss in Architektur der Universidad Politécnica de Cataluña (UPC) mit dem Schwerpunkt nachhaltiges Bauen, Architektur mit geringen Umweltauswirkungen und Bauen mit Erde. Zudem verfügt er auf dem Gebiet der natürlichen Energie in der Architektur über einen Doktortitel der UPC. Sein Tapia-Haus in Ayerbe erhielt den Terra Award 2016, den International Prize for Contemporary Earthen Architecture und den Castilla y León 2015-2016 Prize for Sustainable Construction.

EDRA Arquitectura km0 es un estudio de arquitectura ubicado en el Prepirineo Aragonés. Forma parte del proyecto EDRA cultura y natura, que desarrolla sostenibilidad creativa desde la arquitectura y la agricultura. En EDRA son artesanos y diseñan arquitectura vernácula del siglo XXI, eficiente, saludable y comprometida con su medio natural y social. Su trabajo se basa en la sostenibilidad ambiental, el respeto a la tradición, la investigación y la experimentación que siempre preceden a la acción.

Su fundadora, Àngels Castellarnau Visús, es arquitecta por la UPC, especializada en bioconstrucción, arquitectura de bajo impacto ambiental y construcción con tierra, Phd por la UPC en Energía natural en la Arquitectura. Su casa de Tapia situada en Ayerbe ha sido reconocida con el Terra Award 2016, Premio Internacional de Arquitectura Contemporánea en Tierra Cruda y el Premio de Construcción Sostenible de Castilla y León 2015-2016.

[GISTAÍN]

[CASA TIERRA]

GISTAÍN

One day we dreamed that the forests of the Pyrenees valleys would be managed. That its people could continue to live off local timber and livestock. That the wood was cut in accordance with the phases of the moon to ensure its long life without further treatment. That it would be dried, transformed, and processed for use in buildings in the valleys and the nearby plain. Perhaps it would not be transported by river... That wool would be shorn from sheep, and once cleaned and treated, would be used to isolate any buildings without having to resort petroleum-based products. In Gistaín, in the Valley of Chistau, where Pyrenean wood is managed, handled, prefabricated, and assembled by families in the area, it becomes energy efficient thanks to passive solar architecture. South facing and local material for the win!... and stone, wood, wool... Pure "low-tech mountain architecture" pure "EDRA cultura y natura!".

Einst träumten wir von der Nutzung der Wälder in den Tälern der Pyrenäen. Die Menschen sollten von deren Hölzern und heimischem Vieh leben. Bäume sollten im Einklang mit den Mondphasen zurückgeschnitten werden, um somit die Langlebigkeit des Waldes ohne äußere Unterstützung zu garantieren. Man würde seine Materialien trocknen, verarbeiten und für die Gebäude der Täler und der naheliegenden Ebene verwenden. Vielleicht müsste man sie nicht einmal verschiffen... Schafe würden geschoren und ihre Wolle nach der Reinigung und Verarbeitung zur Isolierung von Gebäuden ohne petroleum-haltige Produkte verwendet. In Gistaín im Tal von Chistau ist dieser Traum wahr geworden. Die Wälder der Pyrenäen werden gepflegt und das Holz verarbeitet, vorgefertigt und von den Familien der Gegend für ihre Häuser verwendet. Zudem sorgt passive Solararchitektur für Energieeffizienz. Nach Süden ausgerichtete Fassaden und lokale Materialien wie Stein, Holz und Wolle sorgen für Einsparungen und Gewinn. Reine "low-tech-Bergarchitektur" - reines "EDRA cultura y natura!".

Un jour nous avons rêvé que les forêts des vallées pyrénéennes seraient gérées. Que ses habitants pourraient continuer à vivre de l'exploitation du bois local et du bétail. Que le bois serait coupé en fonction des phases de la lune pour garantir sa longue vie sans autres traitements. Qu'il serait séché, transformé, et traité pour être utilisé dans des constructions dans les vallées et la plaine avoisinante. Peut-être qu'il ne serait pas transporté par la rivière... Cette laine serait le fruit de la tonte de moutons, et une fois nettoyée et traitée, serait utilisée pour isoler tous les bâtiments sans avoir à utiliser des produits dérivés de pétrole. A Gistaín, dans la vallée de Chistau, où le bois des Pyrénées est géré, manipulé, préfabriqué et assemblé par des familles de la région, celui-ci a un haut rendement énergétique grâce à l'architecture solaire passive. Exposition au Sud et matériaux locaux sont la clé du succès ! Ainsi que la pierre, le bois, la laine... Une pure « architecture montagnarde low-tech », purement « EDRA cultura y natura! ».

Un día soñamos que los valles del Pirineo tenían sus bosques gestionados. Que sus gentes podían seguir viviendo de la madera local y del ganado. Que la madera se cortaba con la luna para asegurar su larga vida sin tratamientos ulteriores. Que ésta se secaba, transformaba y mecanizaba para poder usarla en las edificaciones de los valles y del llano cercanos. Tal vez ya no se transportaba por los ríos... Que de sus ovejas se cosechaba lana, que limpia y tratada servía para aislar los edificios sin utilizar productos derivados del petróleo. En Gistaín, en el valle de Chistau, con madera del Pirineo gestionada, manipulada, prefabricada y montada por familias de la zona, energéticamente eficiente gracias a su arquitectura solar pasiva, ¡southface y material local a tope! ...y piedra, madera, lana de oveja.... Pura «arquitectura lowtech de montaña», ¡pura «EDRA cultura y natura»!

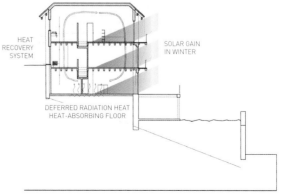

HEAT RECOVERY SYSTEM

SOLAR GAIN IN WINTER

DEFERRED RADIATION HEAT
HEAT-ABSORBING FLOOR

Bioclimatic section

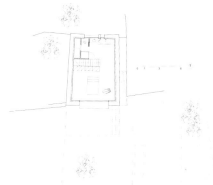

Second floor plan

First floor plan

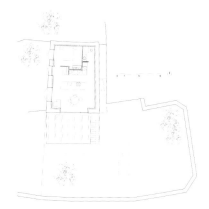

Ground floor plan

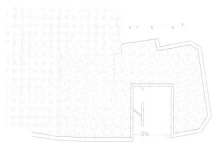

Garage plan

CASA TIERRA

In a rural context devalued by depopulation and the loss of the traditional use of land and building, the concept behind this dwelling is based on local vernacular architecture combined with energy-saving solar and bioclimatic design. Earth was used as a building material, for its low environmental impact and for being part of the local identity, using the "tapia calicostrada" technique, which consists of constructing loadbearing walls using local unprocessed earth, with an inner crust and a lime mortar exterior. The thermal inertia of the earth allows the passive solar energy captured during the day through the large perforations, skylights, and the walls of the southern façade to be accrued and expended throughout the night. A selection of sustainable materials reduced its environmental impact by 60%.

Dieses Haus befindet sich in einem ländlichen Gebiet, in dem die Bevölkerung stetig abnimmt und traditionelle Landnutzung und Bauweisen in Vergessenheit geraten. Es kombiniert den Architekturstil des Ortes mit energiesparender Solartechnik und bioklimatischen Konzepten. Erde wurde aufgrund ihrer geringen Auswirkungen auf die Umwelt und ihres lokalen Vorkommens als Baumaterial verwendet. Mit der Bautechnik „Tapia Calocostrada" wurden starke Mauern aus vor Ort vorhandener Erde mit Innenkruste errichtet und außen mit Kalkmörtel verkleidet. Mit Hilfe der thermischen Trägheit der Erde wird die tagsüber durch die großen Perforierungen, Dachfenster und die Wände der Südfassade eindringende passive Sonnenenergie für die Abend- und Nachtstunden gespeichert. Nachhaltige Baumaterialien konnten den Umwelteinfluss um 60 % verringern.

Dans un contexte rural dévalorisé par le dépeuplement et la perte de l'usage traditionnel de la terre et de la construction, le concept qui sous-tend ce bâtiment est basé sur l'architecture locale vernaculaire mêlée à un design incorporant énergie solaire et bio-climat. La terre a été utilisée comme matériau de construction, pour son faible impact environnemental et sa place dans l'identité locale, en utilisant la technique dite de la « *tapia calicostrada* » ou pisé, qui consiste à construire des murs porteurs en utilisant de la terre brute, avec un corps compacté et une finition de chaux extérieure. L'inertie thermique de la terre permet à l'énergie solaire passive captée au cours de la journée par le biais de larges perforations, de fenêtres de toit et des murs de la façade sud d'être emmagasinée et restituée dans la nuit. Grâce à une sélection de matériaux durables, son impact environnemental a été réduit de 60 %.

En un contexto rural desvalorizado por la despoblación y la pérdida del uso tradicional del suelo y la edificación, el concepto de esta vivienda se basa en la arquitectura vernácula local combinada con un diseño solar pasivo y bioclimático. Se utilizó la tierra como material de construcción, por su bajo impacto ambiental y por formar parte de la identidad local, mediante la técnica de la «tapia calicostrada», que consiste en la construcción de muros de carga a base de tierra Km0 no manufacturada, con costra interior y exterior de mortero de cal. La gran inercia térmica de los elementos masivos de tierra permite acumular de día la energía solar pasiva captada a través de los grandes huecos, los lucernarios y los muros de la fachada sur y cederla a lo largo de la noche. Una selección de materiales sostenibles permite la reducción de más de un 60% del impacto ambiental.

North elevation

West elevation

South elevation

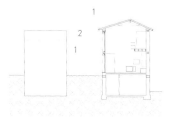

Sections

1. Summer solstice (72º)
2. Winter solstice (27 º)

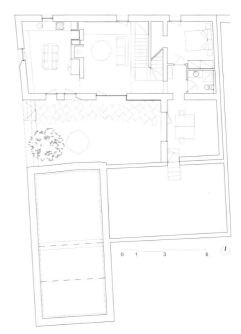

First floor plan

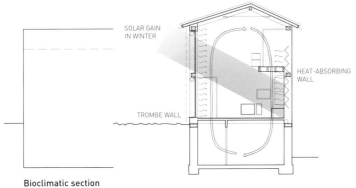

Bioclimatic section

SOLAR GAIN
IN WINTER

HEAT-ABSORBING
WALL

TROMBE WALL

Ground floor plan

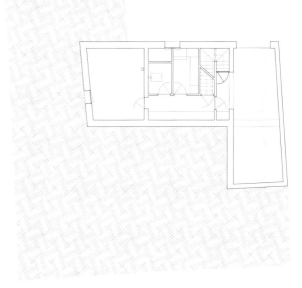

Basement plan

ES ARQUITETURA

WWW.ESARQUITETURA.COM.BR

ES Arquitetura's multidisciplinary team, with offices in Brazil and the US, is focused on obtaining solutions that are more appropriate to the profile and needs of its clients, bringing intelligent solutions, focusing on technologies and materials that do not the environment. With residential, commercial, industrial and corporate projects, as well as interior architecture and furniture design, ES Arquitetura values sustainability from the launch to the detailing of each work, choosing raw materials, products and techniques with lower environmental impact, lower costs of work and maintenance.
Casa 01 project has received several awards: Saint Gobain Sustainability Award, Residential Modality, 2017, Winner; Re-Thinking the Future Awards 2017, Category Residence Built, Second Prize; selected to the ArchDaily's International Building of the Year'18 Awards.

Sous la direction permanente de l'architecte Diego Espirito Santo, avec des bureaux au Brésil et aux USA, l'équipe multidisciplinaire d'ES Arquitetura s'emploie à trouver des solutions plus adaptées au profil et aux besoins de ses clients, apportant des solutions intelligentes en ciblant des technologies et des matériaux qui ne nuisent pas à l'environnement. Avec des projets résidentiels, commerciaux, industriels et d'entreprise, ainsi que de la décoration intérieure et du design de mobilier, ES Architecture valorise la durabilité depuis le lancement jusqu'aux finitions de chaque travail, choisissant des matériaux, des techniques et des produits bruts, à l'impact environnemental plus faible, aux coûts de mise en œuvre et d'entretien moindres.
Le projet Casa 01 a été récompensé plusieurs fois : Gagnant du prix de la durabilité Saint-Gobain, Modalité résidentielle, 2017 ; seconde place pour le Prix « Re-thinking the Future », catégorie résidence construite ; sélectionné pour le prix de la construction internationale de l'année 2018 d'ArchDaily.

ES Arquitetura befindet sich von Beginn an unter der Leitung des Architekten Diego Espiritu Santo und verfügt über Niederlassungen in Brasilien und den USA. Das Team beeindruckt mit Erfahrung in vielen unterschiedlichen Bereichen und orientiert sich dabei besonders an auf Profil und Bedürfnisse der Kunden abgestimmten Lösungen. Die intelligenten Konzepte basieren dabei auf umweltfreundlichen Technologien und Materialien. Zu den Projekten von ES Architecture gehören Wohn-, Geschäfts-, Industrie- und Unternehmenskonzepte sowie Innenarchitektur und Möbeldesign. Hierbei wird schon beim Beginn und der detailgenauen Planung auf Nachhaltigkeit geachtet, was sich in Rohstoffen, Produkten und Techniken mit geringem Umwelteinfluss, geringeren Arbeits- und Instandhaltungskosten wiederspiegelt.
Das Projekt Casa 01 erhielt mehrere Auszeichnungen: Saint Gobain Sustainability Award, Wohngebäude, 2017, Gewinner; Re-Thinking the Future Awards 2017, Kategorie Wohngebäude, zweiter Platz; ausgewählt für ArchDaily's International Building of the Year'18 Awards.

ES Arquitetura, con oficinas en Brasil y Estados Unidos, está formado por un equipo multidisciplinar bajo la dirección permanente del arquitecto Diego Espirito Santo. Su principal objetivo es encontrar las soluciones arquitectónicas más adecuadas al perfil y las necesidades de sus clientes, buscando soluciones inteligentes y usando tecnologías y materiales que no dañan el medio ambiente. Con proyectos residenciales, industriales, comerciales y corporativos así como interiorismo y diseño de mobiliario, ES Architecture valora la sostenibilidad desde el lanzamiento hasta los detalles finales de cada trabajo, eligiendo materias primas, productos y técnicas con bajo impacto ambiental, menores costes de trabajo y mantenimiento.
Casa 01 ha recibido numerosos premios: Premio a la sostenibilidad Saint Gobain 2017, Modalidad residencial, ganador; Premio Re-Thinking the Future 2017, Categoría construcción residencial, segundo premio; seleccionado para los premios International Building of the Year de 2018 otorgados por ArchDaily.

[CASA 01]

CASA 01

The concept of sustainability in its widest sense was applied in the project for this dwelling. From the design to the location in the surroundings, its construction, finishes, use and even its landscaping, everything was conceived according to Cradle to Cradle principles. The sustainable concepts used include universal accessibility for all rooms, the choice and use of materials and the complete preservation of any existing wildlife. The project provides for measures such as the use of titanium dioxide concrete (a material that tackles pollution), technologies to generate energy, the reuse of wastewater, collecting rain water or the efficient control of ventilation and natural light. Materials like bamboo, recycled wood skirting boards, wood from reforestation, leather, linen, or cotton are used for the interior finishes.

Bei diesem Wohnhaus wurde das Konzept der Nachhaltigkeit im strengsten Sinne angewandt. Planung, Standortwahl, Oberflächengestaltung, Nutzung und selbst Landschaftsbau erfolgten nach dem „Cradle-to-Cradle-Prinzip". Zu den Nachhaltigkeitskonzepten gehören die universelle Zugänglichkeit zu allen Räumen, die Wahl und Verwendung der Materialien und der komplette Erhalt der vorherrschenden Flora und Fauna. Einen weiteren Beitrag leisten Materialien wie Titanoxidbeton (der nicht verschmutzt), Techniken zur Energiegewinnung, die Abwasserwiederverwertung, das Auffangen von Regenwasser oder die effiziente Steuerung der Belüftung und des Einfalls natürlichen Lichts. Im Inneren finden sich Materialien wie Bambus, recycelte Holzkehrleisten, Holz aus der Aufforstung, Leder, Leinen oder Baumwolle.

Le concept de la durabilité au sens le plus large du terme a été appliqué dans ce projet d'habitation. De la conception à l'emplacement sur le site, sa construction, ses finitions, et même l'architecture du paysage, tout a été conçu selon le principe du « berceau au berceau ». Les concepts durables utilisés comprennent l'accessibilité universelle à toutes les pièces, le choix et l'usage des matériaux et la conservation intégrale de toute faune existante. Ce projet prévoit des dispositions telles que l'usage de béton au dioxyde de titane (un matériau qui combat la pollution), des technologies qui génèrent de l'énergie, la réutilisation de l'eau de pluie, la récupération d'eau de pluie ou la régulation efficace de l'aération et de la lumière naturelles. Les matériaux tels que du bambou, des plinthes de bois recyclées, du bois de reforestation, du cuir, du lin, ou du coton sont utilisés pour les finitions intérieures.

El concepto de sostenibilidad en su sentido más amplio fue aplicado en el proyecto de esta casa. Desde el diseño hasta la ubicación en el lugar, la construcción, los acabados, el uso e incluso el paisajismo, todo fue concebido según los principios del «cradle to cradle». Las premisas sostenibles utilizadas incluyen la accesibilidad universal en todas las estancias, la elección y uso de los materiales y la preservación total de la naturaleza existente. El proyecto prevé medidas como el uso de hormigón con dióxido de titanio (material que combate la contaminación), tecnologías para generar energía, reutilización de aguas residuales, recogida de agua de lluvia o el control eficiente de la ventilación y la luz natural. Los acabados interiores utilizan materiales como el bambú, zócalos de material reciclado, madera procedente de reforestación, cuero, lino o algodón.

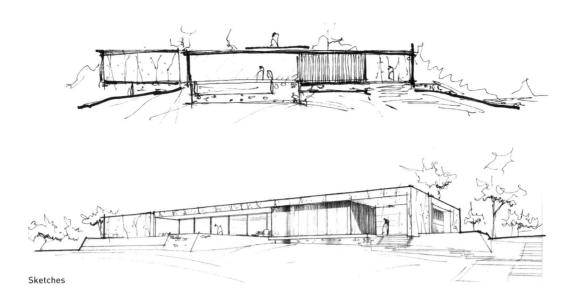

Sketches

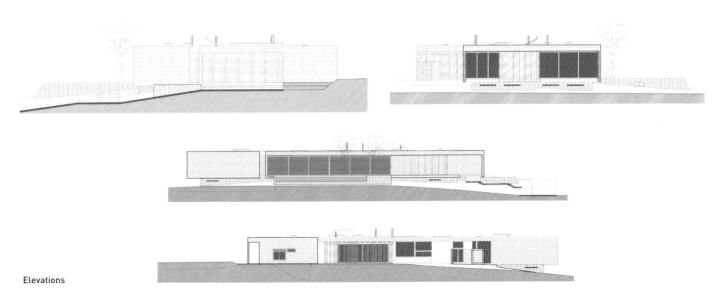

Elevations

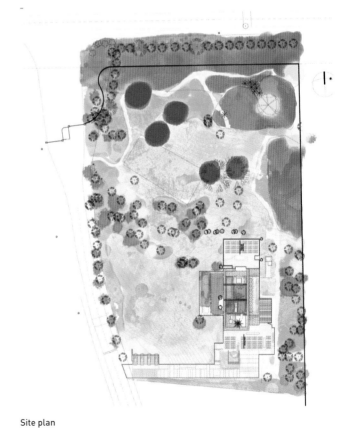

Site plan

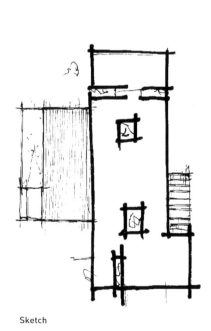

Sketch

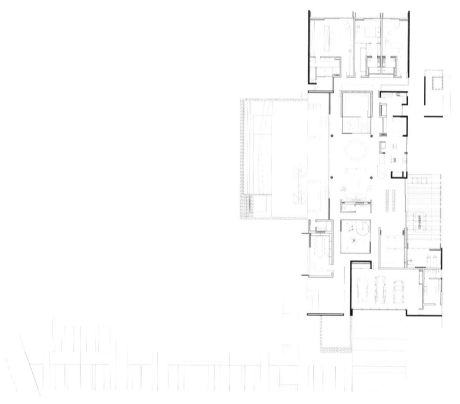

Floor plan

H&P ARCHITECTS

WWW.HPA.VN

H&P Architects was founded by Doan Thanh Ha and Tran Ngoc Phuong, architects who graduated from Hanoi University in 2002. Doan Thanh Ha has worked on social issues within H&P by encouraging the implementation of projects for disadvantaged communities in Vietnam. H&P's social projects aim to create spaces (what Ha calls "necessary spaces") that meet and adapt to the most basic needs of the poor and the disadvantaged. This "necessary space" has been constructed using "necessary materials" (those that are cheap, locally available or recycled), with "appropriate building technology" for specific contexts (traditional craftsmanship combined with modern technology) and with the users taking part in the building work. This approach aims to raise awareness, inspire, and motivate responsible, respectful, and necessary actions from users towards culture, community, and climate.

H&P Architects a été fondé par Doan Thanh Ha et Tran Ngoc Phuong, architectes diplômés de l'Université de Hanoï en 2002. Doan Thanh Ha a travaillé sur les questions sociales au sein de H&P en encourageant la mise en œuvre de projets pour les communautés défavorisées du Vietnam. Les projets sociaux de H&P visent à créer des espaces (ce que Ha appelle des « espaces nécessaires ») qui répondent aux besoins les plus basiques des pauvres et des défavorisés et s'y adaptent. Cet « espace nécessaire » a été construit en utilisant les « matériaux nécessaires » (ceux qui sont bon marché, disponibles localement ou recyclés), avec une « technologie de construction adaptée » à des contextes spécifiques (l'artisanat traditionnel allié à la technologie moderne) et la participation des usagers à la construction. Cette approche vise à sensibiliser, inspirer, et motiver des actions responsables, respectueuses et nécessaires chez les usagers à l'égard de la culture, de la communauté, et du climat.

H&P Architects wurde von den Architekten Doan Thanh Ha und Tran Ngoc Phuong gegründet, die beide 2002 an der Universität Hanoi ihr Studium abschlossen. Doan Thanh Ha leistet mit H&P durch seine Projekte für benachteiligte Gemeinden in Vietnam einen sozialen Beitrag.
Die Sozialprojekte von H&P schaffen Wohnraum (den Ha als „benötigtem Wohnraum" bezeichnet), der speziell an die Grundbedürfnisse der Armen und Bedürftigen angepasst ist. Dieser „benötigte Wohnraum" entsteht durch eine für den jeweiligen Kontext „geeignete Bautechnik" (traditionelles Handwerk kombiniert mit moderner Technologie) aus „benötigtem Material" (billig, vor Ort verfügbar oder recycelt), wobei die Kunden in den Bau miteingebunden werden. Dieses Projekt möchte ein Bewusstsein für einen verantwortungsbewussten und respektvollen Umgang mit Kultur, Gesellschaft und Klima schaffen und Kunden zu den notwendigen Handlungen inspirieren und motivieren.

H&P Architects fue fundada por Doan Thanh Ha y Tran Ngoc Phuong, graduados en Arquitectura por la Universidad Hanoi en 2002. Doan Thanh Ha ha trabajado en aspectos sociales dentro de H&P fomentando la implementación de proyectos en comunidades desfavorecidas en Vietnam. Los proyectos sociales de H&P tienen como objetivo crear espacios (llamados «espacios necesarios» por Ha) que satisfagan y se adapten a las necesidades más fundamentales de los pobres y de los desfavorecidos. El «espacio necesario» está hecho de «materiales necesarios» (baratos, disponibles a nivel local o reciclados), con «tecnología constructiva apropiada» para contextos específicos (artesanía tradicional combinada con tecnología moderna) y con la participación de los usuarios en la construcción. Este enfoque pretende generar conciencia, inspirar y motivar acciones responsables, necesarias y respetuosas de los usuarios hacia la cultura, la comunidad y el clima.

[TERRACES HOME]

[BES PAVILION]

[BB HOME]

TERRACES HOME

As part of a program developing *Agritectura* projects, Terraces Home combines architecture and agriculture as a basis for sustainable development. The idea combines two distinctive features of the Vietnamese countryside: the dwelling and the terraced paddy fields, to create a home that blurs boundaries, inside and out, above, and below, shared, and private. The dwelling's sloped roof consists of planted concrete trays, located at different heights, and provided with irrigation systems. Between those trays, a series of large openings generate different visual angles, providing light and shadow to the inhabited spaces. The project aims to promote the expansion of agricultural lots in urban areas to bring nature closer to city dwellers, providing them with the experience of planting, caring for and sharing their own garden products.

Terraces Home ist Teil des Programms *Agritectura*, das für seine nachhaltige Entwicklung Architektur und Landwirtschaft kombiniert. Das Konzept vereint zwei unterschiedliche Aspekte der vietnamesischen Landschaft. Die Wohnung und die terrassenförmigen Reisfelder schaffen ein Zuhause, das die Grenzen zwischen innen und außen, oben und unten, gemeinschaftlich und privat verschwimmen lässt. Das geneigte Wohnungsdach besteht aus bepflanzten Betonkästen in unterschiedlicher Höhe mit Bewässerungssystemen. Zwischen den Kästen befinden sich mehrere große Öffnungen, die unterschiedliche Blickwinkel erzeugen und für Licht und Schatten in den bewohnten Bereichen sorgen. Das Projekt wirbt für mehr Anbauflächen in städtischen Gebieten, um den Stadtbewohnern die Natur durch das Anpflanzen, Versorgen und Teilen ihrer eigenen Gartenerzeugnisse näherzubringen.

Dans le cadre d'un programme de développement de projets *Agritectura*, Terraces Home mêle architecture et agriculture pour servir de base au développement durable. Cette idée conjugue deux éléments distinctifs de la campagne vietnamienne : l'habitation et les rizières en terrasses, pour créer un lieu qui gomme les frontières entre l'intérieur et l'extérieur, le dessus et le dessous, le partagé et le privé. Le toit pentu de cette habitation est composé de plateaux de béton, disposés à différentes hauteurs, munis de systèmes d'irrigation. Entre ces plateaux, une série de grandes ouvertures génère différents angles de vue, apportant lumière et ombre aux espaces habités. Ce projet vise à promouvoir l'expansion de parcelles agricoles dans des zones urbaines pour rapprocher la nature des citadins, leur procurant l'occasion de planter des produits dans leur propre jardin, d'en prendre soin et de les partager.

Como parte de un programa de proyectos de desarrollo de *Agritectura*, Terraces Home adopta la combinación de Arquitectura y Agricultura como base para un desarrollo sostenible. La idea combina los dos elementos distintivos de las áreas rurales de Vietnam: la casa y el campo de arroz en terrazas, para crear un hogar con límites borrosos, dentro y fuera, encima y debajo, común y privado. La cubierta en pendiente de la casa se compone de bandejas de hormigón con cultivos, situadas a diferentes alturas y dotadas de sistemas de riego. Entre estas bandejas, una serie de amplias aberturas genera diversos ángulos de visión, luz y sombra a los espacios habitados. El proyecto aspira a promover la expansión de las parcelas agrícolas en las áreas urbanas para acercar la naturaleza a sus habitantes, al brindarles la experiencia de plantar, cuidar y compartir sus propios productos.

HOUSE
(ARCHITECTURE)

TERRACES
(AGRICULTURE)

TERRACES HOME
(AGRITECTURE)

Design concept diagram

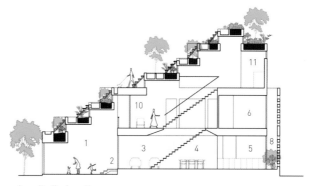

Longitudinal section

Cross section

Elevation

1. Playground
2. Entrance
3. Living room
4. Dining room
5. Kitchen
6. Bedroom
7. Toilet
8. Terrace
9. Multifunction space
10. Workship
11. Study
12. Washing
13. Terraces

Sustainability diagrams

1. Use rainwater for watering vegetation
2. Noise, dust, hot, rainy are minimized when passing vegetation skin
3. Rainwater tank

Roof plan

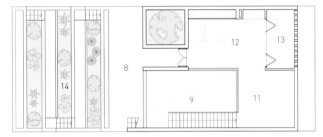

Third floor plan

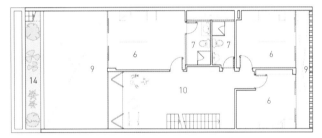

Second floor plan

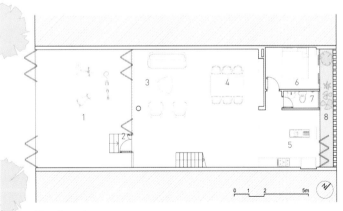

First floor plan

1. Playground /
   garage
2. Entrance
3. Living room
4. Dining room
5. Kitchen
6. Bedroom
7. Toilet
8. Terrace
9. Void
10. Multifunction
    space
11. Workship
12. Study
13. Washing
14. Terraces

BES PAVILION

This communal space focusing on art and culture has been built using local materials and traditional construction methods (BES = Bamboo + Earth
+ Stone). The outcome is comprised of several separate areas, loosely
organised around a central courtyard to produce several viewpoints and
allow light and shadow to interact. This layout helps dilute the boundary
between inner and outer space. The building's users have the opportunity
to learn about its functions and effects regarding nature and the local community. Taking part in the construction process to create their own space,
and learning about ventilation, lighting, or gardening solutions, will help
condition users' future behaviour, and assist the attempt to obtain a far
greener habitable environment.

Dieser monumentale Ort voller Kunst und Kultur wurde mit lokalen Materialien in traditioneller Bauweise errichtet (BES = Bambus + Erde + Stein).
Das Ergebnis sind mehrere um einen zentralen Hof angeordnete Einzel-
elemente. Dies schafft mehrere Aussichtspunkte und sorgt für ein Spiel
aus Licht und Schatten. Dieser Aufbau lässt die Grenzen zwischen innen
und außen verschmelzen. Die Gebäudebenutzer können etwas über seine Funktion und seine Auswirkungen auf die Natur vor Ort lernen. Ihre
Einbindung in Bauprozesse zur Schaffung ihres eigenen Wohnraums und
Wissen über Belüftung, Beleuchtung und Gartenlösungen werden das zukünftige Verhalten der Menschen beeinflussen und so zu einem grüneren
bewohnbaren Planeten beitragen.

Cet espace collectif dédié à l'art et à la culture a été construit en utilisant
des matériaux locaux et des méthodes de construction traditionnelles (BTP
= bambou + terre + pierre). Le résultat est composé de plusieurs zones
séparées, organisées de façon informelle autour d'une cour centrale pour
produire plusieurs points de vue et permettre des jeux d'ombre et de lumière. Cette disposition contribue à diluer les frontières entre les espaces
intérieur et extérieur. L'opportunité est offerte aux usagers de ce bâtiment
de découvrir ses fonctions et effets en rapport avec la nature et la communauté locale. Prendre part au processus de construction pour créer leur
propre espace, et découvrir des solutions de ventilation, d'éclairage, ou de
jardinage contribuera à conditionner le futur comportement des usagers,
et à accompagner la création potentielle d'un environnement habitable
bien plus écologique.

Este espacio comunitario centrado en el arte y la cultura se configura a
partir de materiales locales y métodos de construcción tradicionales
(BES = Bamboo + Earth + Stone). El conjunto se compone de varios espacios separados, organizados libremente entorno a un patio central con el
fin de generar numerosos puntos de vista y la interacción entre luz y sombra. Esta disposición contribuye a diluir el límite entre espacio interior y
exterior. Los usuarios del edificio tienen la oportunidad de aprender acerca de las funciones y efectos del edificio hacia la naturaleza y la comunidad
local. Participar en el proceso constructivo para crear su propio espacio
y aprender de las soluciones de ventilación, iluminación o de jardinería
utilizadas en él ayudará a dirigir el comportamiento de los usuarios en el
futuro, para intentar conseguir un entorno habitable mucho más verde.

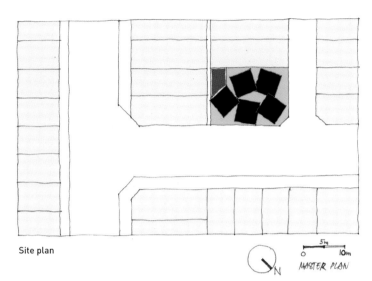

Site plan

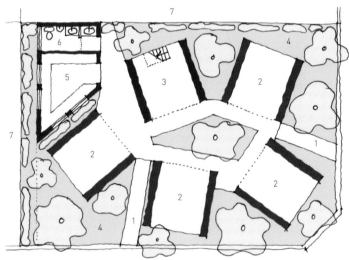

Ground floor plan

1. Entrance
2. Community space
3. Community space
   (2 levels)
4. Garden
5. Service / kitchen
6. Restroom
7. Existing building

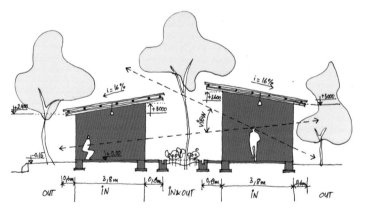

Section

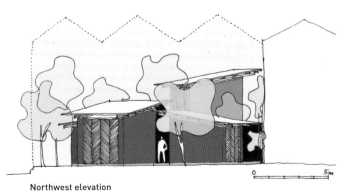

Northwest elevation

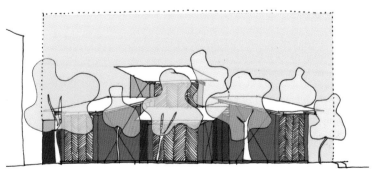

Northeast elevation

BLOOMING BAMBOO HOME

In Vietnam, diverse and severe natural phenomena claim numerous lives every year causing material damage and halting the development of the affected areas. The BB House is intended to be a response to these phenomena through a strong, monolithic architecture based on the use of assembled bamboo modules 8 - 10 cm and 4 - 5 cm in diameter and 3.3 or 6.6 m long, through a sustainable design contributing to ecological development. The result is a space that can be adapted to different applications, which can be extended if necessary and protects its users from the most adverse conditions. The finish of the cladding can be modified depending on the climate and materials in each area, thus creating a vernacular architecture. The dwelling can be built by the users themselves in just 25 days, it is reasonably priced and can be manufactured in bulk.

In Vietnam fordern verschiedene schwere Naturkatastrophen Jahr für Jahr viele Menschenleben, verursachen Sachschäden und beeinträchtigen die Entwicklung der betroffenen Gebiete. Mit seiner starken monolithischen Architektur aus zusammengesetzten Bambusmodulen mit einem Durchmesser von 8 – 10 cm und 4 – 5 cm und einer Länge von 3,3 oder 6,6 m bietet das BB House eine Lösung für dieses Problem und trägt mit seinem ökologischen Design gleichzeitig zu einer nachhaltigen Entwicklung bei. Der Raum kann an verschiedene und bei Bedarf erweiterbare Zwecke angepasst werden und schützt seine Nutzer vor schädlichen Einflüssen. Die Verkleidung kann an Klima und Materialvorkommen im jeweiligen Gebiet angepasst werden und sorgt so für eine funktionale Architektur. Die Wohnstätte kann von den Kunden in nur 25 Tagen selbst aufgebaut werden, ist preiswert und kann in großen Mengen produziert werden.

Au Vietnam, des phénomènes naturels divers et violents font de nombreuses victimes chaque année, provoquant des dommages matériels et stoppant le développement des zones affectées. La BB House est conçue comme une réponse à ces phénomènes par le biais d'une architecture forte, monolithique, basée sur l'assemblage de modules de bambou de 8 à 10 cm et de 4 à 5 cm de diamètre et de 3,3 ou 6, 6 mètres de long, dans un design durable contribuant au développement écologique. Il en résulte un espace qui peut être adapté à différentes applications, qui peut être agrandi si nécessaire et protège ses usagers des conditions les plus défavorables. La finition du bardage peut être modifiée selon le climat et les matériaux de chaque région, créant ainsi une architecture vernaculaire. Cette habitation peut être construite par les usagers eux-mêmes en à peine 25 jours, elle est à un prix abordable et peut être produite en quantités.

En Vietnam, los diversos y severos fenómenos naturales causan cada año numerosas víctimas y daños materiales y frenan el desarrollo de las áreas afectadas. La casa BB pretende ser una solución frente a estos fenómenos a través de una arquitectura monolítica y fuerte, basada en el uso de módulos ensamblados de bambú de 8-10 cm y 4-5 cm de diámetro y 3,3 o 6,6 m de largo, y a través de un diseño sostenible que contribuye al desarrollo ecológico. El resultado es un espacio adaptable a diversos usos, que puede ser ampliado en caso de ser necesario y que protege a los usuarios de las condiciones más adversas. El acabado de la cubierta puede ser modificado en función del clima y de los materiales de cada zona, creando así una arquitectura vernácula. La casa puede ser construida por los propios usuarios en tan solo veinticinco días, tiene un coste asequible y puede producirse en serie.

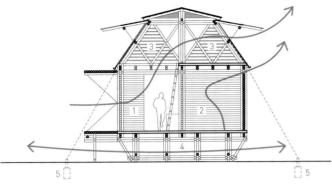

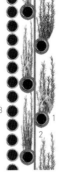
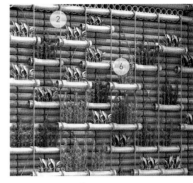

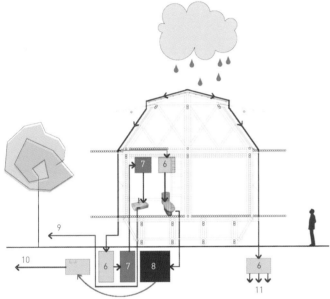

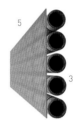

Wall materials

1. Bamboo of 8 -10 cm. diameter
2. Rope
3. Bamboo of 4 -5 cm. diameter
4. Nylon sheet (rain shield)
5. Polycarbonate sheet
6. Vertical garden (vegetable, plant, flower...)

Climatic diagrams

1.	Living room	7.	Clean water tank (filtered)
2	Bedroom	8.	Waste water tank
3.	Indoor terrace (sleeping + learning + workship)	9.	Water for gardening
4.	Area breed animal / plant	10.	Discharged to (after treated)
5.	Anchor steel	11.	Rain water cleaned and returned to the environment (underground reloading)
6.	Rain water tank		

FIRST FLOOR   SECOND FLOOR

House

FIRST FLOOR   SECOND FLOOR

Healthcare

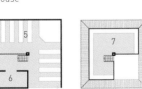

FIRST FLOOR   SECOND FLOOR

Classrooms library

1.	Living room	7.	Library
2	Bedroom	8.	Clinic
3.	Kitchen + WC	9.	Medical treatment
4.	Learning	10.	For healthcare purposes
5.	Study room		
6.	For learning		

Flexible use of space

HIROSHI NAKAMURA & NAP

WWW.NAKAM.INFO

Hiroshi Nakamura graduated from the Graduate School of Science and Technology at Meiji University in 1999. Upon graduation, he started working for Kengo Kuma and Associates and established Hiroshi Nakamura & NAP in 2002. His designs are derived from local contexts such as climate, culture, as well as behaviors of people and natural environment, and aims to create architectures that coexist with both people and nature. Ultimately, this allows people to establish an intimate relationship with nature and appreciate their existence through their own physical experiences, the vision of which accords with that of traditional Japanese architecture that has always valued a harmony with the natural environment and complemented its beauty. The architect has inherited the underlying architectural philosophy of Japanese spirituality towards nature.

Hiroshi Nakamura est diplômé de la Graduate School of Science and Technology de l'Université de Meiji en 1999. Après avoir obtenu son diplôme, il a commencé à travailler pour Kengo Kuma and Associates et a fondé Hiroshi Nakamura & NAP en 2002. Ses conceptions sont dérivées de contextes locaux tels que le climat, la culture, ainsi que les comportements des personnes et de l'environnement naturel, et vise à créer des architectures qui coexistent à la fois avec les personnes et la nature. En fin de compte, cela permet aux gens d'établir une relation intime avec la nature et d'apprécier leur existence à travers leurs propres expériences physiques, dont la vision s'accorde avec celle de l'architecture traditionnelle japonaise qui a toujours valorisé l'harmonie avec l'environnement naturel et complété sa beauté. L'architecte a hérité de la philosophie architecturale sous-jacente de la spiritualité japonaise envers la nature.

Hiroshi Nakamura absolvierte 1999 die Graduate School of Science and Technology an der Meiji Universität. Nach seinem Abschluss arbeitete er für Kengo Kuma and Associates und gründete 2002 Hiroshi Nakamura & NAP. Seine Entwürfe stammen aus lokalen Kontexten wie Klima, Kultur, Verhalten von Menschen und Natur und zielen darauf ab, Architekturen zu schaffen, die mit Mensch und Natur koexistieren. Letztlich ermöglicht dies den Menschen, eine intime Beziehung zur Natur aufzubauen und ihre Existenz durch ihre eigenen körperlichen Erfahrungen zu schätzen, deren Vision mit der der traditionellen japanischen Architektur übereinstimmt, die seit jeher die Harmonie mit der natürlichen Umwelt schätzt und ihre Schönheit ergänzt. Der Architekt hat die zugrunde liegende Architekturphilosophie der japanischen Spiritualität gegenüber der Natur geerbt.

Hiroshi Nakamura se graduó en la Escuela de Postgrado en Ciencia y Tecnología de la Universidad Meiji en 1999. Tras su graduación, comenzó a trabajar para Kengo Kuma and Associates y fundó Hiroshi Nakamura & NAP en 2002. Sus diseños derivan de contextos locales como el clima, la cultura así como el comportamiento de las personas y el entorno natural, que le conducen a crear arquitecturas que coexisten con las personas y con la naturaleza. En definitiva, esto permite a la gente establecer una relación intima con la naturaleza y apreciar su existencia a través de sus propias experiencias físicas, cuya visión va acorde con la arquitectura tradicional japonesa que siempre ha valorado la armonía con el entorno natural y ha complementado su belleza. El arquitecto ha heredado la filosofía arquitectónica subyacente de la espiritualidad japonesa hacia la naturaleza.

[BIRD'S NEST ATAMI]

[KAMIKATZ PUBLIC HOUSE]

BIRD'S NEST ATAMI

The commission consisted of building a teahouse around a tree that could be a showpiece for the Risonare Atami resort. The host tree selected was a 300-year-old camphor tree, 6 m in diameter and 22 m high, located in a lush forest. Considering safety and the tree's health, the structure is independent and does not touch the tree, while blending in with the crowded forest branches. The steep slope and the difficulty in construction in the intertwined branches 10 m above ground prompted the use of smaller and lighter structural elements. A flexible network of mounted steel rods was adapted to the shape of the tree and those branches containing nests were avoided. Components were added or removed during the building process similar to the process of a bird creating its nest. Both the inner space conceived as a swallow's nest and its external appearance transmit a soft and comfortable atmosphere.

Der Auftrag bestand darin, ein Teehaus um einen Baum zu bauen, das ein Vorzeigeobjekt für das Risonare Atami Resort sein könnte. Als Wirtsbaum wurde ein 300 Jahre alter Kampferbaum mit einem Durchmesser von 6 m und einer Höhe von 22 m in einem üppigen Wald ausgewählt. Im Hinblick auf die Sicherheit und die Gesundheit des Baumes ist die Struktur unabhängig und berührt den Baum nicht, während sie sich mit den überfüllten Waldzweigen vermischt. Der steile Hang und die Schwierigkeit der Konstruktion in den ineinander verschlungenen Zweigen in 10 m Höhe führten zum Einsatz von kleineren und leichteren Bauelementen. Ein flexibles Netz von montierten Stahlstäben wurde an die Form des Baumes angepasst und Äste mit Nestern vermieden. Komponenten wurden während des Bauprozesses hinzugefügt oder entfernt, ähnlich wie bei einem Vogel, der sein Nest baut. Sowohl der als Schwalbennest konzipierte Innenraum als auch das äußere Erscheinungsbild vermitteln eine weiche und angenehme Atmosphäre.

La commande consistait à construire une maison de thé autour d'un arbre qui pourrait être une pièce maîtresse de la station balnéaire de Risonare Atami. L'arbre hôte choisi était un camphrier de 300 ans, 6 m de diamètre et 22 m de haut, situé dans une forêt luxuriante. En tenant compte de la sécurité et de la santé de l'arbre, la structure est indépendante et ne touche pas l'arbre, tout en se mêlant aux branches de la forêt encombrées. La forte pente et la difficulté de construction dans les branches entrelacées à 10 m au-dessus du sol ont incité à utiliser des éléments structuraux plus petits et plus légers. Un réseau flexible de tiges d'acier montées a été adapté à la forme de l'arbre et les branches contenant des nids ont été évitées. Des composants ont été ajoutés ou retirés au cours du processus de construction, comme dans le cas d'un oiseau qui crée son nid. L'espace intérieur conçu comme un nid d'hirondelle et son aspect extérieur transmettent une atmosphère douce et confortable.

El encargo consistió en construir una casa de té alrededor de un árbol que sería el foco de atención del resort Risonare Atami. El árbol seleccionado fue un alcanforero de trescientos años, seis metros de diámetro y veintidós metros de altura, ubicado en un exuberante bosque. Teniendo en cuenta la seguridad y la salud del árbol, la estructura es independiente y no toca el árbol, a la vez que se funde con las abundantes ramas. La pronunciada pendiente y la dificultad en la construcción por las ramas entrelazadas diez metros sobre el nivel del suelo hizo necesario el uso de elementos estructurales más pequeños y ligeros. Una red flexible de varillas de acero se adaptó a la forma del árbol y se evitaron las ramas que contenían nidos. Se quitaron o añadieron componentes durante el proceso de construcción de forma similar al proceso de un ave creando su nido. Tanto el espacio interior, concebido como un nido de golondrinas, como su aspecto exterior transmiten una atmósfera suave y confortable.

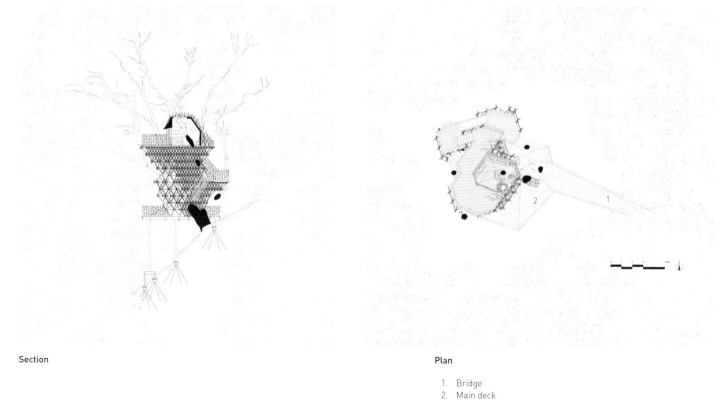

Section

Plan

1. Bridge
2. Main deck

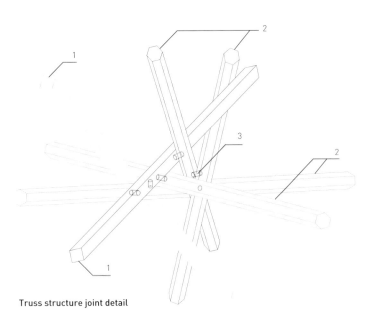

Truss structure joint detail

1. Squear bar (St 28 mm Ø)
2. Hexagonal bar (St 30 mm Ø)
3. High strength hexagon bolt

KAMIKATZ PUBLIC HOUSE

Kamikatsu in Tokushima prefecture is committed to zero waste, aiming to become a sustainable recycling society. The town has already attained an 80% recycling rate. To make the pub a local symbol when looking up from the town, the windows comprising fittings from abandoned houses were set eight meters high. We gathered windows that illuminated the town in the past. We converted and reconstructed furniture such as bridal chests and farm equipment found at the recycle center for use as product display fixtures. Locally-produced cedar board wood waste was colored with naturally derived persimmon tannin paint and applied to the exterior wall. We utilized abandoned items from a tile factory for the floor, empty bottles to create a chandelier, antlers produced in the town for the draft tower, and newspapers as wallpaper.

Kamikatsu in der Präfektur Tokushima hat sich zum Ziel gesetzt, eine nachhaltige Recycling-Gesellschaft zu werden. Die Stadt hat bereits eine Recyclingquote von 80% erreicht. Um die Kneipe zu einem lokalen Symbol zu machen, wenn man von der Stadt aufblickt, wurden die Fenster mit Beschlägen aus verlassenen Häusern acht Meter hoch gesetzt. Wir sammelten Fenster, die die Stadt in der Vergangenheit beleuchteten. Wir haben Möbel wie Brauttruhen und landwirtschaftliche Geräte, die im Recycling-Zentrum gefunden wurden, umgebaut und rekonstruiert, um sie als Ausstellungsstücke zu verwenden. Lokal produzierte Zedernholzabfälle wurden mit natürlich gewonnener Persimmontanninfarbe eingefärbt und auf die Außenwand aufgetragen. Wir benutzten verlassene Gegenstände aus einer Fliesenfabrik für den Boden, leere Flaschen für einen Kronleuchter, in der Stadt produzierte Geweihe für den Entwurfsturm und Zeitungen als Tapete.

Kamikatsu, dans la préfecture de Tokushima, s'est engagé à ne produire aucun déchet, dans le but de devenir une société de recyclage durable. La ville a déjà atteint un taux de recyclage de 80 %. Pour faire du pub un symbole local en regardant depuis la ville, les fenêtres comprenant des ferrures de maisons abandonnées ont été placées à huit mètres de haut. Nous avons rassemblé des fenêtres qui illuminaient la ville dans le passé. Nous avons converti et reconstruit des meubles tels que des coffres de mariage et des équipements agricoles trouvés au centre de recyclage pour les utiliser comme présentoirs de produits. Les déchets de bois de cèdre produits localement ont été colorés avec de la peinture au tanin de kaki d'origine naturelle et appliqués sur le mur extérieur. Nous avons utilisé des articles abandonnés d'une usine de carrelage pour le sol, des bouteilles vides pour créer un lustre, des bois produits dans la ville pour la tour de traite et des journaux comme papier peint.

Kamikatsu en la prefectura de Tokushima tiene el compromiso de residuo cero, con el objetivo de convertirse en una sociedad de reciclaje sostenible. La ciudad ya ha alcanzado una tasa de reciclaje del 80%. Para hacer del pub un símbolo local cuando se mira desde el pueblo, las ventanas, compuestas de materiales de las casas abandonadas, se colocaron a ocho metros de altura. Recolectamos ventanas que abrían las casas al exterior en el pasado. En el centro de reciclaje, convertimos y reconstruimos muebles, tales como baúles de novia, y equipamiento agrícola para su uso como expositores de productos. Los desechos de tableros de madera de cedro producida localmente fueron coloreados con tinte extraído del tanino de caqui y aplicados a la pared exterior. Utilizamos elementos abandonados de una fábrica de azulejos para el suelo, botellas vacías para fabricar una lámpara de techo, astas producidas en la ciudad para el tirador de cerveza y periódicos como papel para la pared.

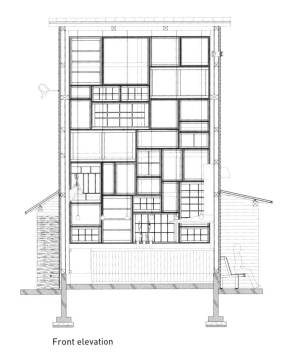

Front elevation

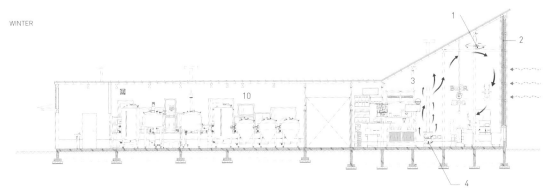

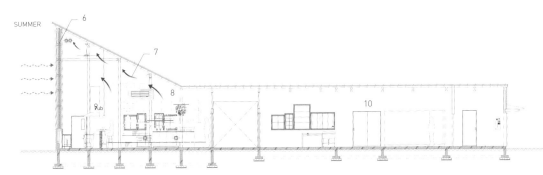

Sections

1. Effectively circulating the warm air that rises upward by using ceiling fans.
2. Reducing heat loss in winter by the double-layered fittings.
3. Sell by weight store
4. A carbon-neutral radiant fireplace that uses tree branches from the local forests.
5. Air-condition load is reduced while acquiring stable natural light by creating a large opening on the northwest side that is rarely exposed to direct sunlight. Moreover, thermal insulation is enhanced by the double layers of fittings and the air space in between.
6. Air-condition load is reduced while acquiring stable natural light by creating a large opening on the northwest side that is rarely exposed to direct sunlight. Moreover, thermal insulation is enhanced by the double layers of fittings and the air space in between.
7. Effectively exhausting the warm air by installing exhaust fans near the top of the roof.
8. Sell by weight store
9. Pub
10. Brewery

147

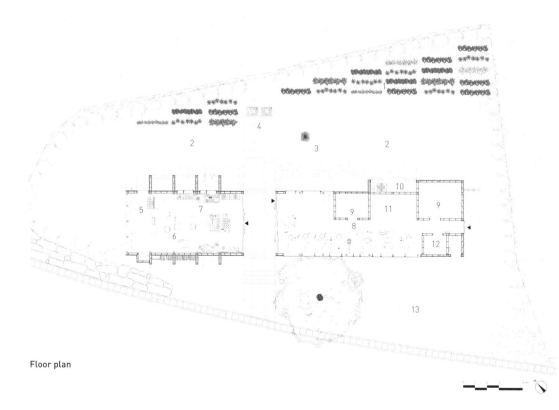

Floor plan

1. Herb garden
2. BBQ garden
3. Outdoor fireplace
4. BBQ booth
5. Kitchen
6. Pub
7. Sell by weight store
8. Brewery
9. Storage
10. Tool room
11. Walk in refrigerator
12. Boiler chamber
13. Guest parking

JURI TROY
ARCHITECTS

WWW.JURITROY.AT

Juri Troy's office was founded in 2003 and looks out into the world from Vienna and Vorarlberg with never forgetting its roots. The intense examination of these strikingly different habitats allows for a constant back and forth where the reflection about the particular qualities and challenges becomes the central element of the architectural discourse. The close contact to craftsmen and to the art of timber construction of the region of Vorarlberg is as essential as the influence and inspiration taken from international teaching assignments. The main focus is a sustainable and holistic approach to architecture and the results are often sculptural structures and differentiated spatial sequences that distinguish themselves through their contextuality as well as their materials and their energy concepts. In 2012, Juri Troy was awarded under Europe's most emerging young architects – 40 under 40.

Le cabinet de Juri Troy a été créé en 2003 et s'ouvre sur le monde entier depuis Vienne et Vorarlberg sans jamais oublier ses racines. En se penchant intensément sur tous ces habitats spectaculairement différents, il se crée un mouvement d'avant en arrière constant dans lequel la réflexion sur les qualités et difficultés spécifiques devient l'élément central du discours architectural. Sa connaissance approfondie des artisans et de l'art de la construction en bois de la région de Vorarlberg est aussi essentielle que l'influence et l'inspiration tirées de son expérience internationale en tant que professeur. Le pivot central de son travail est son approche durable et holistique à l'architecture et les résultats en sont souvent des structures sculpturales et des séquences spatiales différenciées qui se distinguent par leur contextualité aussi bien que par leurs matériaux et leur concept énergétique. En 2012, Juri Troy a été élu parmi les jeunes architectes européens émergents dans la liste des « 40 under 40 » de *Fortune* Magazine.

Juri Troy gründete sein Unternehmen 2003 und vergisst trotz seiner weltweiten Projekte nie seine Wurzeln in Wien und Vorarlberg. Das intensive Studium dieser enorm unterschiedlichen Gebiete erlaubt ihm einen stetigen Blick in alle Richtungen, wobei er sich bei seinem architektonischen Wirken hauptsächlich auf die besonderen Vorzüge und Herausforderungen konzentriert. Der enge Kontakt zu Schreiner- und anderen Handwerksbetrieben der Region Vorarlberg ist ebenso entscheidend wie Einfluss und Inspiration durch internationale Lehrstunden. Sein Schwerpunkt ist ein nachhaltiger und ganzheitlicher Architekturansatz und das Ergebnis sind häufig plastische Strukturen mit verschiedenartigen Raumfolgen, die sich durch Kontextualität, Material und Energiekonzept Auszeichnen. 2012 schaffte es Juri Troy unter die besten jungen und aufstrebenden europäischen Architekten / 40 under 40.

El estudio de Juri Troy se fundó en 2003 y desde sus oficinas en Viena y Vorarlber se abre al mundo sin olvidar nunca sus raíces. El examen exhaustivo de estos hábitats tan asombrosamente distintos permite un constante ir y venir donde la reflexión sobre los retos y cualidades particulares se convierten en el elemento central del discurso arquitectónico. El estrecho contacto con la artesanía y la construcción con madera en la región de Vorarlberg es tan esencial como la influencia e inspiración recibida al impartir clases en el extranjero. El objetivo principal es un enfoque sostenible e integral de la arquitectura y los resultados son a menudo estructuras esculturales y secuencias espaciales diferenciadas que se distinguen por su contextualidad así como por los materiales y conceptos energéticos. En 2012, Juri Troy fue incluido en la lista de los jóvenes arquitectos más prominentes de Europa: «40 under 40».

[HOUSE UNDER THE OAKS]

[HAUS 3B]

[SUNLIGHT HOUSE]

HOUSE UNDER THE OAKS

The house under the oaks is a low budget passive house concept developed for an Austrian family. With a minimum footprint and a wide outstretching wooden box on six columns it offers a living area of about 100m² on a plot of 913m². The whole structure was done in prefabricated timber with ecological wood wool insulation of up to 60 cm. The interior is done in local wood as well, with a simple white pigmented oil cover. A heat pump with a ground collector, a controlled ventilation system with heat exchange and photovoltaic panels on the roof offer a perfect energy concept with a minimum of required external energy – which is provided by eco electricity. It is a new prototype for affordable living on minimal energy standard in Austria.

Das Haus unter den Eichen wurde als günstiges Passivhauskonzept für eine österreichische Familie entwickelt. Dieses Haus hat kaum Einfluss auf die Umwelt und beherbergt in seiner Holzkonstruktion auf sechs Pfeilern einen Wohnbereich mit einer Fläche von 100 m², wobei die Grundstücksfläche 913 m² beträgt. Es handelt sich um ein Holzfertighaus mit einer ökologischen Holzwolleisolierung von bis zu 60 cm. Der Innenbereich besteht ebenfalls aus heimischem Holz mit schlichter weiß pigmentierter Ölung. Eine Wärmepumpe mit Erdkollektor, ein kontrolliertes Lüftungssystem mit Luftaustausch und Photovoltaikplatten auf dem Dach bilden ein perfektes Energiekonzept mit einem minimalen Bedarf an externer Energie, der durch Ökostrom bedient wird. Hierbei handelt es sich um einen neuen Prototypen für erschwingliches Leben bei minimalem Energiebedarf in Österreich.

La « maison sous les chênes » est un concept d'habitation passive à petit budget développé pour une famille autrichienne. Avec une empreinte carbone minimale et un large module de bois étiré sur six colonnes elle offre un espace à vivre d'environ 100 m² sur une parcelle de 913 m². L'intégralité de la structure a été effectuée en pièces de bois préfabriquées avec une isolation en laine de bois allant jusqu'à 60 cm. L'intérieur est également été mis en œuvre en bois local, avec une simple finition d'huile pigmentée blanche. Une pompe à chaleur géothermique, un système de ventilation contrôlée avec échangeur d'air et des panneaux photovoltaïques sur le toit offrent un concept énergétique parfait avec un minimum de besoins en énergie externe – qui est fournie par éco-électricité. C'est un nouveau prototype de vie accessible à partir d'une norme énergétique minimale en Autriche.

Este proyecto de casa pasiva se desarrolló para una familia austriaca, que buscaba una vivienda de coste moderado y que provocase el menor impacto en el entorno. Este amplio volumen rectangular hecho con madera y afianzado en seis columnas proporciona una espacio habitable de aproximadamente 100 m² en una finca de 913 m². La estructura completa se realizó en madera prefabricada con aislamiento ecológico de madera y lana de hasta 60 cm. El interior también se realizó con madera local, tratada simplemente con un aceite blanco. Una bomba de calor geotérmica, un sistema de ventilación controlado con intercambiador de calor y paneles fotovoltáicos en el tejado ofrecen un concepto energético perfecto que precisa de una cantidad de energía externa mínima, que la proporciona electricidad ecológica. Es un nuevo prototipo para viviendas asequibles con mínimo consumo de energía en Austria.

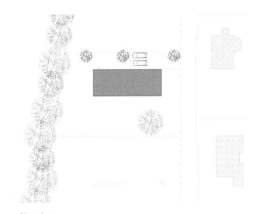

Site plan

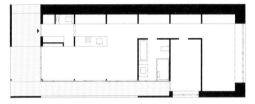

Ground floor plan

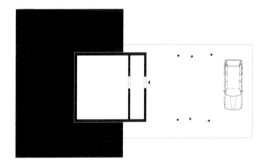

Basement plan

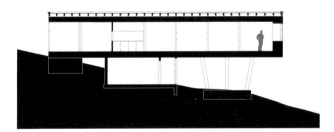

Longitudinal section

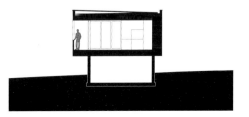

Cross section

HOUSE 3B

The position of this dwelling on the top of a steep plot allows it to take advantage of the views over a small valley and conditioned its design distribution. Access is via the partially buried garage located at street level, from which an underground staircase connects to the dwelling, covering three levels. The upper and lower levels are allocated to bedrooms, and the intermediate one to the shared areas. The use of concrete with pinewood formwork covering its walls should be highlighted here. The House's external appearance is characterised by the fir tile cladding of the façades and the cedar tiles used for the roof. The building constitutes a passive house complying with the Swiss standard *Minergie-P*. It is equipped with a deep drill geothermal heat pump and control of indoor air through heat recuperators.

Die Hanglage des Hauses bietet einen tollen Ausblick auf ein kleines Tal und gibt gleichzeitig die architektonische Aufteilung vor. Der Zugang erfolgt auf Straßenhöhe über die teilweise unterirdisch gelegene Garage. Anschließend gelangt man über eine Treppe in das dreistöckige Wohngebäude. Im ersten und dritten Stockwerk befinden sich die Schlafzimmer, im mittleren Stockwerk liegen die gemeinsamen Wohnräume. Besonders erwähnenswert ist hier die Betonschalung aus seekiefer. Die Außenfassade besteht aus Tannen-, das Dach aus Zedernholz. Das Gebäude ist ein Passivhaus gemäß dem Schweizer Standard Minergie-P. Es verfügt über eine geothermische Erdwärmepumpe und kontrollierte wohneaumlüftung mit Wärmerückgewinnung.

L'emplacement de cette habitation, au sommet d'une parcelle pentue, lui permet de profiter des vues sur une petite vallée et a conditionné la planification de la distribution des pièces. L'accès se fait par le garage partiellement enterré situé au niveau de la rue, d'où un escalier souterrain mène à l'habitation, déployée sur trois niveaux. Les niveaux supérieur et inférieur sont dédiés aux chambres, et l'intermédiaire aux pièces partagées. L'usage du béton avec un coffrage en pin recouvrant les murs doit être souligné. L'apparence extérieure de la Maison est caractérisée par le parement de tuiles de pin sur ses façades et les tuiles de cèdre utilisées pour le toit. Ce bâtiment constitue une maison passive en conformité avec les normes suisses Minergie-P. Elle est équipée d'une pompe à chaleur géothermique à captage vertical et régulation d'air à l'intérieur par le biais de récupérateurs de chaleur.

La posición de esta casa en lo alto de una empinada parcela permitió aprovechar las vistas sobre un pequeño valle y condicionó el diseño de su distribución. El acceso se realiza a través del garaje parcialmente enterrado situado a nivel de la calle, desde el cual una escalera subterránea conecta con la casa, desarrollada en tres niveles. Los niveles superior e inferior se destinan a dormitorios y el intermedio a las zonas comunes, en las que destaca el uso de hormigón visto con encofrado de madera de pino en sus paramentos. La imagen exterior de la casa se caracteriza por el revestimiento de tejas de abeto en las fachadas y tejas de cedro en la cubierta. El edificio constituye una casa pasiva y cumple con el estándar suizo *Minergie-P*; está dotada de una bomba de calor geotérmica con perforación profunda y de control del aire interior mediante recuperadores de calor.

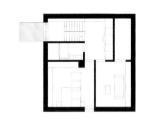

Fourth floor plan

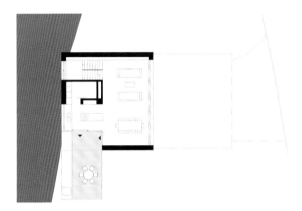

Third floor plan

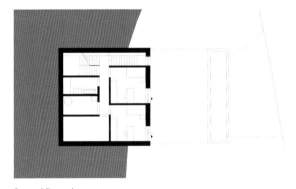

Second floor plan

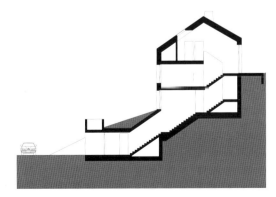

Longitudinal section

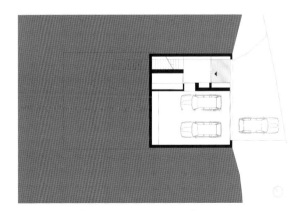

First floor plan / parking

SUNLIGHT HOUSE

This project, promoted by the company Velux as part of an experimental program at the European level, is the first carbon-neutral single-family dwelling in Austria. Its sustainable and efficient design merges with an ambitious architecture leveraging the location's features. It is equipped among other things with a high-performance heat pump, 48 m² of photovoltaic panels, 9 m² of solar panels for hot water and an air control system with a heat recuperator. A strategically placed window area, equivalent to 42% of the dwelling's surface, lets in five times more natural light than normal, improving the energy performance of the interior and providing stunning views. All materials were assessed for their ecological properties prior to being used in the construction.

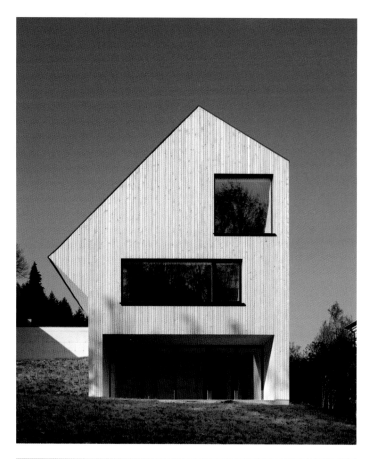

Dieses Projekt ist Teil eines europaweiten Experiments des Unternehmens Velux und das erste CO_2neutrale Einfamilienhaus Österreichs. Das nachhaltige und effiziente Design geht Hand in Hand mit einer ehrgeizigen architektonischen Planung, bei der besonders die Gegebenheiten des Standorts berücksichtigt wurden. Das Haus verfügt unter anderem über eine Hochleistungswärmepumpe, eine 48 m² große Photovoltaikanlage, 9 m² Sonnenkollektoren für Warmwasser und ein System zur Luftregulierung mit Wärmerückgewinnung. 42 % der Hausfassade bestehen aus strategisch günstig platzierten Fensterflächen, die den Einfall von Tageslicht verfünffachen, die Energieeffizienz im Gebäudeinneren verbessern und einen atemberaubenden Ausblick bieten. Das gesamte Baumaterial wurde zuvor auf seine ökologischen Eigenschaften geprüft.

Ce projet, soutenu par la société Velux dans le cadre d'un programme expérimental au niveau européen, représente la première habitation individuelle neutre en carbone d'Autriche. Son design durable et éco-énergétique se mêle à une architecture ambitieuse qui met à profit les caractéristiques de l'emplacement. Elle est équipée, entre autres, d'une pompe à chaleur ultra performante, de 48 m² de panneaux photovoltaïques, de 9 m² de panneaux solaires pour l'eau chaude et d'un système de régulation d'air avec un récupérateur de chaleur. Une zone de fenêtres stratégiquement positionnée, équivalente à 42 % de la surface de l'habitation, fait entrer cinq fois plus de lumière naturelle que la normale, améliorant la performance énergétique de l'intérieur et créant des points de vue remarquables. Tous les matériaux ont été évalués pour leurs propriétés écologiques avant d'être utilisés pour la construction.

Este proyecto, promovido por la empresa Velux como parte de un programa experimental a nivel europeo, constituye la primera vivienda unifamiliar carbono-neutral de Austria. Su diseño sostenible y eficiente energéticamente se combina con una ambiciosa arquitectura que aprovecha las características del emplazamiento. Su equipamiento incluye bomba de calor de alto rendimiento, 48 m² de paneles fotovoltaicos, 9 m² de paneles solares para agua caliente y sistema de control de aire con recuperador de calor. Una superficie de ventanas colocadas estratégicamente, equivalente al 42% de la superficie de la casa, permite una iluminación natural cinco veces superior a la habitual, mejora las prestaciones energéticas del interior y proporciona impresionantes vistas. Todos los materiales fueron evaluados por sus propiedades ecológicas antes de ser utilizados en la construcción.

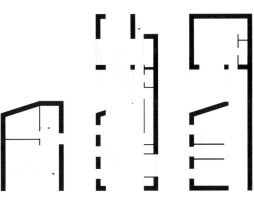

Floor plans

Elevations

Energy

Fresh-water consumption
and waste treatment

Annual energy output

Environmental
impact of emissions
on air, ground and
water

Energy need

Consumption
from non-
renewable
energy sources

Energy supply

Environment

Indoor Climate

Noise
and acoustics

Light and views

Ambient air
quality

Ambient heat

Active house diagram

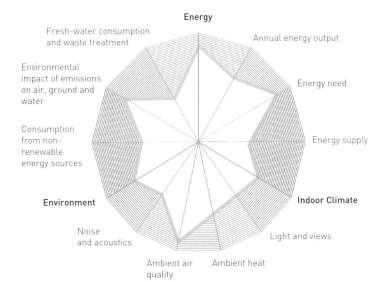

Climatic diagram

1. Energy for solar
   collectors (hot water)
2. Direct energy (heat
   gaine through pane)
3. LED lighting
4. Energy for solar cells
   (electricity)
5. Natural ventilation
   (stack effect)
6. Brine heat exchanger

K20 ARCHITECTURE

WWW.K20ARCHITECTURE.COM

At k20 Architecture we work with our clients to deliver excellence in line with our core values;

Design | Sustainability | Performance

We approach every project with our experience in design innovation, research in sustainability and a focus on best practice to deliver outstanding examples of sustainable architecture.

We have a number of systems and review procedures in place so that each project is designed from the outset to maximise efficiencies and minimise energy loadings. k20 Architecture is Carbon Neutral and certified for the entirety of operations and our clients can benefit that in the first instance we are operating in a sustainably responsive manner. k20 Architecture Director Anthony U is an accredited professional with the Green Building Council of Australia (GBCA) and he contributes to all ESD design ideas within our projects.

Chez k20 Architecture nous travaillons en collaboration avec nos clients pour offrir un service d'excellence dans la lignée de nos valeurs fondamentales ;

Design | Durabilité | Performance

Nous abordons chaque projet armés de notre expérience en innovation et design et en recherche de durabilité, axés sur la meilleure pratique pour pouvoir proposer des exemples modèles pour l'architecture durable.

Nous avons mis en place un grand nombre de procédures de systèmes et de revues de sorte que chaque projet est conçu dès le départ pour optimiser l'efficacité et minimiser les charges énergétiques. k20 Architecture est neutre en carbone et certifié pour l'intégralité de ses opérations. Nos clients peuvent bénéficier du fait que nous opérons en premier lieu d'une manière adaptée et durable. Le directeur de k20, Anthony U, est un professionnel accrédité par le *Green Building Council of Australia* (GBCA) et participe à tous les développements des idées de design ESD et à toutes les questions à résoudre au sein de nos projets.

Bei k20 Architecture arbeiten wir gemeinsam mit unseren Kunden daran, Exzellenz im Einklang mit unseren Kernwerten zu liefern.

Design | Nachhaltigkeit | Leistung

Wir realisieren all unsere Projekte mit Erfahrung in der Designinnovation, Untersuchung der Nachhaltigkeit und Konzentration auf die bestmögliche Lösung für vorbildliche Beispiele nachhaltiger Architektur.

Wir bedienen uns einer Reihe von Systemen und Prüfverfahren, mit denen wir für jedes Projekt von Anfang an maximale Effizienz bei minimalem Energieverlust garantieren können. k20 Architecture ist klimaneutral und für all seine Tätigkeiten zertifiziert. Unsere Kunden profitieren davon, dass wir in erster Linie umweltbewusst arbeiten. Anthony U, Unternehmensleiter von k20 Architecture, verfügt über eine Zertifizierung des australischen Nachhaltigkeitsverbands Green Building Council of Australia (GBCA) und ist ann allen ESD-Designideen und Überlegungen zu unseren Projekten beteiligt.

En k20 Architecture trabajamos con nuestros clientes para conseguir la excelencia en nuestros proyectos en línea con nuestros valores fundamentales:

Diseño | Sostenibilidad | Desempeño

Encaramos cada proyecto con nuestra experiencia en innovación del diseño, la búsqueda de la sostenibilidad y un enfoque en las mejores prácticas para conseguir referentes de la arquitectura sostenible.

Tenemos establecido una serie de procedimientos de sistemas y revisiones para asegurar que cada proyecto se diseña desde el inicio para maximizar las eficiencias y minimizar el consumo energético. k20 es una empresa carbono-neutral y está certificada para todas sus operaciones y nuestros clientes pueden beneficiarse de que operamos desde el principio de forma sostenible. El director de k20 Architecture, Anthony U, es un profesional acreditado por el Green Building Council of Australia (GBCA) y contribuye en todas las ideas de diseño de ESD y se implica en todo el proceso de nuestros proyectos.

[BALLARAT REGIONAL SOCCER FACILITY]

[HINDMARSH SHIRE COUNCIL OFFICES]

[PORT MELBOURNE FOOTBALL CLUB]

BALLARAT REGIONAL SOCCER FACILITY

This building's appearance is inspired by the fence erected by Australian miners in their struggle against the colonial army at the battle of Eureka Stockade in 1854. The project for this stadium, which includes both sports and social facilities is a curved wall emerging from the landscape to give shape to the building protecting it and the pitch from the prevailing winds and hard western Sun. Sustainable design is linked intrinsically to the project through the implementation of passive solar measures such as large eaves, double glazing and high insulation levels and other measures such as solar panels, rainwater recovery, natural ventilation and cooling through solar chimneys or the use of a high percentage of environmentally sustainable, long-lasting local materials.

Dieses Gebäude erhielt seine Inspiration durch den Zaun, den australische Bergarbeiter 1854 zum Schutz vor der kolonialen Armee in der Schlacht von Eureka Stockade errichteten. Das Stadion mit Sport- und Sozialeinrichtungen besteht aus einer zur Landschaft passenden geschwungenen Wand, die das Gebäude vor Stürmen und dem rauen Klima des Westens schützt und ihm gleichzeitig seine Form gibt. Die passive Nutzung der Solarenergie beispielsweise durch große Traufen, Doppelverglasung und sehr gute Isolierung und weitere Vorrichtungen wie Sonnenkollektoren, Regenwasserrückgewinnung, natürliche Belüftung und Kühlung durch Solarkamine und der hohe Anteil an nachhaltigen, langlebigen und lokalen Materialien sorgen für die Nachhaltigkeit des Gebäudes.

L'apparence de ce bâtiment est inspirée par la barricade élevée par les mineurs australiens dans leur lutte contre l'armée coloniale à la bataille de Eureka Stockade en 1854. Ce projet de stade, qui comporte des infrastructures à la fois sportives et sociales, est un mur incurvé émergeant du paysage pour donner forme au bâtiment tout en le protégeant ainsi que le terrain des vents dominants et de l'âpre soleil d'ouest. Un design durable est intrinsèquement lié au projet par le biais de la mise en œuvre de mesures pour une énergie solaire passive telles que de grands avant-toits, du double vitrage et de hauts niveaux d'isolation ainsi que d'autres dispositifs tels que des panneaux solaires, la récupération d'eau de pluie, l'aération et la climatisation naturelles par le biais de cheminées solaires ou l'usage d'un fort pourcentage de matériaux écologiques, locaux et durables.

La imagen de este edificio se inspira en la empalizada levantada por los mineros australianos en su lucha contra las fuerzas coloniales en la batalla de Eureka Stockade, en 1854. En el proyecto de este estadio, que incluye instalaciones deportivas y sociales, es un muro curvilíneo el que emerge del paisaje para dar forma al edificio y proteger a éste y al terreno de juego de los vientos dominantes y del duro sol occidental. El diseño sostenible se vincula de forma intrínseca al proyecto mediante la implementación de medidas solares pasivas como grandes aleros, doble acristalamiento y altos niveles de aislamiento, y de otras medidas como paneles fotovoltaicos, recuperación de agua de lluvia, ventilación natural y refrigeración a través de chimeneas solares o la utilización en un elevado porcentaje de materiales ambientalmente sostenibles, duraderos y de ámbito local.

East elevation

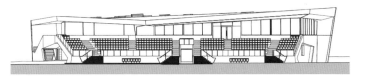

West elevation

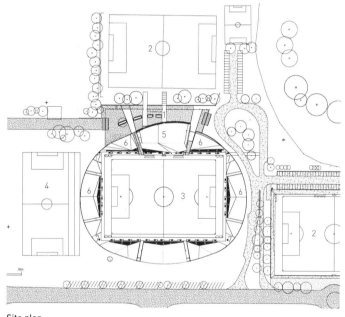

Site plan

1. Forecourt
2. Synthetic fields
3. Star FIFA pitch
4. Small sized soccer
5. Stage 1 - 500 seat community conference facility
6. Future stage 2 - 5000 undercover seats
7. Light towers

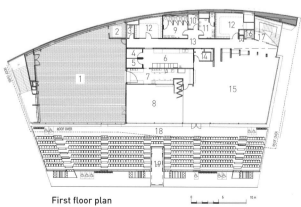

First floor plan

1. Viewing deck (double-sided)
2. Plant room
3. Cleaner's store
4. Dry store
5. Cool room
6. Kitchen
7. Bar
8. Social room south
9. Female WC
10. Accesible WC
11. Male WC
12. Office
13. Corridor
14. AV cabinet
15. Social room north
16. Lift
17. Stairwell
18. 500 seat grandstand
19. Player's race (below)
20. Entry ticketing

HINDMARSH SHIRE COUNCIL OFFICES

With this new civic and administration centre, k20 Architecture sought to create an environmentally-friendly, economically, and culturally sustainable project. Its design incorporates and reuses the existing building, from 1960, and its shape evokes the region's steel silos and agricultural barns. A restricted palette of materials includes wood, steel, and glass also a homage to local agriculture, especially using the artisanal folded metal typical of silos, applied in the form of steel and zinc finishes on the façades. The design of the building follows the ESD principles promoted by the Australian government, introducing innovations reducing energy consumption and carbon emissions during the project's life-cycle and providing high environmental comfort levels to employees.

Mit diesem Verwaltungszentrum gelang den Architekten ein umweltfreundlich, gesellschaftlich und kulturell nachhaltiges Projekt. Die ursprünglichen Gebäude aus dem Jahr 1960 wurden in den Bau eingebunden; seine Form lässt an die Stahlsilos und Scheunen der Region denken. Die sorgfältig ausgewählte Materialkombination aus Holz, Stahl und Glas und vor allem das für Silos typische von Hand gekantete Metallblech, das für die Stahl- und Zinkoberfläche der Fassaden verwendet wurde, würdigen ebenfalls die örtliche Landwirtschaft. Bei der Gebäudeplanung befolgten die Architekten die ESD-Grundsätze für ökologisch nachhaltige Entwicklung der australischen Regierung und übernahmen Innovationen zur Reduzierung des Energieverbrauchs und des CO_2-Ausstoßes während der gesamten Nutzungszeit des Gebäudes. Gleichzeitig wurde natürlich auch auf eine komfortable Umgebung für die Mitarbeiter geachtet.

Avec ce nouveau centre civil et administratif, les architectes ont cherché à créer un projet écologique, économiquement et culturellement durable. Son design incorpore et réutilise le bâtiment d'origine, de 1960, et sa forme évoque les silos d'acier et les granges agricoles de la région. Une palette réduite de matériaux comporte du bois, de l'acier, et du verre, hommage également à l'agriculture locale, en particulier dans l'usage de métal plié artisanal des silos, appliqué sous la forme de finitions en acier et en zinc sur les façades. Le design de ce bâtiment suit les principes de design durable (ESD) promus par le gouvernement australien, introduisant des innovations qui réduisent la consommation énergétique et les émissions de carbone durant le cycle de vie du projet et apportant un confort environnemental considérable aux employés.

Con este nuevo centro cívico y administrativo, los arquitectos buscaron crear un proyecto ambiental, económica y culturalmente sostenible. Su diseño incorpora y reutiliza el edificio existente, de 1960, y su forma hace referencia a los silos de acero y a los cobertizos agrícolas de la región. Su restringida paleta de materiales en madera, acero y vidrio también hace referencia a la agricultura local, en especial a través del uso de la artesanía del metal plegado inherente a los silos, que es aplicada en forma de acabados de acero y cinc en las fachadas. El diseño del edificio sigue los principios ESD (*Ecologically Sustainable Development*) promovidos por el gobierno australiano, introduciendo innovaciones que reducen el consumo de energía y las emisiones de carbono durante la vida del proyecto y que proporcionan un alto nivel de confort ambiental a los empleados.

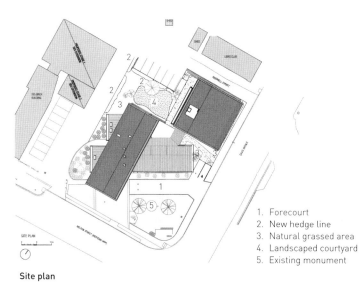

1. Forecourt
2. New hedge line
3. Natural grassed area
4. Landscaped courtyard
5. Existing monument

Site plan

Section

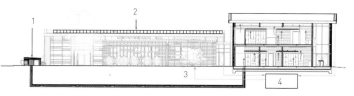

Natural Ventilation Section Hindmarsh Shire Council Office

1. Air intake and earth tube mechanical system
2. Solar panels power generation
3. Rainwater supply to building for toilets, showers and basins
4. Rainwater tanks

PORT MELBOURNE
FOOTBALL CLUB

The slightly elevated location of this sports club's building, together with the pitch, generates extensive views over the lawn through the large openings of the main façade. Its final location was assessed to ensure that healthy trees were not removed during its construction. Sustainability is part of this building's DNA, using prefabricated materials found in the local area and assembled by local labourers together with timber from sustainable sources. Other ESD initiatives include the reuse of rainwater, solar panels for hot drinking water or high-performance air-conditioning systems. The recognition of the intrinsic link between sport and design encouraged architects to create an installation that would inspire users not only on the pitch but also in the stands.

Das Gebäude des Sportvereins liegt etwas höher als das Spielfeld; dementsprechend genießt man durch den großen offenen Bereich der Hauptfassade des Gebäudes einen herrlichen Ausblick auf den Rasen. Der Standort wurde ganz bewusst so gewählt, dass für den Bau keine gesunden Bäume entfernt werden mussten. Nachhaltigkeit ist ein wesentlicher Bestandteil des Gebäudes. Für den Bau wurden vorgefertigte Materialien und nachhaltiges Bauholz aus der Region verwendet und von ansässigen Arbeitern zusammengebaut. Weitere ESD-Maßnahmen sind die Wiederverwertung von Regenwasser, Sonnenkollektoren zur Warmwassererzeugung und Hochleistungsklimaanlagen. Die Architekten wollten Sport und Design in erkennbarer Weise verbinden und schufen daher eine Anlage, die die Besucher nicht nur auf dem Rasen inspirieren soll.

La situation légèrement surélevée du bâtiment de ce club de sport, ainsi que son terrain, génère de larges vues sur la pelouse par les grandes ouvertures de la façade principale. Son emplacement final a été décidé de façon à garantir que des arbres sains ne seraient pas éliminés durant sa construction. La durabilité est inscrite dans l'ADN de ce bâtiment, qui utilise des matériaux préfabriqués sourcés localement et assemblés par des artisans locaux, ainsi que du bois de charpente d'origine durable. Parmi d'autres initiatives ESD on trouve la réutilisation de l'eau de pluie, des panneaux solaires pour l'eau chaude potable ou des systèmes de climatisation de haute performance. La reconnaissance du lien intrinsèque entre le sport et le design a encouragé les architectes à créer une installation qui inspirerait les utilisateurs non seulement sur le terrain mais aussi sur les gradins.

La posición del edificio de este club deportivo, junto al terreno de juego y en una cota ligeramente elevada, genera unas amplias vistas sobre el césped a través de las grandes aberturas de la fachada principal. Su ubicación definitiva fue evaluada para garantizar que no se eliminasen árboles sanos durante la construcción. La sostenibilidad se integra en el ADN del edificio mediante la utilización de materiales prefabricados de la zona que fueron ensamblados por mano de obra local y de madera procedente de fuentes sostenibles. Otras iniciativas ESD incluyen la reutilización del agua de lluvia, paneles solares para ACS o sistemas de aire acondicionado de alto rendimiento. El reconocimiento de la intrínseca vinculación entre deporte y diseño motivó a los arquitectos a crear una instalación que inspirase a los usuarios no sólo en el campo de juego sino también en el club.

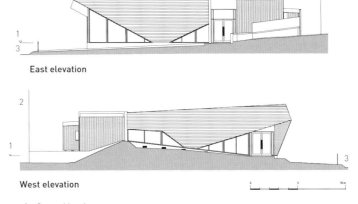

East elevation

West elevation

1. Ground level
2. Title boundary
3. Pitch

KJELLGREN KAMINSKY

WWW.KJELLGRENKAMINSKY.SE

Kjellgren Kaminsky is a multiple award-winning architectural firm recognized for its high level of architecture and sustainability. We have a strong base in environmentally friendly construction and notably designed BREEAM certified projects and several passive houses. We want to design buildings that make people happy and have a minimal ecological footprint, where our expertise is built up through experience of real projects. KK has established partnerships with some of the leading experts on sustainability in Sweden.

We think about our responsibility for the future. Therefore, we want to design builings that can remain for centuries. We hope that in this way we can help to provide a better planet for the next generation.

Some awards: 2017 WA Award Cycle 25, Winner; 2016 Mipim Future Awards, EINNER; 2015 World Architecture Festival, Nominated; 2013 Green Planet Architect, Top 50 Sustainable Architects.

Kjellgren Kaminsky est un cabinet d'architecture aux multiples récompenses reconnu pour son niveau supérieur en architecture et en durabilité. Nous avons de solides bases en construction écologique et avons notamment conçu des projets certifiés BREEAM et plusieurs maisons passives. Nous désirons concevoir des bâtiments qui rendent les gens heureux et ont une empreinte écologique minimale, dans lesquels notre savoir-faire s'accroît par l'expérience de véritables projets. KK a établi des partenariats avec certains des plus grands experts de la durabilité en Suède.

Nous pensons à notre responsabilité pour l'avenir. Par conséquent, nous voulons concevoir des bâtiments qui peuvent perdurer durant des siècles. Nous espérons que de cette façon nous pourrons contribuer à la mise en œuvre d'une planète meilleure pour la prochaine génération.

Quelques prix : Gagnant du WA Award Cycle 25 en 2017 ; Mipim Future Awards 2016, Premier prix du Jeu d'esprit ; Festival mondial de l'architecture 2015, nominés ; Green Planet Architect 2013, dans les 50 premiers architectes durables.

Kjellgren Kaminsky ist ein bereits vielfach ausgezeichnetes Architekturunternehmen, das für seine hohe Qualität bei der Verbindung von Architektur und Nachhaltigkeit bekannt ist. Wir konzentrieren uns besonders auf die umweltfreundliche Bauweise und realisierten bereits beachtenswerte Projekte mit BREEAM-Zertifikat und Passivhäuser. Wir möchten Gebäude bauen, die die Menschen glücklich machen und sich dabei dennoch nur minimal auf die Umwelt auswirken, wobei unsere Erfahrung hier auf zahlreichen Immobilienprojekten beruht. KK arbeitet mit führenden schwedischen Experten im Bereich der Nachhaltigkeit zusammen. Wir sind uns unserer Verantwortung für die Zukunft bewusst. Daher möchten wir Gebäude bauen, die für Jahrhunderte überdauern können. Wir hoffen, der nächsten Generation auf diese Weise einen besseren Planeten hinterlassen zu können.

Einige Auszeichnungen: 2017 WA Award Cycle 25, Gewinner; 2016 Mipim Future Awards, GEWINNER; 2015 World Architecture Festival, nominiert; 2013 Green Planet Architect, Top 50 der nachhaltigen Architekten.

Kjellgren Kaminsky es una firma arquitectónica galardonada con numerosos premios. Es conocida por el gran nivel arquitectónico de sus trabajos y su enfoque en la sostenibilidad. Tenemos una sólida experiencia en construcciones medioambientalmente sostenibles y proyectos notables por su diseño que cuentan con el certificado BREEAM. Asimismo, hemos construido varias casas pasivas. Queremos construir edificios que hagan felices a las personas y tengan el menor impacto ecológico, aquí nuestro saber hacer se basa en la experiencia en proyectos reales. KK ha establecido asociaciones con algunos de los expertos líderes en sostenibilidad de Suecia.

Pensamos en nuestra responsabilidad con el futuro. Por ello, queremos diseñar edificios que duren siglos. Esperamos que de esta manera ayudemos a dejar un planeta mejor a la próxima generación.

Algunos premios: Ganador del premio 2017 *WA Cycle 25*; ganador del premio 2016 *Mipim Future*; nominado al premio *World Architecture Festival* del 2015; incluido entre los 50 primeros arquitectos sostenibles de la lista del 2013 de *Green Planet Architect*.

[KOLLASTADEN SCHOOL]

[ÖIJARED HOTEL]

KOLLASTADEN SCHOOL

The extension to Kollastaden School is one of the largest Passive House buildings in Sweden. The building is strategically placed to envelope a communal schoolyard between the new and the old, providing a playful, inspiring and sustainable school environment centered around the students. The north facades, that face the schoolyard, are clad with fiber cement boards in a colourful and playful pattern, while the street façade has a more restrained expression with the use of brick, establishing a close dialogue with the surrounding park. KK were focused on implementing passive strategies that influenced the design such as the compact volume, durable materials and the angle of the roof which optimises solar gain. Internally, the building is centered around a colourful atrium providing privacy to the classrooms located in the wings.

Der Anbau der Kollastaden School gehört zu den größten Passivhäusern in Schweden. Das Gebäude ist strategisch so ausgerichtet, dass der zentrale Schulhof zwischen altem und neuem Gebäude liegt und so eine verspielte, inspirierende, nachhaltige und auf die Schüler fokussierte Schulumgebung schafft. Die zum Schulhof zeigenden Nordfassaden sind mit Faserzementbauplatten in einem farbigen und verspielten Muster verkleidet, wohingegen die zur Straße zeigende Fassade durch ihre Ziegel etwas unauffälliger daherkommt und perfekt mit dem örtlichen Park harmoniert. KK konzentrierte sich hier hauptsächlich auf Passivstrategien wie das kompakte Volumen, langlebige Materialien und die die Sonneneinstrahlung begünstigende Dachneigung, welche auch das Design beeinflussten. Zentrales Element im Gebäudeinneren ist der farbenfrohe Innenhof, der den Klassenzimmern in den Flügeln Privatsphäre verleiht.

L'extension de l'école Kollastaden est l'un des bâtiments passifs les plus grands de Suède. Il est stratégiquement placé pour englober une cour d'école communale entre anciens et nouveaux locaux, procurant un environnement scolaire ludique, inspirant et durable centré sur les élèves. Les façades nord, qui font face à la cour d'école, sont bardées de panneaux de fibrociment en motifs colorés et joyeux, tandis que la façade côté rue a une expression plus sobre avec l'emploi de la brique, établissant un dialogue étroit avec le parc environnant. KK se sont concentrés sur la mise en œuvre de stratégies passives qui ont influencé la conception, comme le volume compact, des matériaux durables et l'angle du toit qui optimise le gain d'ensoleillement. À l'intérieur, le bâtiment s'organise autour d'un atrium coloré qui procure de l'intimité aux classes situées dans les ailes.

La ampliación de la escuela Kollastaden es uno de los mayores edificios *passivhaus* de Suecia. Este edificio se sitúa estratégicamente para envolver un patio común entre el edificio nuevo y el antiguo, proporcionando un ambiente escolar lúdico, inspirador y sostenible que se centra en los estudiantes. Las fachadas septentrionales, que dan al patio escolar, están revestidas con planchas de fibrocemento que siguen un colorido y lúdico diseño, mientras que la fachada frente a la calle tiene una expresión más restringida con el uso del ladrillo, estableciendo un estrecho diálogo con el parque vecino. KK se centró en implementar estrategias de energía pasiva que influyen en el diseño como el volumen compacto, los materiales resistentes y el ángulo del tejado para optimizar la luz solar. Internamente, el edificio pivota alrededor de un atrio lleno de color, proporcionando privacidad a las clases que se ubican en las alas.

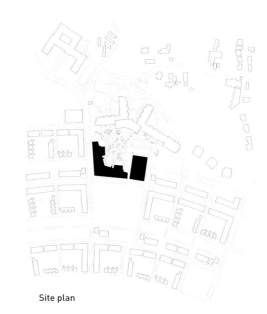

Site plan

First floor plan

Ground floor plan

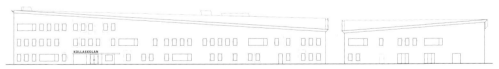

South elevation

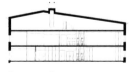

Cross section

West elevation

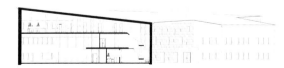

Longitudinal section

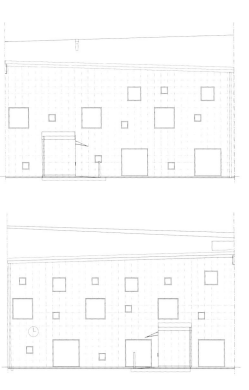

Facade cladding pattern

ÖIJARED HOTEL

The fact that this hotel located in a golf club is mounted on pillars makes the building "float" above the ground, thus generating a close link with the forest. The absence of excavation during construction allowed trees to grow near the building and meant they did not have to be cut down. Its red façade is covered with irregularly textured wooden slats, which come from the neighbouring forest, submerging the hotel in its environment, and giving it a unique appearance. The use of natural materials is abundant in the building's design, combined with a mix of limestone, leather, and brass. The project adopts various measures to ensure the hotel's self-sufficiency, such as the use of biomass for heating, the reuse of wastewater for irrigation, the use of well water, or the future use of wind power produced electricity.

Da sich dieses Hotel – das Teil eines Golfclubs ist – auf Pfeilern befindet, „schwebt" es quasi über dem Boden, was eine enge Verbindung zum Wald schafft. Weil für die Bauarbeiten keine Grabungen erforderlich waren, konnten die Bäume neben dem Gebäude ungehindert weiterwachsen. Die rote Fassade aus Holzlatten in unregelmäßiger Struktur aus den nahegelegenen Wäldern macht das Hotel einzigartig und lässt es mit seiner Umgebung verschmelzen. Bei der Gebäudeplanung wurden viele natürliche Materialien mit einer Kombination aus Kalkstein, Leder und Messing verwendet. Teil des Hotelprojekts sind verschiedene Maßnahmen zu dessen Selbstversorgung, darunter die Verwendung von Biomasse zum Heizen, die Wiederverwertung des Abwassers zur Bewässerung, die Verwendung von Brunnenwasser oder die zukünftige Stromversorgung durch Windkraft.

Le fait que cet hôtel implanté sur le site d'un club de golf soit monté sur des piliers donne l'impression qu'il « flotte » au-dessus du sol, générant ainsi un lien étroit avec la forêt. L'absence d'excavation durant la construction a permis aux arbres de pousser près du bâtiment et fait qu'ils n'ont pas eu à être abattus. Sa façade rouge est recouverte de lamelles de bois de texture irrégulière provenant de la forêt avoisinante, fondant l'hôtel dans son environnement, et lui conférant un caractère unique. Les matériaux naturels sont utilisés abondamment dans le design du bâtiment, associés à un mélange de calcaire, de cuir et de cuivre. Ce projet adopte différentes mesures pour garantir l'autosuffisance du lieu, tels que l'usage de la biomasse pour le chauffage, la réutilisation des eaux usées pour l'irrigation, l'utilisation d'eau de puits, ou l'exploitation future d'énergie générée par éolienne.

La disposición sobre pilares de este hotel situado en un club de golf hace que el edificio «flote» sobre el suelo, generando así un estrecho vínculo con el bosque. La ausencia de excavación durante la construcción permitió a los árboles crecer cerca del edificio y redujo la necesidad de talarlos. Su fachada de color rojo está revestida de listones de madera de texturas irregulares, procedentes del bosque vecino, que sumergen al hotel en el entorno y le otorgan una expresividad única. El uso de materiales naturales es abundante en el diseño de todo el edificio, combinados con una mezcla de piedra caliza, cuero y latón. El proyecto adopta diversas medidas destinadas a hacer autosuficiente al hotel, como el uso de biomasa para calefacción, la reutilización de aguas residuales para riego, el uso de agua de pozo o el futuro uso de electricidad procedente de energía eólica.

Site plan

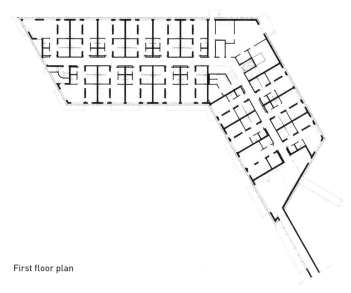

First floor plan

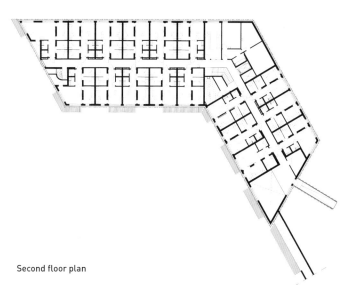

Second floor plan

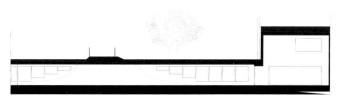

Longitudinal section - Access

Cross section

KWK PROMES
ROBERT KONIECZNY

WWW.KWKPROMES.PL

Robert Konieczny graduated from the University of Technology in Gliwice. In 1996 he graduated from the New Jersey Institute of Technology and in 1999 he founded KWK Promes Studio, which he has directed from that date. In 2007, the studio was among those where the 44 best young architects in the world could be found, according to the Agency "Scalae". In 2016, its National Museum project - the Dialogue Centre Przelomy in Sczecin was chosen as building of the year at the World Architecture Festival international competition and best public space in Europe in the European Prize for Urban Public Space competition, promoted by the CCCB of Barcelona. In 2017, Konieczny's Ark project won the award for the best new private house in the Wallpaper Design Awards. The studio has received 10 nominations for the Foundation Mies Van der Rohe European awards. Robert Konieczny is one of the Polish architects most frequently published overseas.

Robert Konieczny est diplômé de l'Université de technologie de Gliwice. En 1996 il a obtenu un diplôme du New Jersey Institute of Technology et en 1999 il a fondé KWK Promes Studio, qu'il dirige depuis. En 2007, ce studio faisait partie de ceux dans lesquels travaillaient les 44 meilleurs jeunes architectes du monde, selon l'agence « Scalae ». En 2016, son projet de Musée national – le Dialogue Centre Przelomy à Sczecin, a été choisi comme « bâtiment de l'année » au concours international du Festival mondial de l'architecture et « meilleur espace public d'Europe » pour le prix européen du concours de l'espace public urbain, promu par le CCCB de Barcelone. En 2017, le projet d'arche de Konieczny a remporté le prix de la meilleure maison individuelle aux Wallpaper Design Awards. Le studio a été nominé 10 fois pour les European awards de la Fondation Mies Van der Rohe. Robert Konieczny est l'un des architectes polonais les plus fréquemment publiés à l'étranger.

Robert Konieczny verfügt über einen Abschluss der University of Technology in Gliwice. 1996 erlangte er zudem einen Abschluss des New Jersey Institute of Technology. 1999 gründete er das KWK Promes Studio, dessen Unternehmensleiter er nach wie vor ist. 2007 wurde das Studio von der Agentur „Scalae" unter den besten 44 jungen Architekten weltweit gelistet. 2016 wurde das Nationalmuseumsprojekt Dialogue Centre Przelomy in Sczecin beim internationalen Wettbewerb World Architecture Festival zum Gebäude des Jahres gewählt und erhielt zudem die Auszeichnung als Europas bestes öffentliches Gebäude in Form des European Prize for Urban Public Space des CCCB Barcelona. 2017 wurde das Koniecznys-Projekt Ark bei den Wallpaper Design Awards zum besten neuen Privathaus gekürt. Das Studio war zehn Mal für die Foundation Mies Van der Rohe European Awards nominiert. Robert Konieczny gehört zu den am häufigsten in internationalen Veröffentlichungen genannten polnischen Architekten.

Robert Konieczny se graduó en la Universidad de Tecnología de Gliwice. En 1996 recibió el título del New Jersey Institute of Technology y en 1999 fundó el estudio KWK Promes, que dirige desde entonces. En 2007, el estudio figuraba entre los 44 mejores jóvenes arquitectos del mundo según la agencia Scalae. En 2016, su proyecto de Museo Nacional - Centro de Diálogo Przelomy en Sczecin fue elegido edificio del año en el concurso internacional World Architecture Festival y mejor espacio público en Europa en el European Prize for Urban Public Space, promovido por el CCCB de Barcelona. En 2017, el proyecto Konieczny's Ark ganó el premio a la mejor nueva casa privada en los Wallpaper Design Awards. El estudio ha sido nominado diez veces a los premios europeos de la Fundación Mies Van der Rohe. Robert Konieczny es uno de los arquitectos polacos más frecuentemente publicados en el extranjero.

[STANDARD HOUSE]

[LIVING GARDEN HOUSE]

STANDARD HOUSE

Based on an atypical premise, this dwelling was to be built in two different places: Pszczyna and Berlin. The aim was to create a design adapted to both sites, but the second location had not been chosen at the time of implementation of the first part of the task. The result is this round dwelling, a shape that easily adapts to solar energy, with the freedom to choose the type of roof making it universal in landscape terms, and the flexibility in its internal layout allowing it to adjust to family requirements. The house was designed in accordance with sustainable criteria, using natural materials and prefabricated components which reduced building costs while maintaining the quality of the final outcome. The building, helped by its optimal circular shape, is a Passive House thanks to its good thermal insulation and renewable energy installations.

Dieses Haus mit typischen Vorgaben wurde sowohl in Pszczyna als auch in Berlin gebaut. Dementsprechend musste ein zu beiden Standorten passendes Design entwickelt werden, wobei der zweite Standort beim ersten Teil der Arbeit noch gar nicht feststand. Daher entschieden sich die Architekten für ein rundes Gebäude, da dies die Verwendung von Solarenergie begünstigt. Dank des individuell auswählbaren Daches kann es in jede Umgebung integriert werden. Auch der Innenraum kann flexibel an die Bedürfnisse einer Familie angepasst werden. Bei der Planung des Hauses wurde auf Kriterien der Nachhaltigkeit geachtet. Hierfür wurden hochwertige und dennoch günstige Materialien und Fertigbauteile ausgewählt. Die optimale runde Form, die gute Wärmedämmung und die Verwendung erneuerbarer Energien machen das Gebäude zu einem Passivhaus.

Issue d'un postulat atypique, cette habitation devait être construite dans deux endroits différents : Pszczyna et Berlin. Le but était de créer un design adapté aux deux sites, mais le deuxième emplacement n'avait pas été choisi au moment de la mise en œuvre de la première partie de l'opération. Il en est résulté cette maison ronde, forme qui se prête aisément à l'énergie solaire, la liberté de choisir le type de toit la rendant adaptée à tout paysage, et la souplesse de son plan intérieur lui permettant de répondre aux besoins d'une famille. Cette habitation a été conçue en fonction de critères de développement durable, en se servant de matériaux naturels et de composantes préfabriquées qui ont réduit le coût de production tout en maintenant la qualité du résultat final. Ce bâtiment, avec sa forme circulaire optimale, est une Maison Passive grâce à sa bonne isolation thermique et ses installations en énergie renouvelable.

Partiendo de una premisa atípica, esta casa debía ser construida en dos lugares diferentes: Pszczyna y Berlín. El objetivo fue crear un diseño que se adaptara a ambos emplazamientos, ya que el segundo no había sido escogido en el momento de iniciar el encargo. El resultado es esta casa, con una forma redonda fácilmente adaptable al solar, una libertad de elección del tipo de cubierta que la hace universal en términos paisajísticos, y una flexibilidad en su distribución interior que se ajusta a las necesidades de una familia. La casa se diseñó con criterios sostenibles, utilizando materiales naturales y elementos prefabricados que redujeron los costes de construcción manteniendo la calidad del resultado final. El edificio, ayudado por su óptima forma circular, constituye una casa pasiva gracias a su buen aislamiento térmico e instalaciones de energías renovables.

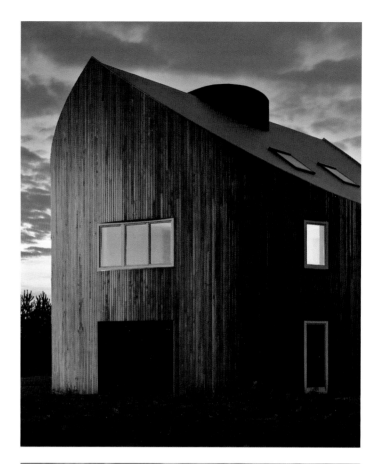

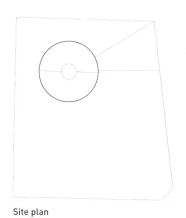

Site plan

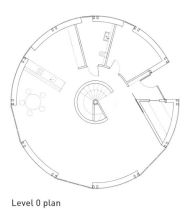

Level 0 plan

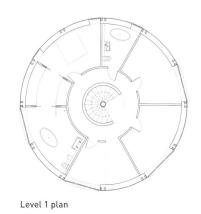

Level 1 plan

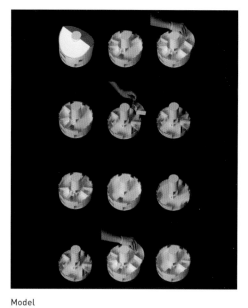

Model

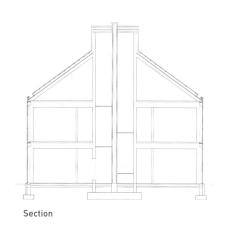

Section

LIVING GARDEN HOUSE

This dwelling is a step in the evolution of the idea of a "living - garden house" from KWK Promes studio, aiming to achieve integration between architecture and nature. Its layout consists of a block on the ground floor, opaque to the outside and open towards the interior garden, isolating the building from the road. There is another block higher up, placed at 90 degrees, which penetrates the plot. Located under the upper block, the living room melds, assisted by its artificial grass flooring and the stainless-steel cladding of its structural walls, with the garden when the windows are opened, producing a dematerialising effect. The first floor, more introverted, contains the bedrooms and access to the terraces. This dwelling is a green building with class A energy efficiency, built with a shape and materials representing local traditions.

Dieses Haus von KWK Promes Studio stellt einen weiteren Schritt bei der Entwicklung des sogenannten „living-garden house" dar, bei dem die Architektur im Einklang mit der Natur stehen soll. Es besteht aus einem opaken ebenerdigen Blockhaus, das durch einen Innengarten von der Straße getrennt wird. Ein höherer Block im 90-Grad-Winkel blickt auf das Anwesen herab. Unterhalb des oberen Blocks befindet sich das Wohnzimmer mit Kunstrasen und tragenden Wänden aus Edelstahl, das bei geöffneten Fenstern perfekt mit dem Garten verschmilzt und für einen entmaterialisierenden Effekt sorgt. Das erste Stockwerk mit den Schlafzimmern, ist eher unauffällig und bietet einen Zugang zur Terrasse. Bei diesem Haus handelt es sich um ein Gebäude mit Energieeffizienzklasse A, wobei Material und Form für lokale Traditionen stehen.

Cette habitation est une étape dans l'évolution de l'idée d'une « maison - jardin à vivre » émanant de KWK Promes studio, visant à rassembler architecture et nature. Son plan est composé d'un module au rez-de-chaussée, opaque pour l'extérieur et ouvert sur le jardin intérieur, isolant le bâtiment de la route. Un autre élément se trouve plus haut, placé à 90 degrés, qui pénètre dans la parcelle. Situé sous le module supérieur, le séjour, grâce à un sol revêtu de pelouse artificielle et au bardage en inox de ses murs porteurs, se fond dans le jardin lorsque les fenêtres sont ouvertes, produisant un effet de dématérialisation. Le premier étage, plus introverti, contient les chambres et l'accès aux terrasses. Cette maison est un bâtiment écologique avec un bilan énergétique de classe A, construit dans une forme et des matériaux évoquant les traditions locales.

Esta casa constituye un paso más en la evolución de la idea «living-garden house» del estudio KWK Promes, dirigida a lograr la integración entre arquitectura y naturaleza. Su esquema consta de un volumen en planta baja, opaco hacia el exterior y abierto hacia el jardín interior, que aisla el edificio de la carretera, y otro volumen superior, colocado a 90°, que penetra en la parcela. Situado bajo el volumen superior, el estar se funde con el jardín al abrir sus ventanales, ayudándose de un pavimento de hierba artificial y del revestimiento de acero inoxidable de sus muros estructurales, que produce un efecto desmaterializador. El primer piso, más introvertido, acoge los dormitorios y los accesos a las terrazas. Esta vivienda constituye un edificio ecológico de eficiencia energética clase A, construido con una forma y materiales representativos de la tradición local.

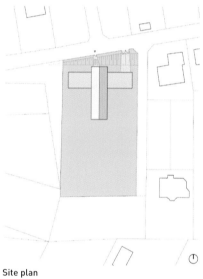

Site plan

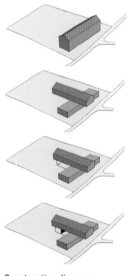

Construction diagram

TYPICAL HOUSE

LIVING-GARDEN HOUSE

Conceptual diagrams

South elevation

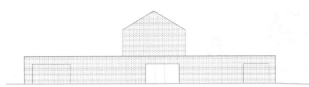

North elevation

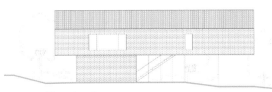

West elevation

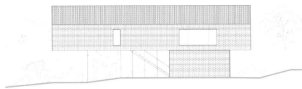

East elevation

Section

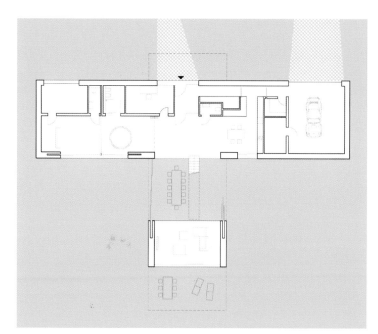
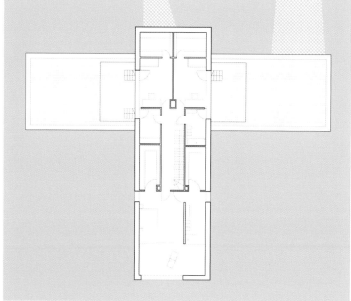

Ground floor plan

First floor plan

LI XIAODONG

Li Xiaodong graduated from Tsinghua University School of Architecture in 1984 and received his doctorate at the School of Architecture of the Technological University of Delft between 1989 and 1993. He is an architect, educator, and architecture researcher. His works include interior design, architecture, and urban spaces. His built works are few due to the dedication and devotion he shows towards his projects, which has led to him winning several national and international awards. Focused on small projects, Li Xiaodong develops proposals for an appropriate "Chinese architecture" bringing together traditional and contemporary expression, technical knowledge, and artistic judgment. His architecture combines the spiritual exploration of ideas with rational thinking and is based on continually researching the underlying concepts of space within a Chinese context.

Li Xiaodong est diplômé de la Tsinghua University School of Architecture (1984) et a reçu son doctorat de l'École d'architecture de l'Université technologique de Delft entre 1989 et 1993. Il est architecte, éducateur, et chercheur en architecture. Ses travaux comportent du design d'intérieur, de l'architecture, et de l'aménagement d'espaces urbains. Ses chantiers sont peu nombreux de par le dévouement et l'implication qu'il mobilise pour chacun de ses projets, ce qui lui a valu de gagner de nombreux prix nationaux et internationaux. Concentré sur des projets à petite échelle, Li Xiaodong développe des propositions d'« architecture chinoise » pertinentes qui rassemblent les expressions traditionnelle et contemporaine, le savoir technique, et le jugement artistique. Son architecture mêle l'exploration spirituelle d'idées avec la pensée rationnelle et elle est basée sur la recherche continuelle de concepts sous-jacents de l'espace dans un contexte chinois.

Li Xiaodong machte 1984 seinen Abschluss an der Tsinghua University School of Architecture und anschließend zwischen 1989 und 1993 seinen Doktortitel an der School of Architecture of the Technological University of Delft. Er arbeitet als Architekt, Ausbilder und Architekturforscher. Zu seinen Arbeiten gehören Inneneinrichtung, Architektur und städtische Räume. Da er sich all seinen Projekten, für die er bereits nationale und internationale Auszeichnungen erhielt, mit äußerster Sorgfalt und Genauigkeit widmet, ist deren Anzahl eher gering. Li Xiaodong konzentriert sich hauptsächlich auf kleine Projekte und entwickelt Konzepte für eine passende "chinesische Architektur", bei denen er traditionelle und zeitgemäße Ausdrucksformen, technisches Wissens und künstlerisches Urteil vereint. Bei seiner Architektur kombiniert er die Spiritualität einer Idee mit rationalem Denken und untersucht dabei fortwährend die zugrundeliegenden Raukonzepte innerhalb des chinesischen Kontexts.

Li Xiaodong se graduó en la Escuela de Arquitectura de la Universidad de Tsinghua en 1984 y se doctoró en la Escuela de Arquitectura de la Universidad Tecnológica de Delft entre 1989-1993. Es arquitecto, educador e investigador en arquitectura. Sus trabajos abarcan el diseño interior, la arquitectura y los espacios urbanos. Sus obras construidas son pocas debido a la gran dedicación y la devoción que vuelca en sus proyectos, hecho que le ha llevado a ganar diversos premios nacionales e internacionales. Centrado en proyectos pequeños, Li Xiaodong desarrolla propuestas sobre una «arquitectura china» apropiada que reúne los modos de expresión tradicionales y contemporáneos, el conocimiento técnico y el juicio artístico. Su arquitectura combina una exploración espiritual de las ideas con el pensamiento racional y se basa en una investigación continua de los conceptos subyacentes del espacio en el contexto chino.

[THE SCREEN]

[THE LIYUAN LIBRARY]

THE SCREEN

Framed within a grouping of architectural interventions aimed at creating a scenic route, this service building sustainably fuses nature and architecture. Its location on a natural mountain platform shows respect for the prevailing conditions of its site. Compositionally, the building is diffused within its environment through a surrounding curtain generating an interaction between its interior and its exterior. This curtain, seemingly simple in appearance, is a complex brick façade combining the artisanal techniques of local builders with modern construction expertise. Inside, the concept of curtain is prolonged with a warmer appearance, by using a local material: bamboo. The interior layout is organised around two courtyards creating a sense of community directed towards the beauty of its natural surroundings.

Umrahmt von einer Gruppierung architektonischer Projekte, die auf eine landschaftlich reizvolle Route abzielen, verbindet dieses Dienstleistungs-gebäude nachhaltig Natur und Architektur. Das Gebäude respektiert die natürlichen Gegebenheiten der Bergplattform, auf der es sich befindet, wodurch ein fortwährender Austausch zwischen innen und außen besteht. Bei dieser einfach wirkenden Trennwand handelt es sich um eine komplexe Ziegelfassade, die lokales Bauhandwerk mit modernen Konstruktions-techniken kombiniert. Im Inneren besteht das Trennwandkonzept in einer wärmer wirkenden Form mit heimischem Bambus fort. Der Innenbereich ist um zwei Innenhöfe herum angeordnet, die ein Gefühl der Verbunden-heit mit der Schönheit der natürlichen Umgebung erwecken.

Dans le cadre d'un groupement d'interventions architecturales vouées à créer une route touristique, ce bâtiment de service opère une fusion du-rable entre nature et architecture. Son emplacement sur une plateforme montagneuse naturelle est une marque de respect pour les conditions ori-ginelles du site. Au niveau de sa composition, ce bâtiment est en commu-nication avec son environnement par le biais d'un écran extérieur générant une interaction entre son intérieur et son extérieur. Cet écran, simple au premier abord, est une façade de briques complexe mêlant les techniques artisanales de maçons locaux avec le savoir-faire de la construction mo-derne. À l'intérieur, ce concept d'écran est prolongé de façon plus cha-leureuse, en utilisant un matériau local : le bambou. Le plan intérieur est organisé autour de deux cours, ce qui crée un sentiment d'appartenance à une communauté orienté vers la beauté de son environnement naturel.

Enmarcado en un conjunto de intervenciones arquitectónicas destinadas a crear una ruta paisajística, este edificio de servicios integra de forma sostenible naturaleza y arquitectura. Su emplazamiento sobre una pla-taforma natural de la montaña muestra respeto hacia los condicionan-tes del lugar. Compositivamente, el edificio se difumina en el entorno a través de una cortina que lo envuelve y que genera una interacción entre interior y exterior. Esta cortina, en apariencia simple, es una compleja fachada de ladrillo que aúna técnicas artesanas de constructores locales y técnicas modernas. En el interior, el concepto de cortina se prolonga con una apariencia más cálida, mediante el uso de otro material local: el bambú. La distribución interior se organiza alrededor de dos patios que crean un sentimiento de comunidad y que se orientan hacia la belleza del entorno natural.

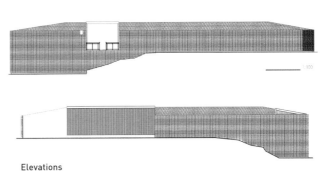

Elevations

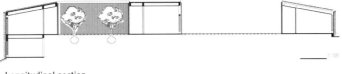

Longitudinal section

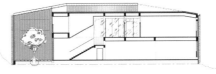

Cross section

THE LIYUAN LIBRARY

The idea of the project focused on forming a spiritual qichang (a flow of energy) concentrating the natural landscape. The building, very simply shaped, is integrated into its environment using various components, notably the fine wood lining covering the façades which gives the project its name (Liyuan). The use of this material provides the library with a local feel, at the same time as allowing and sifting the entry of natural light throughout all its enclosed spaces. The interior represents a single space without partitions or furniture, where steps and small slopes delimit different areas. Its ventilation was designed to be in keeping with its surroundings, taking advantage of the coolness of the water during the summer and the heat provided by the double glazing of the cladding in winter. The library encourages social sustainability, becoming a platform for the exchange of ideas.

Die Idee hinter dem Projekt war die Schaffung eines spirituellen Qichang (Energiefluss) durch die natürliche Landschaft. Das einfach geformte Gebäude wurde mit Hilfe unterschiedlicher Komponenten in seine Umgebung integriert. Hierzu gehört besonders die feine Holzverkleidung der Fassaden, die dem Projekt den Namen „Liyuan" gab. Das Material verleiht der Bibliothek einen lokalen Anstrich und lässt natürliches Licht in jeden Winkel dringen. Im Inneren besteht die Bibliothek aus einem einzigen Raum ohne Aufteilung und Mobiliar; stattdessen sorgen Stufen und Rampen für die Abgrenzung der einzelnen Bereiche. Die Belüftung steht im Einklang mit der Umgebung und nutzt im Sommer die Vorzüge des kalten Wassers und im Winter die Wärme durch die Doppelverglasung. Die Bibliothek soll eine Plattform zum Austausch von Ideen zur gesellschaftlichen Nachhaltigkeit sein.

L'idée derrière ce projet était axée sur la formation d'un *qichang* (flot d'énergie) spirituel concentrant le paysage naturel. Ce bâtiment, d'une forme très simple, est intégré dans son environnement par le biais de diverses composantes, notamment le fin bardage de bois recouvrant les façades qui a donné son nom au projet (*Liyuan*). L'utilisation de ce matériau confère à la bibliothèque un aspect local, tout en favorisant et diffusant l'afflux de lumière naturelle dans tous les espaces fermés. L'intérieur représente un espace unique sans cloison ni mobilier, où les marches et petites pentes délimitent les différentes zones. Son aération a été conçue pour être dans la continuité de son environnement, profitant de la fraîcheur de l'eau au cours de l'été et de la chaleur apportée par la double épaisseur de bardage en hiver. Cette bibliothèque, devenue plateforme pour les échanges d'idées, encourage la durabilité sociale.

La idea del proyecto se centró en formar un *qichang* (flujo de energía) espiritual que concentrara el paisaje natural. El edificio, de formas simples, se integra en su entorno mediante diversos factores, entre los que destaca el revestimiento de leña menuda que envuelve las fachadas y que da nombre al proyecto, *liyuan*. El uso de este material aporta carácter local a la biblioteca, a la vez que permite y tamiza la entrada de luz natural a través de todos sus cerramientos. El interior representa un único espacio sin particiones ni mobiliario, en el que escalones y pequeños desniveles delimitan las zonas. Su ventilación se diseñó acorde con el entorno, aprovechando el frescor del agua para el verano y el calor del doble acristalamiento de la cubierta en invierno. La biblioteca fomenta la sostenibilidad social, convirtiéndose en una plataforma para el intercambio de ideas.

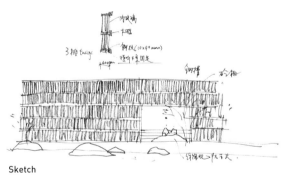

Sketch

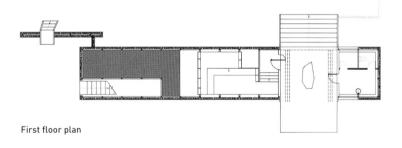

First floor plan

East elevation

South elevation

West elevation

North elevation

OHLAB

WWW.OHLAB.NET

OHLAB is an award-winning office devoted to urban analysis and cultural research of contemporary society through design, architectural practice and urban strategy. The office, directed by Paloma Hernaiz and Jaime Oliver, was originally established in Shanghai, moved to Madrid and currently its main office is in Palma de Mallorca where a varied team of architects and interior designers are working in international projects of very different scales and requirements. Their work has been published extensively worldwide in specialized and general media and in recent years it has received numerous international awards such as World Architecture Festival, Best of the Year Awards from New York or Great Indoor Awards. The office has also received other recognitions such as the nomination to Mies Van der Rohe Awards or being selected by the Chicago Atheneum as "one of Europe's most important and emerging young architects of 2014".

OHLAB est un cabinet récompensé voué à l'analyse urbaine et à la recherche culturelle de la société contemporaine par le biais du design, de la pratique architecturale et de la stratégie urbaine. Ce cabinet, dirigé par Paloma Hernaiz et Jaime Oliver, a été originellement fondé à Shanghai, puis a déménagé à Madrid et ses bureaux principaux sont maintenant à Palma de Majorque où une équipe de 12 architectes et designers d'intérieur travaillent sur des projets à Majorque, Madrid, New York, L.A. et Miami. Paloma et Jaime sont actuellement professeurs de design au Master de design des environnements de travail, de vente et d'apprentissage de la IE School of Architecture de Londres et Madrid. Leur travail a été publié dans le monde entier dans les médias spécialisés et génériques.
Cet office a été sélectionné comme étant l'un des « 40 under 40 » parmi les jeunes architectes et designers européens émergents par le European Centre for Architecture Art Design and Urban Studies et le Chicago Athenaeum Museum of Architecture and Design en 2014.

OHLAB ist ein preisgekröntes Unternehmen, das sich der Stadtanalyse und kulturellen Erforschung unserer derzeitigen Gesellschaft durch Design, Architektur und urbane Strategie verschrieben hat.
Das Unternehmen unter der Leitung von Paloma Hernaiz und Jaime Oliver wurde ursprünglich in Shanghai gegründet, zog später nach Madrid um und hat inzwischen seinen Hauptsitz in Palma de Mallorca, wo ein Team aus 12 Architekten und Raumausstattern an Projekten auf Mallorca, in Madrid, New York, LA und Miami arbeitet. Paloma und Jaime sind zudem Professoren für Design für den Master-Abschluss in Design für Arbeits-, Geschäfts- und Lernumgebungen (Design for Work, Retail and Learning environments) der IE School of Architecture in London und Madrid. Zu ihrer Arbeit gibt es weltweit Veröffentlichungen in allgemeinen und Fachmedien.
Das Unternehmen wurde 2014 vom European Centre for Architecture Art Design and Urban Studies und dem The Chicago Athenaeum Museum of Architecture and Design zu einem von „Europas 40 besten" fortschrittlichen jungen Architekten und Designern gewählt.

OHLAB es una oficina dedicada al análisis urbano y la investigación cultural de la sociedad contemporánea a través de la práctica del diseño, la arquitectura y la estrategia urbana.
El estudio, dirigido por Paloma Hernaiz y Jaime Oliver, se estableció originalmente en Shanghai, se trasladó a Madrid y actualmente su oficina principal se ubica en Palma de Mallorca donde un equipo multidisciplinar trabaja en proyectos internacionales de muy diferentes escalas y requerimientos. Su trabajo se ha publicado ampliamente tanto en prensa general como especializada y en los últimos años han recibido numerosos premios internacionales como los World Architecture Festival, Best of the Year Awards de Nueva York o Great Indoor Awards. También han recibido otras distinciones como la nominación al Premio Mies Van der Rohe o ser nombrados por el Chicago Atheneum como "Uno de los estudios de arquitectura emergentes más importantes de Europa en 2014".

[PASEO MALLORCA 15]

[MM HOUSE]

PASEO MALLORCA 15

This new residential complex acquired its identity through its own context, taking the form of a set of abstract urban blocks with two types of differentiated cladding. The first is located in the chamfered corner, in the area facing the best direction and with the best views, it consists of an inner glass skin and an outdoor one of wooden slats representing an organic veil, permeable and ever-changing for the building's energy efficiency. The second is solid and hermetic and contains the most private dwelling areas. The different levels of the inner courtyard, with its landscaped terraces, act as a green lung connecting the building from the roof to the first basement. The project has been designed following *Passivhaus* standards to achieve maximum efficiency and minimum demand for air conditioning.

Das Design für diesen Wohnkomplex ergab sich aus seinem ganz eigenen Kontext. Er hat die Form eines abstrakten städtischen Gebäudeblocks mit zwei unterschiedlichen Verkleidungen. Die erste besteht innen aus einer Glasschicht und außen aus Holzplatten und umschließt die Schrägkante, also den Bereich mit der besten Ausrichtung und Aussicht. Sie ist organisch, durchlässig und – wie für die Energieeffizienz erforderlich – sehr anpassungsfähig. Die zweite Verkleidung ist fest und undurchlässig und umgibt die privaten Wohnbereiche. Die unterschiedlichen Ebenen des Innenhofs mit ihren Gartenterrassen verbinden das Gebäude vom Dach bis zum ersten Kellergeschoss und fungieren als grüne Lunge. Das Projekt erfüllt die Passivhaus-Standards für maximale Energieeffizienz und benötigt kaum Klimatisierung.

Ce nouveau complexe résidentiel a trouvé son identité à travers son propre contexte, sous la forme d'un ensemble d'îlots urbains abstraits habillés de deux types de revêtement différents. Le premier est situé dans l'angle biseauté, dans la zone la mieux orientée et bénéficiant des meilleures vues, composé d'un habillage intérieur en verre et d'un extérieur de lattes en bois représentant un voile organique, perméable et évolutif pour l'efficacité énergétique du bâtiment. Le second est massif et hermétique et contient les zones les plus privées de l'habitation. Les différents niveaux de la cour intérieure, avec ses terrasses paysagées, sert de poumon vert reliant le bâtiment du toit au premier sous-sol. Ce projet a été conçu en conformité avec les normes Passivhaus pour une efficacité maximale et des besoins de climatisation minimaux.

Este nuevo conjunto residencial adquiere su identidad a través de su propio contexto, configurándose mediante un juego de volúmenes urbanos abstractos y dos tipos de envolventes diferenciadas. La primera se sitúa en el chaflán, en la zona con mejor orientación y mejores vistas, y se compone de una piel interior de vidrio y una exterior de lamas de madera que representa un velo orgánico, permeable y cambiante, clave para la eficiencia energética del edificio. La segunda es sólida y hermética y contiene las zonas más privadas de las viviendas. Los diferentes niveles del patio interior, con sus terrazas ajardinadas, actúan como un pulmón verde que conecta el edificio desde la cubierta hasta el primer sótano. El proyecto se ha diseñado según los estándares *Passivhaus* para conseguir una máxima eficiencia energética y una mínima demanda de climatización.

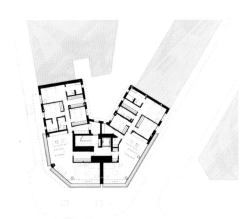
Site plan

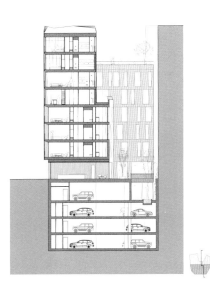
Building sections

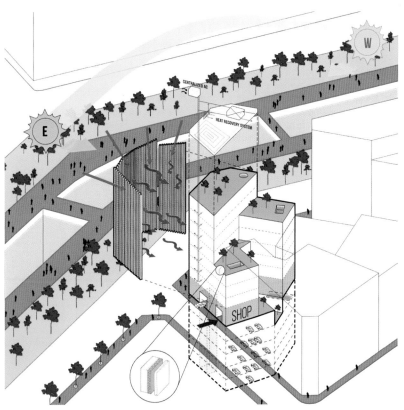
Sustainability diagram

MM HOUSE

This house seeks maximum energy efficiency to adapt to the program, orientation towards the sun, the views, and the slope of the terrain. The project optimises the program by grouping it into four boxes - kitchen, living/dining room, master bedroom and guest rooms – which can work together or independently. Each of the boxes is placed carefully on the ground and turns on its axis to find the best views and the best direction according to its use. The large openings in the main façade and some smaller hollows on the opposite side allow for cross-ventilation. The dwelling has been designed in accordance with Passivhaus standards to achieve maximum energy efficiency. Its design promotes environmental and sustainability values, providing savings and comfort without implying additional financial effort.

Bei der Planung des Hauses ging es, wie bei diesem Programm vorgesehen, um maximale Energieeffizienz. Hierbei wurden die Ausrichtung zur Sonne und die Neigung des Untergrunds berücksichtigt. Das Projekt optimiert das Programm durch die Aufteilung in die vier Bereiche Küche, Wohn- und Esszimmer, Hauptschlafzimmer und Gästezimmer, die unabhängig voneinander oder gemeinsam genutzt werden können. Jeder Bereich wurde sorgsam auf dem Untergrund platziert und dreht sich auf seiner Achse, um jeweils die beste Aussicht und die beste Ausrichtung je nach Nutzung zu erreichen. Für die Querlüftung sorgen die großen Öffnungen der Hauptfassade und mehrere kleine Hohlräume an der gegenüberliegenden Seite. Das Wohngebäude entspricht den Passivhaus-Standards für maximale Energieeffizienz. Hauptmerkmale des Designs sind Umweltfreundlichkeit und Nachhaltigkeit, um ohne zusätzliche Ausgaben für Einsparungen und Komfort zu sorgen.

Cette maison recherche une efficacité énergétique maximale pour s'adapter au programme : l'orientation vers le soleil, les vues, et la pente du terrain. Ce projet optimise celui-ci en le groupant en quatre modules - cuisine, séjour/salle-à-manger, chambre principale et chambres d'invités – qui peuvent fonctionner ensemble ou indépendamment. Chacun des modules est soigneusement placé sur le sol et tourné sur son axe de façon à choisir la meilleure vue et la meilleure direction selon son utilisation. Les grandes ouvertures de la façade principale et de petits creux du côté opposé permettent une aération transversale. Ce bâtiment a été conçu en conformité avec les normes *Passivhaus* pour une efficacité énergétique optimale. Sa conception met en avant des valeurs écologiques et durables, apportant économies et confort sans impliquer d'effort financier supplémentaire.

Esta vivienda busca la máxima eficiencia energética adaptándose al programa, las orientaciones solares, las vistas y la pendiente del terreno. El proyecto optimiza el programa agrupándolo en cuatro cajas –cocina, estar/comedor, habitación principal y habitaciones de invitados– que pueden funcionar en conjunto o independientemente. Cada una de las cajas se coloca cuidadosamente sobre el terreno y gira sobre su eje para buscar las mejores vistas y la mejor orientación según su uso. Las grandes aberturas de las fachadas principales y unos huecos más pequeños en su cara opuesta permiten la ventilación cruzada. La vivienda se ha proyectado según los estándares *Passivhaus* para conseguir una máxima eficiencia energética. Su diseño promueve los valores medioambientales y de sostenibilidad, reportando ahorro y confort sin que ello implique un esfuerzo económico adicional.

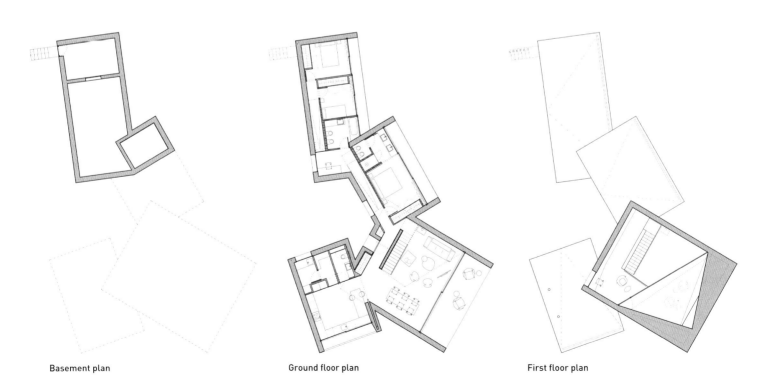

Basement plan

Ground floor plan

First floor plan

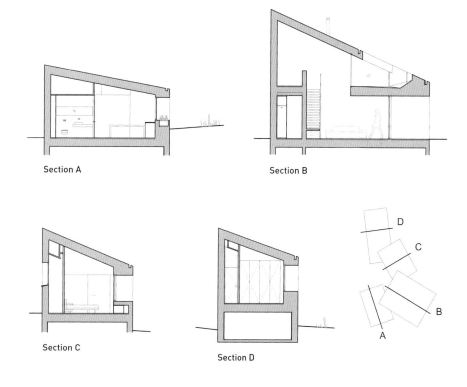

Section A

Section B

Section C

Section D

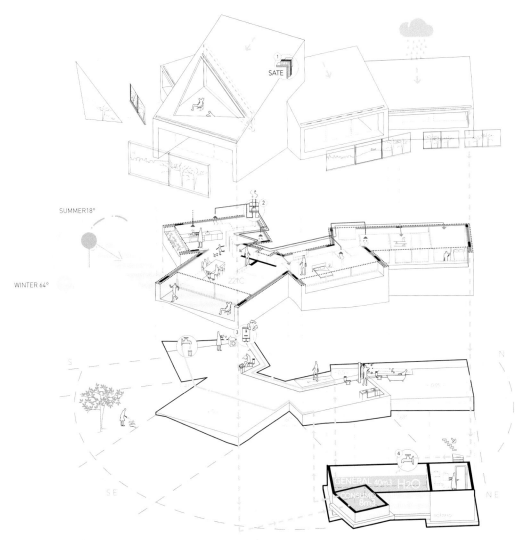

SUMMER18°

WINTER 64°

SATE

1. Exterior Insulating and
   Finishing System (EIFIS)
   ·············· Insulation

2. Air renewal system
   —— Indoor air
   —— Fresh air

3. Rainwater distribution
   system
   —— Direct
   —— SHW

4. Rainwater storage system

Sustainability diagram

PDP LONDON

WWW.PDPLONDON.COM

PDP London is a 100 strong London, Madrid and Hong Kong based international architectural practice known for skilful integration of contemporary architecture within historic environments and expertise through the whole spectrum of residential, commercial, hospitality, civic and mixed-use projects.

With a mindfulness and inherent understanding of traditional values and architectural heritage, and a desire to create world class architecture, PDP London has been pivotal in shaping the built landscape and public realm both in London and further afield, designing great places to live, work and play.

PDP London's projects are developed with sound environmental principles and sustainability in mind from the very start.

PDP London est un cabinet d'architecture international de 100 employés, basé à Londres, Madrid et à Hong Kong, renommé pour son intégration experte d'architecture contemporaine dans des environnements historiques et son savoir-faire dans tous les domaines, projets résidentiels, commerciaux, hôteliers, civils ou à destinations diverses.

Avec sa réflexion attentive et sa compréhension intrinsèque des valeurs traditionnelles et du patrimoine architectural, ainsi que son désir de créer une architecture de calibre international, PDP London a eu un rôle crucial dans la formation du paysage bâti et du domaine public à la fois à Londres et au-delà de ses frontières, concevant des endroits superbes où vivre, travailler et se divertir.

Dès le début de leur conception, les projets de PDP London sont développés en prenant en compte principes environnementaux sains et durabilité.

PDP London ist ein internationales Architekturunternehmen mit 100 Mitarbeitern in London, Madrid und Hong Kong, das für die gute Einbindung zeitgemäßer Architektur in historische Umgebungen und seine allumfassende Erfahrung mit Wohn- und Geschäftsgebäuden, Krankenhäusern, Verwaltungs- und Mehrzweckgebäuden bekannt ist.

Durch sein bedachtes und tiefgreifendes Verständnis für traditionelle Werte und architektonisches Erbe und den Wunsch, Architektur von Weltklasse zu schaffen, spielt PDP London eine entscheidende Rolle bei der Prägung der Baulandschaft und öffentlichen Gebäude sowohl in London als auch andernorts. Hieraus entstanden tolle Orte zum Leben, Arbeiten und Spielen.

PDP London berücksichtigt bei seinen Projekten von Anfang an strenge Umwelt- und Nachhaltigkeitsprinzipien.

PDP London es un estudio arquitectónico con oficinas en Londres, Madrid y Hong Kong conocido por su delicada integración de arquitectura contemporánea en emplazamientos históricos y su experiencia en todo tipo de proyectos: desde hoteleros y comerciales a edificios residenciales y públicos así como proyectos mixtos.

Su conocimiento y aceptación de los valores tradicionales y la herencia arquitectónica y el deseo de crear arquitectura de gran calidad le han otorgado un papel clave para modelar el paisaje constructivo y el patrimonio público tanto en Londres como en otras ciudades, diseñando grandes lugares para vivir, trabajar y jugar.

Los proyectos de PDP London se rigen por unos sólidos principios medioambientales y tienen en cuenta desde el primer momento su sostenibilidad.

[ONE CHURCH SQUARE]

ONE CHURCH SQUARE

This five-storey building in the Centre of London, the outcome of a contest promoted by the charity Dolphin Living, consists of 39 affordable quality homes, designed in accordance with environmental criteria. The project is integrated into a rich urban context and visually and physically connects to the square with the neighbouring church. Its approach shows a strong sense of community due to the covered central courtyard which gives access to dwellings, and the roof terrace, open to all tenants. The building is placed at grade 4 of the Code for Sustainable Homes through approaches such as using a CHP (Combined Heat and Power) system to generate heating and hot water, mechanical ventilation with a heat recuperator or photovoltaic cells for producing electricity, as well as the inclusion of passive measures in its design.

Dieses fünfstöckige Gebäude im Zentrum Londons gehört zu den 39 erschwinglichen und dennoch hochwertigen und umweltfreundlichen Häusern des Charity Dolphin Living-Konzepts. Das Projekt musste in die vielfältige städtische Umgebung eingebunden werden und passt optisch und physikalisch zum benachbarten Kirchenplatz. Durch den überdachten zentralen Innenhof sind sowohl die Wohnungen als auch die Gemeinschaftsdachterrasse zu erreichen, was den Sinn für Zusammengehörigkeit des Konzepts betont. Laut dem Gesetz für nachhaltige Häuser (Code for Sustainable Homes) erreicht das Gebäude durch sein System zur Kraft-Wärme-Kopplung (KWK) für Heizung und Warmwasser, die mechanische Belüftung mit Wärmerückgewinnung, die Photovoltaik-Anlage zur Stromerzeugung und die Maßnahmen zur Entwicklung eines Passivhauses den Energieeffizienzgrad 4.

Cet immeuble de cinq étages au centre de Londres, résultat d'un concours lancé par la société caritative Dolphin Living, est composé de 39 appartements abordables de qualité, conçus en conformité avec des critères environnementaux. Ce projet est intégré dans un riche contexte urbain et il est relié visuellement et physiquement à la place du quartier et à son église. Son approche montre un sentiment d'appartenance à une communauté de par la cour centrale couverte qui donne accès aux habitations, et le toit-terrasse ouvert à tous les locataires. Ce bâtiment est classé au grade 4 du code de l'habitat durable (Code for Sustainable Homes) par le biais d'approches telles que l'utilisation d'un CHP (système combiné de chauffage et d'énergie) pour générer chaleur et eau chaude, d'une ventilation mécanique avec récupérateur de chaleur ou de cellules photovoltaïques pour la production d'électricité, ainsi que l'inclusion de mesures passives dans sa conception.

Este edificio de cinco plantas, resultado de un concurso promovido por la entidad benéfica Dolphin Living en el centro de Londres, se compone de 39 viviendas asequibles de calidad, diseñadas con criterios medioambientales. El proyecto se integra en un rico contexto urbano y se conecta visual y físicamente con la plaza de la iglesia vecina. Su planteamiento encierra un fuerte sentido de la comunidad gracias al patio central cubierto, que da acceso a las viviendas, y a la terraza de la cubierta, abierta a todos los inquilinos. El edificio alcanza el grado 4 del *Code for Sustainable Homes* mediante estrategias como el uso del sistema CHP (*Combined Heat and Power*) para generar calefacción y agua caliente, de ventilación mecánica con recuperador de calor, o de células fotovoltaicas para producción de electricidad, además de la integración de medidas pasivas en su diseño.

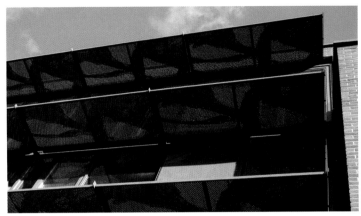

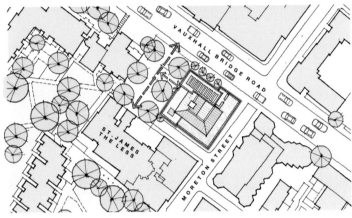

Site plan

Sketch

Sketch

Vauxhall Bridge Road elevation

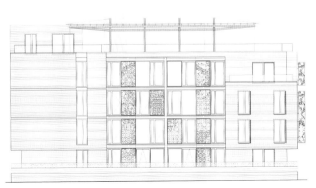

Thorndike Street elevation

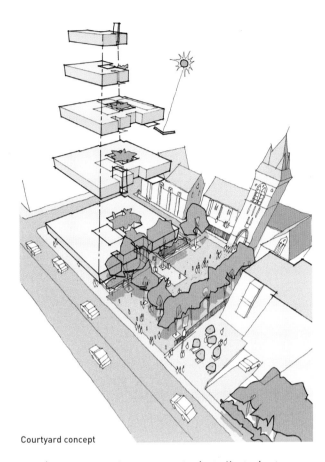

Courtyard concept

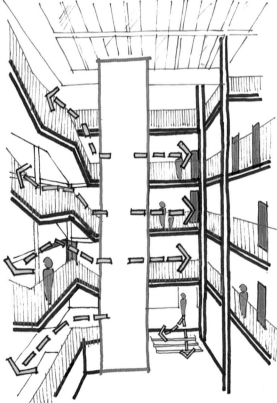

Community sketch

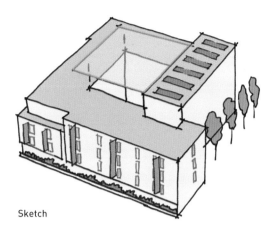

Sketch

First floor plan C7

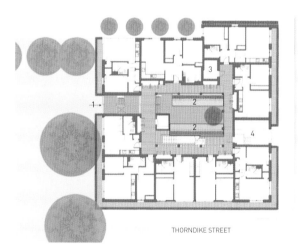

THORNDIKE STREET

MORETON STREET

Ground floor plan

1. Entrance
2. Bike storage
3. General store
4. Bin store

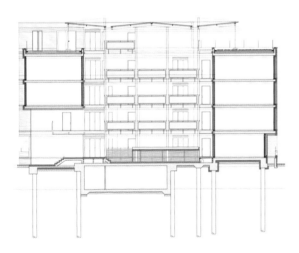

Section

PKdM

WWW.PKDM.IS

PKdM is a Nordic architecture and Design Studio based in Iceland. Its founder, Pálmar Kristmundsson, is inspired by the impressive Icelandic countryside and his encounters with vernacular Japanese architecture. His partner, Fernando de Mendonça, provides a dynamic international perspective originating from large-scale architecture projects in South America and Europe.
In PKdM, an international team of architects works on projects that include development and urban planning, skyscrapers, public buildings, and housing. Clients and the PKdM staff are committed to experimentation and the quest for exciting architectural experiences.
PKdM's design philosophy includes an unwavering commitment to the natural environment. To ensure the quality and the environmental development of its buildings, PKdM applies environmental management and quality standards throughout the design process.

PKdM est un studio d'architecture et de design nordique basé en Islande. Son fondateur, Pálmar Kristmundsson, est inspiré par l'impressionnante campagne islandaise et ses rencontres avec l'architecture vernaculaire japonaise. Son partenaire, Fernando de Mendonça, apporte une perspective internationale dynamique provenant de projets architecturaux à grande échelle en Amérique du Sud et en Europe.
Chez PKdM, une équipe internationale d'architectes œuvre sur des projets qui comportent du développement et de la planification urbaine, des gratte-ciels, des bâtiments publics, et des habitations. Les clients et le personnel de PKdM sont engagés dans l'expérimentation et la quête d'expériences architecturales palpitantes.
La philosophie du design de PKdM comprend un engagement indéfectible envers l'environnement naturel. Pour garantir la qualité et le développement écologique de ses constructions, PKdM applique une gestion environnementale et des normes de qualité tout au long du processus de conception.

PKdM ist ein nordisches Architektur- und Designstudio in Island. Gründer Pálmar Kristmundsson erhält seine Inspiration durch die beeindruckende Landschaft Islands und seine Begegnungen mit der typisch japanischen Architektur. Sein Partner Fernando de Mendonça verfügt durch große Architekturprojekte in Südamerika und Europa über einen dynamischen, internationalen Weitblick.
Bei FKdM arbeitet ein internationales Architektenteam an Projekten zur Entwicklung und Städteplanung, Wolkenkratzern, öffentlichen Gebäuden und Wohnhäusern. Die PKdM-Mitarbeiter sind ebenso wie ihre Kunden äußerst experimentierfreudig und stets auf der Suche nach spannenden architektonischen Möglichkeiten.
Die Designphilosophie von PKdM fußt auf einer unerschütterlichen Verpflichtung gegenüber unserer Umwelt. Durch die Einbindung von Umweltmanagement und Qualitätsstandards während des gesamten Planungsprozesses garantiert PKdM Qualität und Umweltfreundlichkeit seiner Gebäude.

PKdM es un estudio nórdico de arquitectura y diseño con sede en Islandia. Su fundador, Pálmar Kristmundsson, se inspira en el impresionante paisaje natural islandés y en sus encuentros con la arquitectura vernácula japonesa. Su socio, Fernando de Mendonça, aporta una dinámica perspectiva internacional desde proyectos arquitectónicos a gran escala en América del Sur y Europa.
En PKdM, un equipo internacional de arquitectos trabaja en proyectos que incluyen desarrollo y planificación urbana, rascacielos, edificios públicos y viviendas. Los clientes y el personal de PKdM están comprometidos con la experimentación y la búsqueda de experiencias arquitectónicas emocionantes.
La filosofía de diseño de PKdM incluye un compromiso inquebrantable con el entorno natural. Para asegurar la calidad y el desarrollo ambiental de sus edificios, PKdM aplica estándares de gestión ambiental y de calidad durante todo el proceso de diseño.

[BHM VACATION RENTAL COTTAGES]

[BRÆÐRAHÚS SUMMERHOUSES 1 AND 2]

[ARBORG]

BHM
VACATION RENTAL COTTAGES

The main aim of the design of these holiday cottages was to create a semi-rural architecture in tune with the landscape. The earth from the excavation was used to create a bunker protecting the buildings from the wind and to merge the planted roofs with the slope of the terrain, following the traditional approach of Icelandic turf houses. The façades are covered with seared wood panels, using a Japanese technique that improves the material's durability. The interior presents a simple and effective distribution limiting circulation and minimising complex details. The cabins use geothermal energy from the area. Their design conforms to recognised environmental standards, with the aim of promoting a minimal environmental impact and creating dwellings with almost zero carbon footprint.

Diese Häuser befinden sich in einem Wald unterhalb von beeindruckenden Bergen und wurden für zwei Brüder und deren Familien erbaut. Ein schmaler Holzfußweg führt zwischen Birken hindurch zu den Blockhütten. Somit bemerkt man die atemberaubende Schönheit der Landschaft erst beim Erreichen der Gebäude, deren Terrassen einen weitläufigen Ausblick auf den Fluss und das ihn umgebende Tal bieten. Die Hauptbereiche sind nach Süden hin ausgerichtet und durch Terrassen verbunden, die den eigentlichen Hausmittelpunkt darstellen. Die Gebäude sind so angeordnet, dass sie die Terrassen vor starkem Wind schützen. Die für den Bau entfernten Pflanzen wurden auf den Dächern wieder angepflanzt. Die Fassaden bestehen aus hellen Holzbrettern, die nach und nach ausbleichen und so die Farbschattierungen der umliegenden Birken annehmen.

L'objectif principal du concept de ces cottages de vacances était de créer une architecture semi-rurale en harmonie avec le paysage. La terre de l'excavation a été utilisée pour créer une butte pour protéger les bâtiments du vent et fondre les toits végétaux dans la pente du terrain, selon l'approche des maisons traditionnelles islandaises. Les façades sont recouvertes de panneaux de bois calciné, à partir d'une technique japonaise qui améliore la durabilité du matériau. L'intérieur offre une distribution simple et efficace limitant la circulation et minimisant les détails complexes. Ces cabanes utilisent l'énergie géothermique de leur propre emplacement. Leur conception est conforme aux normes écologiques, avec l'objectif de promouvoir un impact environnemental minimal et de créer des habitations ayant une empreinte carbone quasiment nulle.

El principal objetivo del diseño de estas cabañas de vacaciones fue crear una arquitectura semirrural que se mezclase con el paisaje. La tierra procedente de la excavación se utilizó para crear un búnker que protege al edificio del viento y para fusionar las cubiertas vegetales con la pendiente del terreno, siguiendo el método tradicional de las casas de césped islandesas. Las fachadas están revestidas de paneles de madera quemada, utilizando un sistema procedente de Japón que mejora la durabilidad del material. El interior alberga una distribución sencilla y eficiente, que limita las circulaciones y minimiza los detalles complejos. Las cabañas utilizan energía geotérmica procedente de las propias parcelas. Su diseño se ajusta a estándares ecológicos reconocidos, con el objetivo de promover un mínimo impacto ambiental y crear así cabañas con huella de carbono casi nula.

North elevation

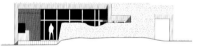

South elevation

East elevation

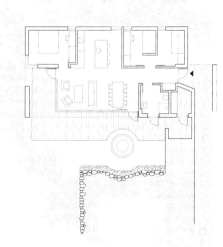

West elevation

Cross section

Ground floor plan

5   10m

BRÆÐRAHÚS
SUMMERHOUSES 1 AND 2

Located in a forest under impressive mountains, these houses built for two brothers merge with their surroundings. The pathway to the cabins is a narrow wooden footbridge surrounded by birches which prevents people from appreciating the grandiosity of the landscape until the buildings are reached, where large terraces offer sweeping views of the river and the valley surrounding them. The main areas face southwards and are connected by terraces, representing the true centres of the dwellings. The buildings are also designed as barriers protecting the terraces from the strong local winds. Their roofs replace the vegetation from the footprint left by the dwellings and their concrete façades are covered with light wooden boards which will gradually degrade until they reach a colour level similar to the shades of seasonal birch.

Hauptziel bei der Planung dieser Ferienhäuser war ein halbländlicher Architekturstil im Einklang mit der Landschaft. Aus der durch die Grabungen gewonnenen Erde wurde ein Windschutz für die Gebäude errichtet, der die bepflanzten Dächer mit der Neigung des Grundstücks verbindet und den traditionellen isländischen Torfhäusern nachempfunden ist. Die Widerstandsfähigkeit der Paneele aus verkohltem Holz an den Fassaden wurde mit Hilfe einer japanischen Technik verbessert. Die Raumaufteilung ist einfach und zweckdienlich mit wenig Durchgangsmöglichkeiten und kaum komplexen Details. Die Häuser nutzen die Erdwärme des Grundstücks. Bei der Planung wurden anerkannte Umweltstandards berücksichtigt, um die Umweltauswirkungen zu minimieren und Wohnungen mit kaum CO2-Fußabdruck zu schaffen.

Situées dans une forêt au pied de montagnes impressionnantes, ces maisons construites pour deux frères se fondent dans leur environnement. Le chemin qui y mène est une passerelle étroite entourée de bouleaux qui empêchent d'appréhender l'aspect grandiose du paysage jusqu'à ce qu'on atteigne les bâtisses, où de larges terrasses offrent des vues imprenables sur la rivière et la vallée tout autour. Les espaces principaux sont orientés au sud et sont connectés par des terrasses, qui représentent le véritable cœur des habitations. Celles-ci sont également conçues comme des barrières protégeant les terrasses des violents vents de la région. Leur toit remplace dans l'empreinte carbone la végétation retirée pour les maisons et leur façade de béton est couverte d'un bardage de bois clair qui se patinera progressivement jusqu'à avoir une teinte similaire à celle du bouleau saisonnier.

Situadas en un bosque bajo impresionantes montañas, estas casas para dos hermanos se funden con su entorno. El recorrido de acceso hasta las cabañas es una estrecha pasarela de madera rodeada de abedules que impide apreciar la magnitud del paisaje hasta llegar a los edificios, donde unas grandes terrazas ofrecen amplias vistas del río y del valle que los rodean. Los espacios principales están orientados hacia el sur y se conectan con las terrazas, que representan los verdaderos núcleos de las casas. Los edificios también se han diseñado como barreras que protegen las terrazas de los fuertes vientos de la zona. Sus cubiertas reponen la vegetación procedente de la huella dejada por la casas y sus fachadas de hormigón están revestidas con tableros de madera liviana que se degradarán gradualmente hasta alcanzar un grado de color similar a los tonos estacionales del abedul.

Site plan

Floor plan - Bræðrahús 1

East elevation

North elevation

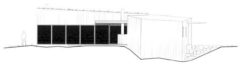

South elevation

West elevation

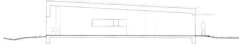

Section

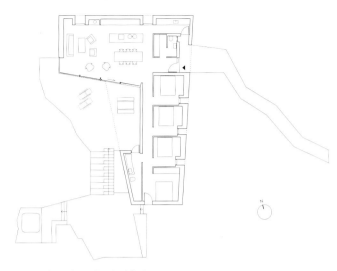

Ground floor plan - Bræðrahús 2

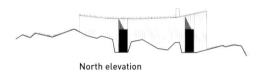

North elevation

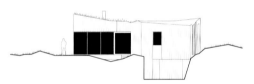

South elevation

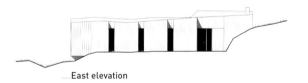

East elevation

West elevation

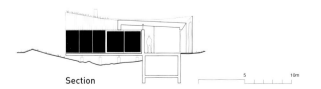

Section

ARBORG HOUSE

The location of this villa on a hill provides spectacular views of a river formed by glaciers and towards the mountains to the west. It is organised as a succession of spaces, from the front porch to the living room through an enclosed courtyard, and finally to the terrace. The building's external appearance is that of a rough concrete surface incorporating the texture of river gravel and in tune with the moss of the surrounding landscape. Any moss existing on the site before the dwelling's construction was preserved and replanted over the new roof. Doors and terraces are covered with teak panels which will gradually age until they reach a colour matching that of the concrete surfaces, and, together with the seasonal moss, help the dwelling to integrate fully with the landscape.

Diese Villa liegt auf einem Hügel und bietet einen spektakulären Ausblick über einen, durch Gletscher rauschenden, Fluss und die Berge im Westen. Im Inneren gelangt man durch aneinandergereihte Räume von der Veranda über das Wohnzimmer zu einem Innenhof und schließlich auf die Terrasse. Außen besteht das Gebäude aus einer rauen Betonwand in der Struktur von Flusskies und im Einklang mit der umliegenden Landschaft. Das vor dem Bau auf dem Gebiet vorhandene Moos wurde aufbewahrt und auf das neue Dach gepflanzt. Türen und Terrassen bestehen aus Teakholzpaneelen, die nach und nach die Farbe der Betonwand annehmen werden und zusammen mit dem saisonal vorhandenen Moos dafür sorgen, dass sich das Wohnhaus perfekt in das Landschaftsbild einfügt.

L'emplacement de cette villa sur une colline offre des vues spectaculaires sur une rivière formée par des glaciers et à l'ouest vers les montagnes. Elle est organisée comme une succession d'espaces, du porche d'entrée au séjour, par une cour intérieure, pour arriver à la terrasse. L'apparence extérieure du bâtiment est celle d'une surface brute en béton incorporant la texture du gravier de rivière et en harmonie avec la mousse du paysage environnant. Toute la sphaigne présente sur le site avant les travaux a été conservée et replantée sur le nouveau toit. Les portes et terrasses sont recouvertes de panneaux de teck qui vont progressivement vieillir jusqu'à avoir une couleur assortie à celle des surfaces bétonnées et, avec la mousse saisonnière, contribuer à l'intégration complète de cette habitation dans le paysage.

La ubicación de esta casa de vacaciones sobre una colina proporciona espectaculares vistas hacia un río formado por glaciares y hacia las montañas orientadas al oeste. El programa se organiza como una sucesión de espacios, desde el porche de entrada hacia la sala de estar a través de un patio cerrado, y finalmente hasta la terraza. La imagen exterior del edificio es una superficie rugosa de hormigón visto que incorpora la textura de la grava del río y armoniza con el musgo del paisaje circundante. El musgo existente en el solar antes de la construcción de la casa fue conservado y recolocado en la nueva cubierta. Las puertas y las terrazas están revestidas con paneles de teca que envejecerán gradualmente hasta alcanzar un grado de color que coincida con las superficies de hormigón y con el musgo estacional, consiguiendo la plena integración de la casa en el paisaje.

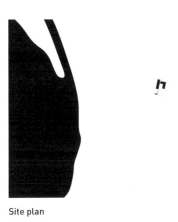

Site plan

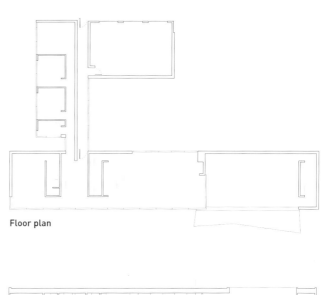

Floor plan

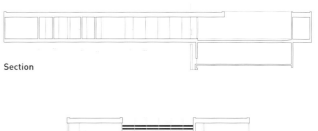

Section

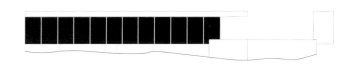

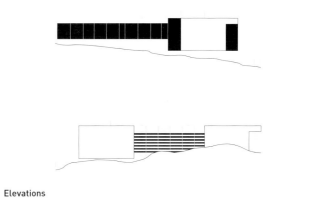

Elevations

PROARH

Proarh is an architectural office founded in 1992 in Zagreb. Under the management of its founder and principal architect Davor Matekovic, the firm has evolved into a multidisciplinary workshop, creating projects of various functions, typologies, as well as programmatic and spatial dimensions. Architecture is approached as a diversely complex topic, where all its individual elements are formative and the design process is all encompassing.

Proarh's innovative approach, creativity, as well as dedicated work and acquired experience through relentless market conditions, have created a great number of successful projects and finished work of a wide spectrum. Its signature architectural work and progressive ideas have been recognized outside the local architectural scene. Proarh's works have been nominated and awarded with a wide variety of architectural prizes, presented in many exhibitions and published in renown publications.

Proarh est un cabinet d'architecte fondé en 1992 à Zagreb. Sous la direction de son fondateur et principal architecte Davor Matekovic, cette entreprise est devenue un atelier multidisciplinaire, créant des projets aux diverses fonctions et typologies, ainsi que dimensions de programmation et d'espace. L'architecture est abordée comme un sujet aux nombreuses facettes, dans lequel tous ses éléments individuels sont formatifs et tout est englobé dans le processus de conception.

L'approche innovante de Proarh, sa créativité, ainsi que son travail acharné et son expérience acquise dans des conditions de marché implacables, ont donné lieu à un grand nombre de projets réussis et un large éventail de réalisations. Son travail architectural distinctif et ses idées progressistes ont été reconnus en dehors de la scène architecturale locale. Les travaux de Proarh ont été nominés et récompensés par une grande variété de prix d'architecture, présentés dans de nombreuses expositions et publiés dans des ouvrages renommés.

Das Architekturstudio Proarh wurde 1992 in Zagreb gegründet. Gründer und Hauptarchitekt Davor Matekovic machte das Unternehmen zu einer multidisziplinären Werkstatt für Projekte mit unterschiedlicher Funktion und Art und verschiedenen programmatischen und räumlichen Dimensionen. Das Unternehmen geht die Architektur als ein Thema vielfältiger Komplexität an, bei dem jedes einzelne Element prägend ist und in den Designprozess eingebunden werden muss.

Der innovative Ansatz, Kreativität, sorgfältige Arbeit und Erfahrung mit schwierigen Marktsituationen brachten Proarh eine Vielzahl von Projekten und abgeschlossenen Aufträgen in einem weiten Spektrum ein. Seine charakteristische architektonische Arbeit und fortschrittliche Ideen fanden auch außerhalb der Architektenszene Anerkennung. Die Arbeiten des Unternehmens Proarh wurden bei einer Vielzahl von Architekturpreisen nominiert und ausgezeichnet, auf Messen präsentiert und in angesehenen Veröffentlichungen gewürdigt.

Proarh es un estudio arquitectónico fundado en 1992 en Zagreb. Bajo la gestión de su fundador y arquitecto principal Davor Matekovic, el estudio ha evolucionado hasta convertirse en un taller multidisciplinar, que crea proyectos de distintos tipos y con diversas funciones, así como con diferentes dimensiones espaciales y programas. En Proarh, la arquitectura es un campo vasto y complejo, donde todos los elementos individuales son formativos y el proceso de diseño lo incluye todo.

Gracias a su método de trabajo y su creatividad, así como a su dedicación y la experiencia adquirida en un mercado implacable, Proarh ha creado un gran número de proyectos de éxito y trabajos finalizados de muchos tipos. Su trabajo arquitectónico e ideas progresivas se han reconocido más allá de la esfera arquitectónica nacional. El trabajo de esta firma ha recibido nominaciones y galardones de una gran variedad de premios arquitectónicos. Su trabajo está presente en muchas exposiciones y se ha incluido en reconocidas publicaciones.

[HIZA]

[ISSA MEGARON]

HIZA

The discrete and simple spaces of the architecture of the traditional cabins of the Zagorje region inspired the refurbishment of this dwelling. The project retains the original shape, replacing the porch with a glass cube which slides out of the main block allowing for southern exposure. The building sits on a pre-existing stone base and combines its construction and wood finishes with an innovative use of straw on the roof and façade, fruit of field and documentary research. The dwelling consists of a basement, a ground floor including the shared areas, organised traditionally around the "hearth", and a first floor with bedrooms. The cabin becomes an "organic" entity, easily renewable using local resources and labour, breathing and mutating over time, creating a healthy living environment.

Bei der Renovierung dieses Wohnhauses orientierten sich die Architekten an den unauffälligen und schlichten Räumen der traditionellen Blockhütten der Region Zagorje. Die ursprüngliche Gebäudeform wurde beibehalten, man ersetzte lediglich die Veranda durch eine würfelförmige Glaskonstroukion, die aus der Gebäudeform ausbricht und für dessen südliche Ausrichtung sorgt. Der Steinuntergrund war bereits vor der Gebäudeerrichtung vorhanden. Der Bau und seine Holzflächen werden beim Dach und den Fassaden durch Stroh ergänzt. Diese Innovation ist das Ergebnis von Feldforschung und dokumentarischer Recherche. Das Wohngebäude besteht aus einem Keller, einem Erdgeschoss, in dem die Gemeinschaftsbereiche auf traditionelle Weise um das „Herz" angeordnet sind, und dem ersten Stockwerk mit den Schlafzimmern. Die Blockhütte wird zu einer „organischen" Einheit, die durch lokale Ressourcen und Arbeit jederzeit erneuert werden kann, mit der Zeit lebt und sich entsprechend verändert und somit ein gesundes Lebensumfeld darstellt.

Les espaces discrets et simples de l'architecture des cabanes traditionnelles de la région du Zagorje ont inspiré la rénovation de ce bâtiment. Ce projet conserve la forme d'origine, remplaçant le porche d'entrée par un cube de verre qui coulisse hors du module principal pour permettre l'exposition au sud. La bâtisse est posée sur une base rocheuse préexistante et mêle sa construction et des finitions en bois avec un usage créatif de la paille sur le toit et la façade, fruit d'une recherche de terrain et documentaire. Cette habitation est composée d'un sous-sol, d'un rez-de-chaussée contenant les zones partagées, organisées traditionnellement autour du « foyer », et d'un premier étage avec des chambres. Cette cabane devient une entité « organique », facilement renouvelable en utilisant de ressources et de la main d'œuvre locales, respirant et se transformant au fil du temps, créant un environnement de vie sain.

La arquitectura discreta y de espacios sencillos de las cabañas tradicionales de la región de Zagorje inspiró la reforma de esta casa. El proyecto conserva la forma original, sustituyendo el porche por un cubo de vidrio que se desliza fuera del volumen principal y permite la exposición a sur. El edificio se asienta sobre una base de piedra existente y combina la construcción y los acabados de madera con un uso innovador de la paja en la cubierta y en la fachada, fruto de una investigación de campo y documental. La vivienda se compone de un sótano, una planta baja que incluye las zonas comunes, organizadas en función del «hogar» según un sistema tradicional, y una planta piso con los dormitorios. La cabaña deviene un elemento «orgánico», fácilmente renovable mediante recursos y mano de obra locales, que respira y muta con el tiempo, creando un entorno de vida saludable.

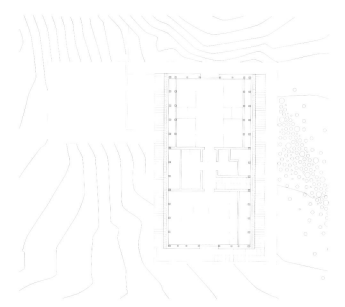

First floor plan

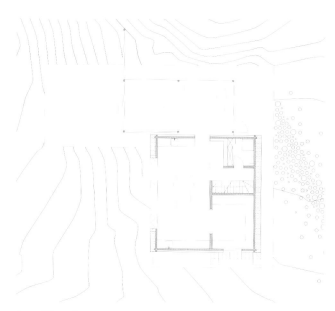

Ground floor plan

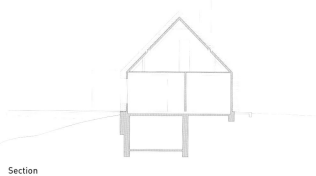

Section

ISSA MEGARON

This dwelling's design reinterprets the traditional country's stone walls (suhozid) to create a new topography integrating the building by making minimal changes in the terrain. Conceived as a reinvention of Socrates's Megaron, the dwelling can be visualised as a block excavated over two levels, a discreet design, creating a subtle symbiosis with the landscape. Sustainable criteria, adapting traditional techniques and using local materials was used in its construction. The absence of infrastructure meant the dwelling had to be 100% self-sufficient, which is why several forms of exploiting natural resources were considered, such as CSP (concentrated solar power) systems, photovoltaic panels, recycling of rainwater for domestic use and for irrigation through natural filters, and passive ventilation and cooling systems.

Teil des Designs dieses Hauses ist eine Neuinterpretation der traditionellen Steinmauern des Landes (Suhozid). Hierbei sollte das Gebäude durch minimale Änderungen im Untergrund in die Topographie integriert werden. Das Haus ist eine Neuerfindung von Sokrates´ Megaron und erweckt optisch den Anschein eines in den Boden eingelassenen Blocks auf zwei Ebenen; das diskrete Design geht hier eine subtile Symbiose mit der umliegenden Landschaft ein. Für den nachhaltigen Bau wurden traditionelle Techniken und lokale Materialien verwendet. Aufgrund der fehlenden Infrastruktur musste das Haus vollkommen energieautark sein. Daher bediente man sich verschiedener Formen zur Nutzung natürlicher Ressourcen, wie beispielsweise eines CSP-Systems (gebündelte Solarenergie), Sonnenkollektoren, Wiederaufbereitung des Regenwassers für Hausgebrauch und Bewässerung durch natürliche Filter und passiver Belüftungs- und Kühlsysteme.

Le design de cette habitation réinterprète les murs de pierre traditionnels du pays (suhozid) pour créer une nouvelle topographie intégrant le bâtiment en ayant un impact minimal au niveau du terrain. Conçue comme une réinvention du Mégaron de Socrate, cette habitation peut être visualisée comme un immeuble creusé sur deux niveaux, d'un design discret, créant une symbiose subtile avec le paysage. Des critères durables, l'adaptation de techniques traditionnelles et l'utilisation de matériaux locaux ont été adoptés pour sa construction. L'absence d'infrastructures signifiait qu'elle devait être auto-suffisante, ce qui explique que plusieurs formes d'exploitations aient été considérées, comme des systèmes de centrale solaire thermodynamique, des panneaux photovoltaïques, le recyclage de l'eau de pluie pour usage domestique et pour l'irrigation par le biais de filtres naturels, ainsi qu'une aération et des systèmes de refroidissement passifs.

El diseño de esta casa reinterpreta los muros de piedra tradicionales del país (*suhozid*) para crear una nueva topografía que integra el edificio realizando mínimas alteraciones en el terreno. Concebida como reinvención del Megarón de Sócrates, la casa se visualiza como un volumen excavado de dos niveles y exhibe un diseño discreto que crea una sutil simbiosis con la topografía. En su construcción se emplearon criterios sostenibles, adaptando técnicas tradicionales y utilizando materiales de la zona. La ausencia de infraestructuras implicó plantear una casa 100% autosuficiente, para lo cual se consideraron diversas formas de explotación de los recursos naturales, como sistemas CSP (concentrated solar power), paneles fotovoltaicos, reciclaje del agua de lluvia para uso doméstico mediante filtros naturales y para riego, y sistemas de ventilación y refrigeración pasiva.

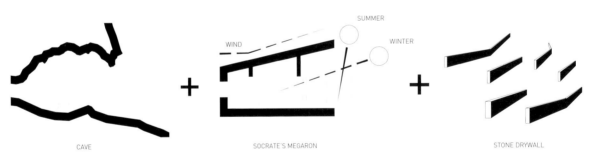

CAVE   SOCRATE'S MEGARON   STONE DRYWALL

SUMMER

WIND   WINTER

Concept scheme

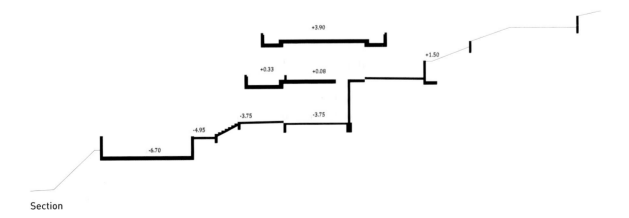

+3.90

+1.50

+0.33   +0.08

-3.75   -3.75

-4.95

-6.70

Section

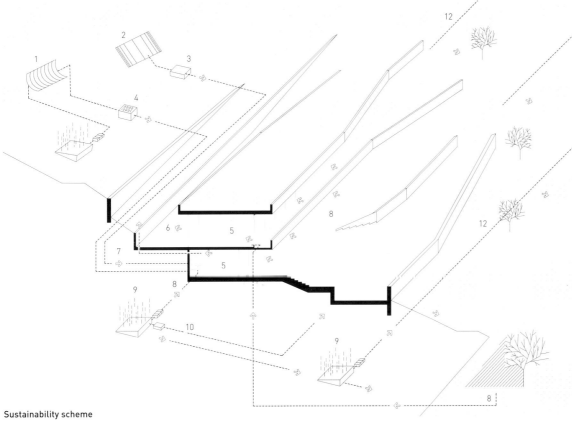

Sustainability scheme

1. Concetrating solar power system
2. Photovoltaic panels
3. DC/AC converter
4. Thermal storage container
5. Negative pressure
6. Hot air
7. Distribution box
8. Cool air
9. Rainwater collection tank
10. Gravel filters
11. Shade
12. Irrigation

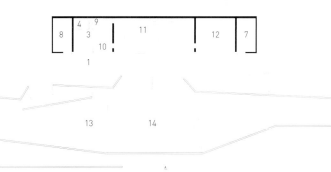

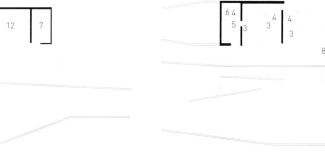

Ground floor plan

First floor plan

1. Terrace
2. Living room
3. Bedroom
4. Bathroom
5. Office
6. Wardrobe
7. Storage
8. Green roof
9. WC
10. Laundry / storage
11. Dining room / kitchen / lounge
12. Game room / gym
13. Pool deck
14. Pool

RICHARD +
SCHOELLER

WWW.RICHARDSCHOELLER.EU

Richard + Schoeller is an architectural studio established in the 4e arrondissement of Paris, founded in 1989 by Isabelle Richard and Frédéric Schoeller, both graduates of the Paris-Belleville School of Architecture.

The studio has a multi-disciplinary team working together to develop an approach to architectural practice based on innovative concepts, applied in the creation of public cultural facilities such as libraries, art centres educational facilities, city councils and diplomatic campuses.

Its objective is to design new worlds by linking different scales through light, space, and form, from the architectural landscape to the urban one. Using the poetry of any location as a strategy, Richard + Schoeller conceive a project as an efficient attraction in the city, a place where the daily activity of citizens can shine, a place of well-being.

Das Architekturstudio Richard + Schoeller wurde 1989 von den Absolventen der Paris-Belleville School of Architecture Isabelle Richard und Frédéric Schoeller gegründet und hat seinen Sitz im 4. Arrondissement von Paris.

Das breit aufgestellte Team des Studios entwickelt mit seinem Architekturansatz aus innovativen Konzepten öffentliche Kulturstäten wie Bibliotheken und Kunstzentren, Bildungseinrichtungen, Rathäuser und stilvolle Universitätsgebäude.

Sein Ziel ist die Erschaffung neuer Welten durch eine Verbindung von unterschiedlichen Facetten durch Licht, Raum und Form, wobei es dabei auf das architektonische und das städtische Bild gleichermaßen achtet. Richard + Schoeller nimmt die Struktur des jeweiligen Ortes als Grundlage und betrachtet seine Projekte als wirkungsvolle Stadtattraktion, einen Platz für die täglichen Aktivitäten der Stadtbewohnern und einen Ort des Wohlbefindens.

Richard + Schoeller est un studio d'architecture établi dans le 4ème arrondissement de Paris, fondé en 1989 par Isabelle Richard et Frédéric Schoeller, tous deux diplômés de l'École d'architecture de Paris-Belleville.

Ce studio possède une équipe multidisciplinaire qui travaille ensemble pour développer une approche de la pratique architecturale axée sur des concepts novateurs, appliqués à la création d'infrastructures culturelles publiques comme des bibliothèques, des infrastructures pédagogiques dans les centres d'art, des mairies et des campus diplomatiques.

Son objectif est de concevoir de nouveaux mondes en reliant différentes échelles par le biais de la lumière, de l'espace, et de la forme, du paysage architectural au paysage urbain. Leur stratégie étant de puiser dans la poésie d'un site, Richard + Schoeller conçoivent un projet comme une attraction performante dans la ville, un lieu où les activités quotidiennes des citoyens peuvent s'éclairer, un lieu de bien-être.

Richard + Schoeller es un estudio de arquitectura establecido en el 4e arrondissement de París, fundado en 1989 por Isabelle Richard y Frédéric Schoeller, diplomados ambos en la Escuela de Arquitectura de Paris-Belleville.

El estudio está formado por un equipo multidisciplinar que trabaja en conjunto para desarrollar un enfoque de la práctica arquitectónica basado en conceptos innovadores, aplicado en la realización de equipamientos culturales públicos como mediatecas, centros de arte, instalaciones educativas, ayuntamientos y campus diplomáticos.

Su objetivo es diseñar nuevos mundos vinculando diferentes escalas a través de la luz, el espacio y la forma, desde el paisaje arquitectónico al urbano. Usando la poesía del sitio como una estrategia, Richard + Schoeller concibe un proyecto como un polo de atracción eficiente en la ciudad, un lugar donde brilla la actividad diaria de los ciudadanos, un lugar de bienestar.

[CULTURAL CENTRE GARENNE-COLOMBES]

[JEAN MOULIN SCHOOL]

CULTURAL CENTRE GARENNE-COLOMBES

A geometry closed by two symmetrical curves forming a leaf shape defines the main block of this media library inserting the building in its urban context. A concrete curve at the rear shapes the envelope while the glass exterior opens towards the neighbouring Place de la Liberté, glimpsed through a few screen-printed brise-soleils lines covering the entire façade. In this project, the architects transmit the idea that light and proportion are the two components that come together to create spaces. Its transparency and depth can be perceived from the entrance, the double height of the ground floor spaces, opening onto the rear garden, the skylight over the exhibition hall or the effects of the brise-soleils inside the building reflect the importance of light as a project driver.

Zwei symmetrische Kurven verleihen dem Hauptblock dieser Mediathek die Form eines Blattes, welches perfekt zum Stadtbild passt. Die Betonkurve an der Vorderseite ist formgebend für die Außenwand und durch die Glaswand blickt man auf den benachbarten Place de la Liberté, der nur durch die wenigen, die komplette Fassade überziehenden Brise-Soleil-Streifen getrübt wird. Mit diesem Projekt möchte der Architekt die Vorstellung vermitteln, dass Licht und Proportionen gemeinsam einen Raum schaffen. Der Eingangsbereich, die doppelte Höhe der zum Garten an der Vorderseite hin offenen Räume im Erdgeschoss, das Dachfenster über der Ausstellungshalle und die Brise-Soleils im Gebäudeinneren vermitteln Transparenz und Tiefe und zeigen die Bedeutung des Lichts für das Projekt.

Une forme géométrique fermée par deux courbes symétriques prenant la forme d'une feuille définit le bâtiment principal de cette médiathèque, insérant l'ensemble dans son contexte urbain. Un arc de béton à l'arrière façonne l'enveloppe tandis que l'extérieur vitré s'ouvre sur la Place de la Liberté voisine, aperçue au travers de quelques rangées de brise-soleils sérigraphiés recouvrant l'intégralité de la façade. Dans ce projet, les architectes transmettent l'idée que lumière et proportions sont les deux composantes qui s'accordent pour créer des espaces. Sa transparence et sa profondeur peuvent se percevoir depuis l'entrée ; la double hauteur des espaces du rez-de-chaussée, ouvrant sur le jardin à l'arrière, la fenêtre de toit au-dessus du hall d'exposition ou les effets des brise-soleils à l'intérieur du bâtiment sont un miroir de l'importance de la lumière en tant que moteur du projet.

Una geometría cerrada por dos curvas simétricas que dibujan una hoja vegetal define el volumen principal de esta mediateca e inserta el edificio en el contexto urbano. La curva de hormigón de la parte posterior conforma el contenedor mientras que la exterior, de vidrio, se abre hacia la vecina Place de la Liberté, vislumbrada a través de unas líneas de brise-soleils serigrafiados que cubren toda la fachada. En este proyecto, los arquitectos transmiten la idea de que la luz y la medida son los dos componentes que confluyen para crear espacios; la transparencia y profundidad que se perciben desde la entrada, los espacios a doble altura de la planta baja, las aberturas hacia el jardín posterior, la iluminación cenital sobre la sala de exposiciones o los efectos de los brise-soleils en el interior del edificio plasman la importancia de la luz como motor del proyecto.

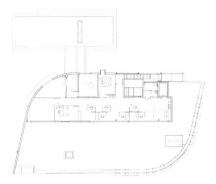

Fourth floor plan

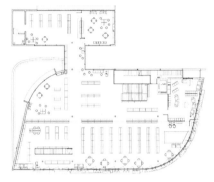

Second floor plan

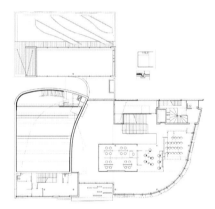

First floor plan

Ground floor plan

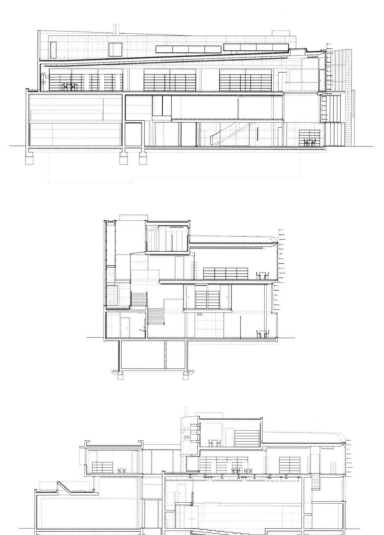

Sections

JEAN MOULIN SCHOOL

Compared to the parallelepipeds warming the buildings surrounding it, this primary school and nursery has been conceived as the superposition of two closed arcs, forming a simple shape organising the different spaces and unifying it. Its white concrete in-situ façade covers an innovative structure both in terms of design and execution, whose intermediate section of pre-assembled wood constitutes an important environmental asset for the building. The project is sensitive to mandatory environmental requirements for state schools and achieves an energy balance meeting the highest standards. Multiple measures favouring sustainability have been incorporated into the design, completed with a plant cover providing character to the building. Likewise, managing and assessing power consumption have now become part of the school's educational project.

Im Gegensatz zu den umliegenden quaderförmigen Gebäuden besteht diese Vor- und Grundschule aus zwei geschlossenen Bögen, wobei ihre einfach gehaltene Form die unterschiedlichen Räume anordnet und verbindet. Die Struktur hinter der weißen Betonwand überzeugt durch Innovation bei Design und Ausführung. Der hölzerne Mittelabschnitt verleiht dem Gebäude eine wichtige und umweltbewusste Komponente. Das Gebäude erfüllt die geforderten Umweltnormen für staatliche Schulen und seine Energiebilanz entspricht den höchsten Standards. Bei der Planung wurden vielfältige Maßnahmen zur Nachhaltigkeit berücksichtigt und eine Pflanzendecke verleiht dem Gebäude Charakter. Zudem gehören Management und Bewertung des Stromverbrauchs zum Lehrplan der Schule.

Comparée aux bâtiments environnants, en forme de parallélépipèdes, cette école primaire et maternelle a été conçue comme la superposition de deux arches fermées formant une forme simple organisant les différents espaces et les harmonisant. Sa façade en béton blanc coulé sur place recouvre une structure novatrice en termes d'exécution, dont la section intermédiaire pré-assemblée en bois constitue un atout écologique pour le bâtiment. Ce projet est sensible aux exigences environnementales obligatoires pour les écoles publiques et atteint un équilibre énergétique répondant aux normes les plus exigeantes. De multiples mesures en faveur de la durabilité ont été incorporées au design, complétées par une végétalisation de la couverture, donnant du caractère à la bâtisse. De même, la gestion et l'évaluation de la consommation énergétique font maintenant partie du projet pédagogique de cet établissement.

Frente a los paralelepípedos que conforman los edificios que la rodean, esta escuela primaria y guardería se concibe como la superposición de dos curvas cerradas, generadoras de una forma simple que organiza los diferentes espacios y da unidad al lugar. Su fachada de hormigón blanco in situ envuelve una estructura innovadora en diseño y realización, cuyo forjado intermedio de madera preensamblada supone un importante activo medioambiental para el edificio. El proyecto es sensible a los requisitos medioambientales preceptivos en una escuela pública y logra un balance energético que responde a las demandas más exigentes. Múltiples medidas favorecedoras de la sostenibilidad se integran en el diseño, completadas con la cubierta vegetal que da carácter al edificio. Así mismo, la gestión y evaluación de los consumos se han incorporado al proyecto educativo de la escuela.

Renderings

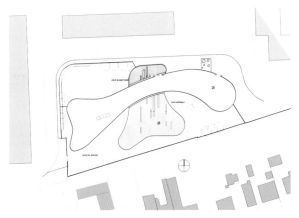

Massing plan

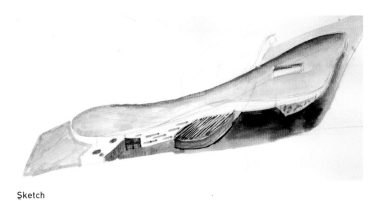

Sketch

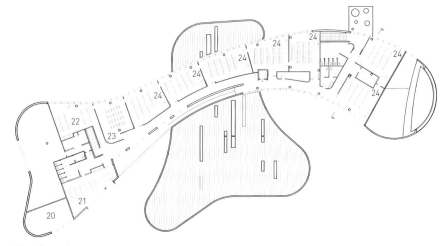

First floor plan

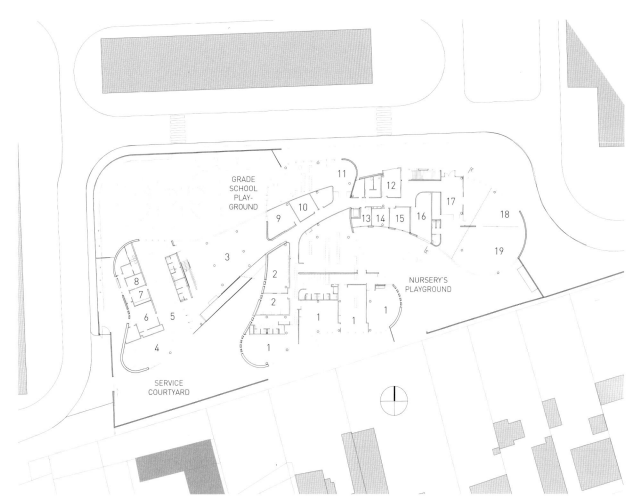

Ground floor plan

1. Nursery classroom	6. Reheating	12. Management
2. Break room	7. Laundry room	13. Infirmary
3. Grade school's covered playground	8. Rubbish	14. Psychology
4. Nursery school's refectory	9. Nursery school assistant room and linen room	15. Teachers' assistants
		16. Teachers
5. Grade school refectory	10. Physical education	17. Reception hall
	11. Library	18. Day-care

19. Nursery's covered playground	
20. Void over restaurant	
21. Plastic arts room	
22. Music room	
23. Computer room	
24. Grade school classroom	

SIGURD LARSEN

WWW.SIGURDLARSEN.COM

Sigurd Larsen is a Berlin based Danish architect within the fields of architecture and furniture design. He has a master degree from The Royal Academy of Fine Arts, School of Architecture in Copenhagen and previously been employed at OMA, MVRDV and Topotek1. Sigurd Larsen founded the design studio in 2010 and recently completed several single-family houses in Denmark and New York as well as a series of loft rooms at Michelberger hotel in Berlin. Currently the studio is building in Austria, Greece, Denmark and Germany. His furniture is available in stores and galleries in Berlin, Copenhagen and 12 other cities. The work of the design studio combines the aesthetics of high quality materials with concepts focusing on functionality in complex spaces. Since 2016 Sigurd Larsen is Professor at BAU International University in Berlin where building design and visual communication is explored through teaching and research.

Sigurd Larsen est un architecte danois basé à Berlin qui travaille dans les domaines de l'architecture et du design de mobilier. Il a un Master de l'école d'architecture de l'Académie royale des beaux-arts de Copenhague et a travaillé pour OMA, MVRDV et Topotek1. Il a fondé son studio d'architecture en 2010 et a récemment terminé plusieurs maisons individuelles au Danemark et à New York ainsi qu'une série de chambres lofts pour l'Hotel Michelberger à Berlin. Actuellement son studio est chargé de constructions en Autriche, en Grèce, au Danemark et en Allemagne. Ses meubles sont visibles dans des magazines et des galeries à Berlin, à Copenhague et dans 12 autres villes. Le travail du studio de design mêle l'esthétique de matériaux de grande qualité avec des concepts axés sur la fonctionnalité des espaces complexes. Depuis 2016 Sigurd Larsen est professeur à l'Université internationale BAU de Berlin où le design de construction et la communication visuelle sont explorés par le biais de l'enseignement et la recherche.

Sigurd Larsen ist ein in Berlin ansässiger dänischer Architekt, der auf den Gebieten Architektur und Möbeldesign arbeitet. Er verfügt über einen Master der Königlichen Akademie der bildenden Künste in Kopenhagen und arbeitete zuvor bei OMA, MVRDV und Topotek1. Sigurd Larsen gründete 2010 sein Architekturstudio und baute in letzter Zeit mehrere Einfamilienhäuser in Dänemark und New York sowie eine Reihe von Dachgeschossapartments für das Michelberger Hotel in Berlin. Derzeit realisiert das Studio Bauprojekte in Österreich, Griechenland, Dänemark und Deutschland. Seine Möbel sind in Geschäften und Galerien in Berlin, Kopenhagen und 12 weiteren Städten erhältlich. Die Arbeit des Architekturstudios kombiniert die Ästhetik hochwertiger Materialien mit funktionalen Konzepten für komplexe Räume. Seit 2016 ist Sigurd Larsen Professor an der BAU International-Universität in Berlin, an der Gebäudeplanung und visuelle Kommunikation durch Lehren und Forschen untersucht werden.

Sigurd Larsen es un arquitecto danés afincado en Berlín que trabaja en el campo de la arquitectura y el diseño de mobiliario. Tiene un máster de la Royal Academy of Fine Arts, en la escuela de arquitectura de Copenhague y anteriormente trabajó en OMA, MVRDV y Topotek1. Sigurd Larsen creó su estudio en 2010 y ha terminado recientemente varias casas unifamiliares en Dinamarca y Nueva York, así como una serie de estancias tipo *loft* en el hotel Michelberger en Berlín. Actualmente su estudio está trabajando en Austria, Grecia, Dinamarca y Alemania. Su mobiliario está disponible en tiendas y galerías en Berlín, Copenhague y otras doce ciudades. El trabajo del estudio de diseño combina la estética de materiales de gran calidad con conceptos orientados a la funcionalidad de espacios complejos. Desde 2016 Sigurd Larsen es profesor en la universidad DAU International de Berlín donde el diseño de edificios y la comunicación visual se exploran a través de la enseñanza y la investigación.

[THE GREEN HOUSE]

[THE LIGHT HOUSE]

[THE ROOF HOUSE]

THE GREEN HOUSE

This project represents the first in a series of "affordably sustainable" townhouses designed for the company Frikøbing, offering generous living spaces within a range comprised of a few simple prototypes with low construction costs. This dwelling's main feature is its 32 m² greenhouse attached to the southern façade, which in winter captures solar heat during the day and provides it to the dwelling at night, it also guarantees that natural light can access the shared areas. The dwelling is naturally ventilated with the help of a triple glazed window which regulates temperature and air flow. The interior is lined with birch plywood, while the exterior finish is comprised of vertical panels of untreated larch that over time will acquire a lighter silver tone, allowing the dwelling to adapt to its environment.

Hierbei handelt es sich um das erste Gebäude in einer Projektreihe „erschwinglicher und nachhaltiger" Stadthäuser des Unternehmens Frikøbing, die großzügigen Raum in einfachen Prototypen mit geringen Baukosten bietet. Hauptmerkmal dieses Wohnhauses ist das 32 m² große Gewächshaus an der Südseite, das im Winter tagsüber Sonnenwärme aufnimmt, mit der es das Wohngebäude nachts versorgt. Zudem begünstigt es das Eindringen natürlichen Lichts in die Gemeinschaftsräume. Ein Fenster mit Dreifachverglasung reguliert Temperatur und Luftstrom und sorgt für die natürliche Belüftung des Hauses. Das Gebäudeinnere besteht aus Birkensperrholz, die Außenfassade aus vertikalen Platten aus unbehandeltem Lärchenholz, das mit der Zeit einen leichten Silberton annehmen wird, wodurch sich das Gebäude noch besser in seine Umgebung einfügt.

Ce projet représente la première d'une série de maisons « durables et abordables » conçues par la société Frikøbing, proposant des espaces de vie aux dimensions généreuses dans une gamme composée de quelques prototypes simples au coût de construction réduits. La caractéristique principale de cette habitation est sa véranda de 32 m² reliée à la façade sud, qui en hiver capte la chaleur du soleil pendant la journée et la renvoie dans la maison la nuit ; elle garantit également l'accès de lumière naturelle dans les zones partagées. Cette habitation est naturellement aérée à l'aide d'une fenêtre à triple vitrage qui régule température et flux d'air. L'intérieur est revêtu de contreplaqué en bouleau, alors que la finition extérieure est composée de panneaux verticaux de mélèze non traités qui au fil du temps prendront une teinte argentée plus claire, permettant à la maison de se fondre dans son environnement.

Este proyecto supone la primera de una serie de casas unifamiliares de «sostenibilidad asequible» diseñadas para la empresa Frikøbing, que ofrecen unos generosos espacios habitables dentro de unas tipologías sencillas y con bajos costes de construcción. La principal característica de esta casa es su invernadero de 32 m² adosado a la fachada sur, que en invierno retiene el calor del sol durante el día y lo cede a la casa durante la noche, y que garantiza la entrada de luz natural a las zonas comunes. La casa se ventila de forma natural con la ayuda de una ventana de tres capas que regula la temperatura y el flujo de aire. El interior está revestido con madera contrachapada de abedul, mientras que el acabado exterior se compone de paneles verticales de alerce sin tratar que con el tiempo adquirirán un tono plateado más claro, permitiendo a la casa adaptarse a su entorno.

South elevation

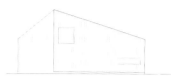

East elevation

North elevation

West elevation

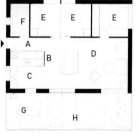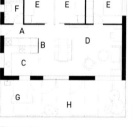

Floor plan

A. Entry
B. Rise to the loft
C. Kitchen
D. Living room
E. Bedroom
F. Bathroom
G. Workbench
H. Greenhouse

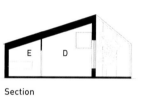

Section

Axonometry

THE LIGHT HOUSE

The second type of "affordably sustainable" dwelling has a large dining/living room on the ground floor, flanked by two bedrooms on one side, and a bathroom and the master bedroom on the other. its single sloping roof generates a very high space in the shared area and allows a bedroom and an extra lounge to be located on the second floor. On the façade, differently-sized windows are carefully placed to frame views of the surrounding landscape or capture a ray of sunlight at a specific time of day. The dwelling is naturally ventilated through a triple glazed window regulating the temperature and ensuring good air circulation. The interior is painted white to reflect the light, while the exterior façade, similar to the first prototype, is covered with vertical panels of untreated larch.

Der zweite Prototyp des „erschwinglichen und nachhaltigen" Wohnhauses verfügt über einen großen Wohn- und Essbereich im Erdgeschoss, von dem zwei Schlafzimmer an der einen und das Hauptschlafzimmer und das Badezimmer an der anderen Seite abzweigen. Das durchgehende Schrägdach bietet Platz für einen sehr hohen Gemeinschaftsraum, sowie ein zusätzliches Schlafzimmer und eine Lounge im zweiten Stockwerk. Die unterschiedlich großen Fenster der Fassade sind so platziert, dass sie einerseits einen tollen Ausblick auf die Umgebung ermöglichen und andererseits zur gewünschten Tageszeit Sonnenlicht eindringen lassen. Fenster mit Dreifachverglasung regeln auf natürliche Weise Temperatur und Luftzirkulation. Das Gebäudeinnere ist weiß gestrichen, um das Licht zu reflektieren. Wie schon beim ersten Prototyp besteht auch bei diesem Modell die Außenfassade aus vertikalen Platten aus unbehandelter Lärche.

Le second type d'habitation « durable et abordable » comprend un grand séjour/salle-à-manger au rez-de-chaussée, flanqué par deux chambres d'un côté, et d'une salle-de-bain et d'une chambre parentale de l'autre. Son toit à une seule pente génère un espace très haut dans la partie partagée et permet l'inclusion d'une chambre et d'un salon supplémentaire au deuxième étage. Sur la façade, des fenêtres de diverses tailles sont placées soigneusement pour encadrer des vues du paysage environnant ou capter un rayon de soleil à un moment spécifique de la journée. Cette maison profite d'une aération naturelle par le biais d'une fenêtre à triple vitrage régulant la température et garantissant une bonne circulation de l'air. L'intérieur en est peint en blanc pour réfléchir la lumière, tandis que la façade extérieure, comme sur le premier prototype, est recouverte de panneaux verticaux de mélèze non traité.

La segunda tipología de casa de «sostenibilidad asequible» presenta en planta baja un gran salón-comedor central flanqueado por dos dormitorios en un lado, y un baño y el dormitorio principal en el otro. Su cubierta de una sola pendiente genera un espacio de gran altura en la zona común y permite ubicar un dormitorio y una sala de estar adicionales en un segundo piso. En la fachada, los distintos tamaños de ventanas se colocan cuidadosamente para enmarcar vistas del paisaje circundante o capturar un rayo de sol en un momento específico del día. La casa se ventila naturalmente mediante una ventana de tres capas que regula la temperatura y garantiza una buena circulación del aire. El interior está pintado de blanco para reflejar la luz, mientras que la fachada exterior, al igual que en la primera tipología, está revestida de paneles verticales de alerce sin tratar.

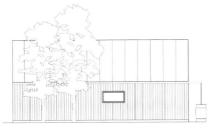

North elevation

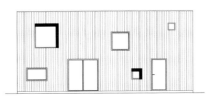

South elevation

West elevation

East elevation

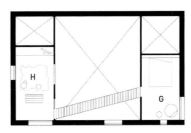

Mezzanine plan

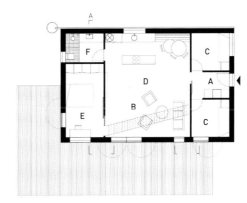

Ground floor plan

A. Entrance hall
B. Living room
C. Bedroom
D. Kitchen
E. Master bedroom
F. Bathroom
G. Guest bedroom
H. TV room

THE ROOF HOUSE

Located on an orthogonal base consisting of a grid formed by 16 rectangles, this dwelling's cladding is presented as a set of planes slanting in different directions. The project's main aim is to capture direct and indirect natural light and channel it into every room, making the inner circulation within the dwelling a constantly changeable experience. To achieve this, a series of sloping roofs and skylights is joined to a series of courtyards and terraces separated from the street by an outside wood covered wall, whose openings give the spaces varying degrees of privacy. Behind the entrance door, located at the end of a small courtyard, accesses to bedrooms and bathrooms flank the way towards the dwelling's shared areas, where the juxtaposition of the various sections of the roof become more apparent.

Dieses Wohngebäude ruht auf einem orthogonalen Gitter aus 16 Rechtecken und besteht aus mehreren, sich in unterschiedliche Richtungen neigenden, Ebenen. Die Hauptaufgabe des Projekts bestand darin, direktes und indirektes natürliches Licht einzufangen und in alle Räume zu leiten, um das Gebäudeinnere in ein sich stetig wandelndes Lichterspiel zu tauchen. Hierzu bedienten sich die Architekten Schrägdächern, Dachfenstern, Höfen und Terrassen. Eine mit Holz verkleidete Wand, deren Öffnungen den einzelnen Räumen ein unterschiedliches Maß an Intimität verleihen, trennt das Anwesen von der Straße. Über die Haustür am Ende eines kleinen Hofes gelangt man in den Gemeinschaftsbereich, von dem zu beiden Seiten die Schlaf- und Badezimmer abzweigen und in dem die aneinandergereihten einzelnen Dachabschnitte deutlich sichtbar werden.

Situé sur une base orthogonale faite d'une grille formée de 16 rectangles, cette maison est entourée d'un bardage qui est présenté comme une série de plans inclinés à différents angles. L'objectif principal de ce projet est de capter la lumière, directe et indirecte, et de la canaliser pour la renvoyer dans chaque pièce, ce qui fait de la circulation intérieure dans l'habitation une expérience constamment changeante. À cette fin, une série de toits pentus et de fenêtres de toit est reliée à une série de cours et de terrasses séparées de la rue par un mur extérieur recouvert d'un bardage de bois, dont les ouvertures procurent aux espaces des degrés d'intimité variables. Derrière la porte d'entrée, situés au bout d'une petite cour, les accès aux chambres et aux salles-de-bain bordent l'accès aux zones partagées de l'habitation, là où la juxtaposition des différentes sections du toit devient plus visible.

Situada sobre una planta ortogonal formada por una cuadrícula de dieciséis rectángulos, la cubierta de esta vivienda se presenta como un conjunto de planos inclinados en diferentes direcciones. La propuesta tiene como objetivo principal atrapar la luz natural directa e indirecta y conducirla a todas las estancias, convirtiendo la circulación interior de la casa en una experiencia en constante cambio. Para conseguirlo, al juego de cubiertas inclinadas y claraboyas se une una serie de patios y terrazas separada de la calle por un muro exterior revestido de madera, cuyas aberturas confieren diferentes grados de privacidad a los espacios. Tras la puerta de entrada, situada al final de un pequeño patio, los accesos a dormitorios y baños flanquean el paso hacia el espacio común de la casa, donde la yuxtaposición de las diversas secciones de la cubierta se hace más evidente.

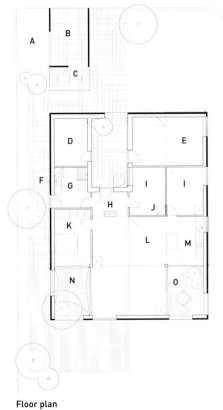

A. Garage
B. Carport
C. Bikes
D. Workshop
E. Annex with loft
F. Shower
G. Bathroom
H. Entry
 I. Room with loft
J. Sliding door between
   lofts
K. Bedroom
L. Living room
M. Kitchen
N. Farm with evening sun
O. Farm with morning sun

Floor plan

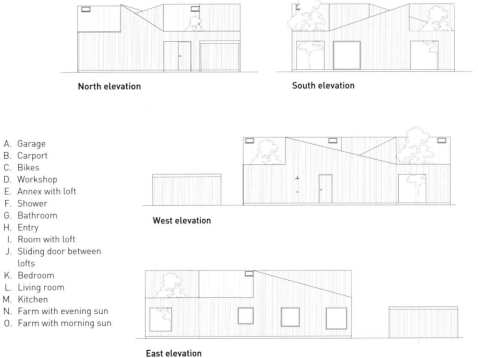

North elevation

South elevation

West elevation

East elevation

STUDIO DELBOCA&PARTNERS

WWW.DELBOCAPARTNERS.COM

Studio DelBoca&Partners is based in Milan and Parma. It was founded by Giovanni del Boca and Alessandra Amoretti and specialises in the development of complex and multidisciplinary projects related to urban design, architecture and the conservation of historical buildings and monuments. The studio has completed several residential complexes, offices, and public buildings. From the year 2000 onwards, it has also worked in the fields of retail and interior design, building more than 100 shops around the world. Its projects have received awards and been covered by the most important Italian architecture magazines. The team consists of ten architects, engineers, and designers. Its most recent works include the new Parma station (with MBM arquitectos) (2015) or the STU109B (2013) residential building, winner of the first prize of the "la Ceramica e il Progetto" competition.

Studio DelBoca&Partners est basé à Milan et à Parme. Il a été fondé par Giovanni del Boca et Alessandra Amoretti et il est spécialisé dans le développement de projets complexes et multidisciplinaires liés à l'aménagement urbain, à l'architecture et à la conservation de bâtiments et monuments historiques. Ce studio a réalisé plusieurs complexes résidentiels, des bureaux et des bâtiments publics. Depuis l'an 2000, il a également travaillé dans le domaine de la vente et de l'aménagement d'intérieur, créant plus de 100 boutiques dans le monde entier. Ses projets ont été récompensés par des prix et ont été couverts par la plupart des magazines d'architectures majeurs d'Italie. Son équipe est composée de dix architectes, ingénieurs, et designers. Ses plus récents travaux comptent la nouvelle gare de Parme (avec MBM arquitectos) (2015) ou l'immeuble résidentiel STU109B (2013), vainqueur du premier prix du concours d'architecture de l'industrie céramique italienne « La Ceramica e il Progetto ».

Studio DelBoca&Partners hat seinen Sitz in Mailand und Parma. Das von Giovanni del Boca und Alessandra Amoretti gegründete Unternehmen hat sich auf komplexe und vielschichtige Projekte der Städteplanung und Architektur und den Erhalt historischer Gebäude und Denkmäler spezialisiert. Boca&Partners entwarfen bereits zahlreiche Wohnanlagen, Büros und öffentliche Gebäude. 2000 begannen sie ihre Tätigkeit im Bereich Einzelhandel und Inneneinrichtung und bauten seitdem mehr als 100 Geschäfte weltweit. Die Projekte des Studios erhielten Auszeichnungen und fanden Eingang in die wichtigsten italienischen Architekturzeitschriften. Das Team besteht aus zehn Architekten, Ingenieuren und Designern. Zu ihren aktuellen Projekten gehörten der neue Bahnhof von Parma (mit MBM arquitectos) (2015), sowie das Wohngebäude STU109B (2013), Gewinner des ersten Preises beim Wettbewerb „la Ceramica e il Progetto".

Studio DelBoca&Partners es un estudio de arquitectura con sede en Milán y Parma, fundado por Giovanni del Boca y Alessandra Amoretti, especializado en el desarrollo de proyectos complejos y multidisciplinares relacionados con el diseño urbano, la arquitectura y la conservación del patrimonio histórico y monumental. El estudio ha completado diversos complejos residenciales, oficinas y edificios públicos. Desde el año 2000 trabaja también en el ámbito del *retail* y del diseño interior, con más de cien tiendas construidas alrededor de todo el mundo. Sus proyectos han sido galardonados y publicados en las más importantes revistas de arquitectura italianas. El equipo está compuesto por diez arquitectos, ingenieros y diseñadores. Sus obras más recientes incluyen la Nueva Estación de Parma (con MBM arquitectos) (2015) o el edificio residencial STU109B (2013), ganador del primer premio del concurso «la Ceramica e il Progetto».

[CASA SUL PARCO]

CASA SUL PARCO

The building is comprised of three blocks organised around a vertical communications core and provides 10 different types of dwelling. Its access hall communicates with the public space and is characterised by the six inclined columns evoking the trunks of the lime trees found in the neighbouring Rimembranze Park. The project prioritises using natural light and controlling solar radiation for each of the dwellings. The Passivhaus certification for its cladding and the use of geothermal and photovoltaic renewable energy guarantee the building's indoor comfort and energy efficiency. Environmental issues are reflected in aspects such as the integration of vegetation with façades and its relationship with the park, developed via flying terraces, or the implementation of water-saving measures.

Das Gebäude besteht aus drei Blöcken, die um ein vertikales Kommunikationszentrum angeordnet sind, und beherbergt 10 unterschiedliche Wohnungsarten. Die Eingangshalle steht in Verbindung mit dem öffentlichen Bereich und überzeugt mit sechs geneigten Säulen - ähnlich der Stämme der Linden im benachbarten Rimembranze Park. Die Verwendung natürlichen Lichts und die Kontrolle der Sonneneinstrahlung für die einzelnen Wohnungen hatten bei diesem Projekt oberste Priorität. Der Komfort im Gebäudeinneren und die Energieeffizienz werden durch die Passivhaus-Zertifizierung der Verkleidung sowie die Verwendung von geothermischer Energie und erneuerbarer Energie durch Photovoltaik garantiert. Das Umweltbewusstsein spiegelt sich in Aspekten wie der Einbindung der Vegetation in die Fassaden, der Verbindung zum Park durch fliegende Terrassen oder den Wassersparsystemen wider.

Ce bâtiment est composé de trois immeubles organisés autour d'un noyau de communication vertical et offre 10 types d'habitation différents. Son hall d'accès communique avec l'espace public et il se caractérise par les six colonnes inclinées évoquant les troncs des tilleuls du Rimembranze Park, tout près de là. Ce projet donne la priorité à l'usage de la lumière naturelle et à la régulation du rayonnement solaire pour chacune des habitations. La certification Passivhaus de ses bardages et l'utilisation de l'énergie renouvelable géothermique et photovoltaïque garantissent le confort intérieur et la performance énergétique du bâtiment. Les problèmes environnementaux sont reflétés dans des aspects comme l'intégration de la végétation sur les façades et sa relation au parc, développée par le biais de terrasses flottantes, ou l'application de mesures d'économie d'eau.

El edificio se compone de tres volúmenes organizados alrededor de un núcleo vertical de comunicaciones y alberga diez viviendas de tipologías diferentes. Su vestíbulo de acceso dialoga con el espacio público y se caracteriza por las seis columnas inclinadas que evocan los troncos de las tilias del vecino parque Rimembranze. El proyecto da prioridad a la iluminación natural de cada una de las viviendas y al control de la radiación solar. La certificación *Passivhaus* de la envolvente y el uso de energías renovables como la geotérmica y la fotovoltaica garantizan el confort interior y la eficiencia energética del edificio. La atención hacia los temas medioambientales se refleja en aspectos como la integración de la vegetación en las fachadas y su relación con el parque, desarrollada en amplias terrazas en vuelo, o la implantación de medidas de ahorro en el consumo de agua.

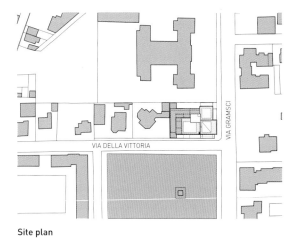

Site plan

Sketch

South elevation

East elevation

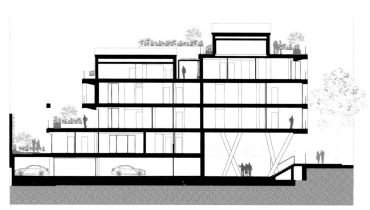

Section

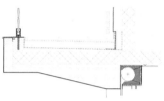

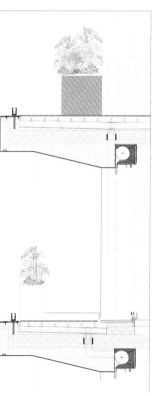

Balcony details

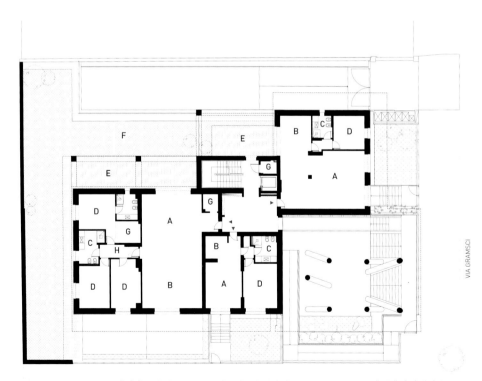

Floor plan

VIA GRAMSCI

A. Living room
B. Kitchen
C. Bathroom
D. Bedroom
E. Terrace
F. Garden
G. Closet
H. Hallway

TERRITORI 24

WWW.TERRITORI24.COM

T24 are a group of architects who share research, tenders, and projects, as well as a common trait driving us to share our professional career paths: concentrating creativity on making resource savings - both natural and financial - making sustainability our overarching value in all our work.

In T24, we have always opted for understanding architecture as an opportunity to improve and develop the society in which we live. Thus, it is our understanding that sustainability should no longer be a value-added factor but become an inbuilt and essential characteristic both of our work processes as well as the outcomes of the same.

Transverse sustainability is only possible if all those taking part in the project work towards delivering it. For this reason, T24 has as its mission carrying out collective work with a multidisciplinary team ensuring diversity both in scale and typology.

T24 est un groupe d'architectes partageant recherche, appels d'offres, et projets. Nous avons également comme trait commun, nous poussant à partager nos trajectoires professionnelles, celui de concentrer la créativité sur l'économie de ressources – naturelles comme financières – faisant de la durabilité une valeur primordiale de notre travail.

Chez T24, nous avons toujours voulu comprendre l'architecture comme une opportunité d'améliorer et de développer la société dans laquelle nous vivons. Ainsi, il nous semble que la durabilité ne devrait plus être un facteur de valeur ajoutée mais devrait devenir une caractéristique essentielle et intégrée à la fois dans nos processus de travail et les résultats qui en découlent.

La durabilité transversale est seulement possible si tous les participants au projet œuvrent pour l'obtenir. C'est pour cette raison que T24 s'est donné pour mission de travailler collectivement avec une équipe multidisciplinaire pour garantir de la diversité au niveau de l'échelle comme de la typologie.

T24 sind ein Architektenteam, das gemeinsam forscht, sich an Ausschreibungen beteiligt und Projekte übernimmt. Allen gemeinsam ist ein, uns bereits während unserer gesamten beruflichen Laufbahn begleitender, Ansatz: die Einsparung von natürlichen und finanziellen Ressourcen und die Nachhaltigkeit als oberste Priorität in all unserem Wirken.

Für uns war die Architektur stets eine Möglichkeit, unsere Gesellschaft zu verbessern und weiterzuentwickeln. Nachhaltigkeit sollte nicht länger nur ein Mehrwert, sondern ein fester und essentieller Bestandteil in unseren Arbeitsprozessen und deren Ergebnissen sein.

Eine bereichsübergreifende Nachhaltigkeit bedarf der Unterstützung durch alle am Projekt beteiligten Personen und Unternehmen. Dank unseres breit aufgestellten Teams können wir von T24 Projekte aller Art und Größe annehmen.

T24 somos un grupo de arquitectos que comparten investigación, concursos y proyectos, así como un rasgo en común que nos impulsa a converger en un trayectoria profesional conjunta: focalizar la creatividad en la economía de recursos –naturales y financieros– con el fin de que la Sostenibilidad sea un valor global en todos los trabajos.

En T24 hemos apostado siempre por una manera de entender la arquitectura como una oportunidad para la mejora y desarrollo de la sociedad en la que vivimos. Así entendemos que la Sostenibilidad deja de ser un valor añadido para pasar a ser parte integrante e imprescindible tanto de nuestros procesos de trabajo como del resultado final de los mismos.

La Sostenibilidad transversal solo es posible si todos los participantes están comprometidos. Para ello, T24 fundamenta su misión en el desarrollo del trabajo colectivo con un equipo multidisciplinar que hace posible la diversidad en escala y tipología.

[CENTRE CÍVIC BARÓ DE VIVER]

CENTRE CÍVIC
BARÓ DE VIVER

This is the first newly constructed LEED Platinum certified building in Catalonia and the first with Social Facilities in Spain. It is a compact block whose utilities are distributed over the ground floor and with a façade covered by plants allowing it to blend in with the neighbourhood's green spaces. The building uses 48% less power than a standard one. It produces much of the energy it consumes with photovoltaic panels and uses rainwater for irrigation and sanitation. The inner spaces have natural light thus reducing power consumption and expenditure and improving comfort. The construction is aimed at optimising the different building systems to achieve sustainability goals without increasing the overall budget. It is completely prefabricated and dry built, reducing by 41% any environmental impacts and emissions throughout its lifecycle.

Dieses Gebäude ist der erste Neubau in Katalonien und die erste Sozialeinrichtung in Spanien mit LED Platinium-Zertifikat. Es handelt sich um einen kompakten Block, dessen Räumlichkeiten über das Erdgeschoss verteilt sind. Die mit Pflanzen bewachsene Fassade passt perfekt zur Grünfläche des Nachbargebäudes. Das Gebäude braucht 48% weniger Strom als ein Standardgebäude. Es produziert einen Großteil seines Energiebedarfs über Solarzellen und verwendet Regenwasser für die Bewässerung und die Sanitäranlagen. Das natürliche Licht im Innenbereich reduziert ebenfalls den Stromverbrauch und die damit verbundenen Ausgaben und sorgt für zusätzlichen Komfort. Das Konzept widmet sich der Optimierung der Nachhaltigkeit verschiedener Gebäudetypen, ohne dabei das verfügbare Budget zu übersteigen. Es handelt sich um eine komplett vorgefertigte und trocken gebaute Konstruktion, die während ihrer gesamten Bestandszeit 41% weniger Umweltbelastung verursacht.

Voici le premier bâtiment neuf certifié LEED de Catalogne et, en Espagne, le premier de cette catégorie à être équipé d'infrastructures sociales. Il s'agit d'un pâté de maison compact dont les infrastructures sont distribuées sur le rez-de-chaussée, avec une façade végétalisée lui permettant de se fondre dans les espaces verts environnants. Cette bâtisse utilise 49 % d'énergie de moins que son équivalent classique. Elle produit beaucoup de l'énergie qu'elle consomme grâce à des panneaux photovoltaïques et utilise l'eau de pluie pour l'irrigation et les installations sanitaires. Les espaces intérieurs profitent de la lumière naturelle, ce qui réduit la consommation et les dépenses énergétiques et améliore le confort. Cette mise en œuvre vise à optimiser les différents systèmes de construction pour atteindre des objectifs de durabilité sans augmenter le budget global. Elle est complètement préfabriquée et bâtie à sec, ce qui réduit de 41 % toute émission et impact environnemental durant son cycle de vie.

Se trata del primer edificio con certificado LEED Platinum de Nueva Construcción de Cataluña y el primer Equipamiento Social de España, un volumen compacto con los usos distribuidos en planta baja y una fachada vegetal que le permite integrarse al sistema de espacios verdes del barrio. El edificio consume un 48% menos que un edificio estándar. Produce buena parte de la energía consumida mediante placas fotovoltaicas y utiliza agua de lluvia para riego y uso sanitario. Los espacios interiores tienen luz natural disminuyendo así consumo y gasto de energía y mejorando el confort de su interior. La construcción se focaliza en optimizar los diferentes sistemas constructivos para lograr los objetivos de sostenibilidad sin incrementar el presupuesto global. Completamente prefabricado y construido en seco, disminuye el impacto y las emisiones de todo su ciclo de vida en un 41%.

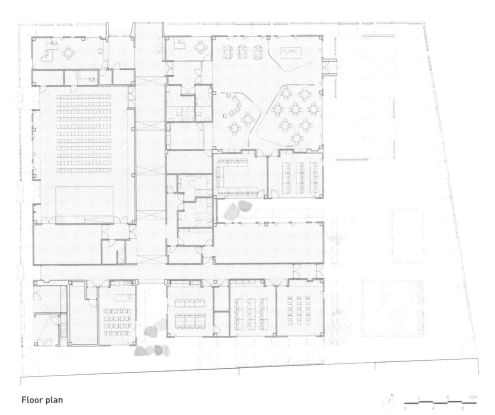

Floor plan

N
0 2 4 6 8 10m

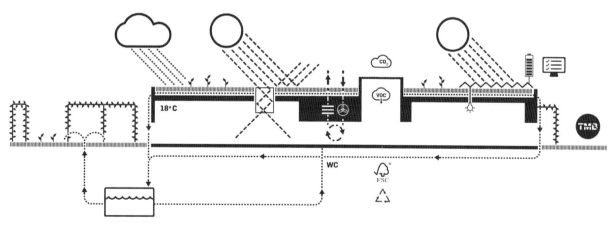

Biodiversity and environment:
- Green island
- Green wall
- Green roof

Water cycle. Water saving. Rainwater harvest for:
- Use for sanitary water
- Use for irrigation permeable site

Interior comfort special attention for users:
- Thermal insulation
- Cross ventilation
- Air renewal and filtering
- Optimal temperature
- Natural light
- Exterior views

Environmentally friendly construction and materials:
- Recycled materials
- Sustainable wood (FSC)
- Free of volatile organic compounds (VOCs)
- Mercury-free lamps
- Heating and cooling free of polluting refrigerants
- Selective waste collection

Energy optimization. Energy saving:
- Renewable energy: solar
- Consumption measurement and control
- Recovery of energy surplus by air conditioning
- Management connected to the Barcelona City Council's central system

Urban connectivity:
- Access to public transportation
- Ease of alternative transportation
- Proximity to basic services

TONI YLI-SUVANTO ARCHITECTS

WWW.TONIYLISUVANTO.COM

Toni Yli-Suvanto Architects was founded in 2007, when Mr. Yli-Suvanto relocated his design studio from London to Helsinki. The company focuses on designing healthy built environment promoting social well-being whilst being economical and ecologically sustainable. It promotes functional and flexible low carbon design solutions, respecting and taking advantage of the environment in terms of functionality, performance,
and appearance. Its holistic approach gives buildings a lasting value and an embedded quality creating a cycle of positive influence on the individual, society, the environment and nature. The company has won several international awards for its sustainable and innovative designs, and articles on its works have been published in the European, American, and Asian media. In 2016 Toni received an Architect of the Year award in Britain and in 2018 he was invited to take part in the exhibition Time Space Existence for the Venice Biennale.

Toni Yli-Suvanto Architects a été fondé en 2007. Le siège de ce cabinet est à Helsinki. Son travail est axé sur le design d'un environnement physique sain encourageant le bien-être social tout en étant économiquement et écologiquement durable. Il fait la promotion de solutions de design à faible empreinte carbone, souples et fonctionnelles, respectant l'environnement naturel et en bénéficiant en matière de fonctionnalité, de performance, et d'aspect. Son approche holistique confère aux bâtiments une valeur stable et une qualité profonde qui crée un cycle d'influence positive sur l'individu, la société, l'environnement et la nature.
Cette société a gagné plusieurs prix internationaux pour ses designs durables et novateurs et des articles sur ses réalisations ont été publiés dans les médias d'Europe, d'Amérique et d'Asie. En 2016, Toni a reçu le prix de l'architecte britannique de l'année et en 2018 il a été invité à prendre part à l'exposition Time Space Existence pour la biennale de Venise.

Toni Yli-Suvanto Architects wurde 2007 gegründet und hat seinen Hauptsitz in Helsinki. Das Unternehmen setzt seinen Schwerpunkt auf die Planung eines physikalisch gesunden, ökonomisch und ökologisch nachhaltigen Umfelds, ohne dabei den Wohlfühlfaktor außer Acht zu lassen. Es steht für niedrigen CO2-Ausstoß, flexible und funktionale Designlösungen, einen respektvollen Umgang mit Umwelt und Natur und die Nutzung ihrer Vorteile bei Funktionalität, Leistung und Erscheinungsbild. Sein ganzheitlicher Ansatz verleiht Gebäuden einen fortdauernden Wert und sorgt für das notwendige Maß an Qualität mit positiven Auswirkungen auf Mensch, Gesellschaft, Umwelt und Natur.
Das Unternehmen erhielt für seine nachhaltigen und innovativen Architekturprojekte bereits nationale und internationale Auszeichnungen und fand in europäischen, amerikanischen und asiatischen Medien Erwähnung. 2016 erhielt Toni die Auszeichnung British Architect of the Year; 2018 wurde er eingeladen seine Arbeit auf der Austellung Time Space Existence der Biennale Venedig zu präsentieren.

Toni Yli-Suvanto Architects es una empresa fundada en 2007, con sede en Helsinki, centrada en el diseño de un entorno físico saludable que promueva el bienestar social y sea económica y ecológicamente sostenible. La empresa promueve soluciones de diseño funcionales y flexibles con bajo contenido de carbono, que respeten y aprovechen su entorno natural en términos de funcionalidad, rendimiento y apariencia. Su enfoque holístico otorga a los edificios un valor duradero y cualidades integradas que crean un ciclo de influencia positiva en el individuo, la sociedad, el medio ambiente y la naturaleza.
La empresa ha ganado varios premios internacionales por sus diseños sostenibles e innovadores y sus trabajos han sido publicados en medios de Europa, América del Norte y Asia. En 2016 recibió en Gran Bretaña el premio Architect of the Year y en 2018 fue invitado a participar en la exposición Time Space Existence de la Bienal de Venecia.

[BAMIYAN CULTURAL CENTRE]

[WOODEN SAUNA PAVILION]

[ECOLOGICAL ENGINEERING CENTRE]

BAMIYAN CULTURAL CENTRE

By following a concept of traditional Afghan architecture, and by taking advantage of the climatic conditions and the local materials, a self-sufficient centre with flexible cultural spaces and pleasant indoor environment is proposed to support the ongoing efforts for peaceful and independent development of local communities and tribes. The building is divided into units organised around courtyards with gardens, where plants provide colour, shade and a moderated microclimate. The succession of spaces leads the visitor gradually towards the panoramic views of the Buddhas, the world heritage monuments. The use of compacted earth contributes thermal inertia to the interior. The building's design takes advantage of natural light avoiding excessive heat, allowing for natural ventilation according to the local winds and it thrives on solar energy, supplying both the centre and the community.

Dieses Gebäude wurde im traditionellen afghanischen Architekturstil erbaut und gehörte zu den Angeboten einer Ausschreibung für den Bau eines energieautarken Kulturzentrums. Mehrere kleine Einheiten sind um Höfe angeordnet, was besser zum Gemeinschaftssinn des Landes passt. Zu jedem Hof gehört ein Garten mit Farben und Schatten in moderatem Mikroklima. Beim Durchschreiten der Räume kann der Besucher jeweils einen tollen Ausblick auf die zum Weltkulturerbe erklärten Buddha-Statuen genießen. Wände aus kompakter Erde und erschwingliches und lokales Baumaterial unterstützen die thermische Trägheit im komfortablen Inneren. Bei der Gebäudeplanung bediente man sich der Vorteile des natürlichen Lichts, um enorme Hitze zu vermeiden und eine natürliche Belüftung durch den Wind zu ermöglichen. Warmwasserkollektoren und eine Photovoltaikanlage versorgen das Zentrum und die Gemeinschaft mit Solarenergie.

Selon un concept d'architecture afghane traditionnelle, ce bâtiment est issu d'une proposition de construction d'un centre culturel auto-suffisant. Il est divisé en petites entités organisées autour de cours, très usitées dans la communauté locale. Chaque cour renferme un jardin qui apporte de la couleur, de l'ombre et un microclimat tempéré. La succession d'espaces mène progressivement le visiteur vers les vues panoramiques des Bouddhas, monument inscrit au patrimoine mondial. L'usage de murs de terre compactée, matériau économique et disponible localement, apporte une inertie thermique à cet intérieur confortable. Le design de ce bâtiment profite de la lumière naturelle en évitant une chaleur excessive, en permettant une aération naturelle en fonction des vents régionaux et il bénéficie amplement de l'énergie solaire des récupérateurs d'eau potable chaude et des panneaux voltaïques qui approvisionnent le centre comme la communauté.

Siguiendo un concepto de la arquitectura tradicional afgana, esta propuesta resultante de un concurso para edificar un centro cultural autosuficiente se estructura en pequeñas unidades organizadas en torno a patios, más familiares para la comunidad local. Cada patio encierra un jardín que aporta color, genera sombra y modera el microclima. La sucesión de espacios conduce de manera gradual al visitante hacia las vistas panorámicas sobre los budas declarados Patrimonio Mundial. El uso de muros de tierra compactada, material económico y disponible a nivel local, aporta su inercia térmica al confort interior. El diseño del edificio aprovecha la luz natural evitando el calor excesivo, permite una ventilación natural acorde a los vientos locales y se nutre de energía solar mediante colectores para ACS y paneles fotovoltaicos que abastecen al centro y a la comunidad.

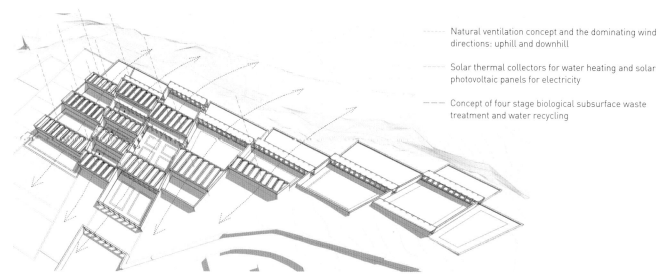

------ Natural ventilation concept and the dominating wind directions: uphill and downhill

------ Solar thermal collectors for water heating and solar photovoltaic panels for electricity

——— Concept of four stage biological subsurface waste treatment and water recycling

Energy, ventilation, waste treatment and water recycling concepts

WOODEN SAUNA PAVILION

This pavilion serves as a centre of socializing during the warmer seasons, following the tradition in Lapland of decentralising the living spaces into several buildings after the cold winter. Its interior follows the traditional layout of locating the bath and sauna in the same space, and taking advantage of the natural airflow. Therefore, the bath is on the cooler, lower level whereas hot steam can be enjoyed above. The building's main opening, framed by a porch, captures the view over the lake and allows the light reflected from the water to enter. In order to minimise its carbon footprint and support the local economy, more than 95% of the materials used were obtained, processed, and built locally. The structure and finishes are made of local wood, cellulose is used for insulation and any waste produced during building was reused for heating.

Dieses Clubhaus spiegelt die Tradition der Häuser Lapplands, bei denen der Wohnbereich für die warmen Jahreszeiten auf mehrere Gebäude verteilt ist, wider. Bad und Sauna befinden sich wie in dieser Tradition üblich im selben Raum, um dem Fluss der Natur zu folgen. Das Bad liegt im unteren und kühleren Bereich, oben kann hingegen heißer Dampf genossen werden. Der Haupteingang des Gebäudes liegt auf einer Veranda, von der aus man den See betrachten kann, dessen Wasser das Licht in wunderbarer Weise reflektiert. Mehr als 95% des verwendeten Materials stammt aus der Region und wurde vor Ort für den Bau verarbeitet. So wird der CO2-Fußabdruck minimiert und die lokale Wirtschaft unterstützt. Struktur und Oberflächen bestehen aus einheimischen Hölzern, für die Isolierung wurde Zellstoff verwendet und Bauabfälle wurden für die Beheizung wiederverwertet.

Ce pavillon s'inscrit dans la tradition des maisons lapones en ce qu'il décentralise les espaces à vivre dans plusieurs bâtiments durant les saisons les plus chaudes. Son intérieur suit le plan traditionnel dans lequel le bain et le sauna sont dans le même espace de par la circulation naturelle de l'air. Par conséquent, le bain se situe au niveau inférieur, le plus frais, tandis qu'on peut profiter de la vapeur chaude au-dessus. L'ouverture principale du bâtiment, encadrée par un porche, procure une vue sur le lac et fait entrer la lumière réfléchie par l'eau. Pour minimiser l'empreinte carbone et soutenir l'économie locale, plus de 95 % des matériaux utilisés ont été sourcés, élaborés, et construits localement. La structure et les finitions sont faites de bois local, la cellulose utilisée pour l'isolation et tous les déchets produits durant les travaux ont été réutilisés pour le chauffage.

Este pabellón se enmarca dentro de la tradición de las casas laponas, que descentraliza los espacios habitables en varios edificios durante las temporadas más cálidas. Su interior sigue el esquema tradicional de situar baño y sauna en un mismo espacio, colocados según el flujo natural del aire: el baño en un nivel inferior más fresco y el disfrute de los vapores calientes en la parte superior. La abertura principal del edificio, enmarcada por un porche, captura la vista sobre el lago y permite la entrada de la luz reflejada sobre el agua. Con el fin de minimizar la huella de carbono y respaldar la economía local, más del 95% de los materiales utilizados se obtuvieron, procesaron y construyeron localmente. La estructura y los acabados son de madera de la zona, el aislamiento es de celulosa y los residuos de la construcción fueron reutilizados para la calefacción.

Site plan

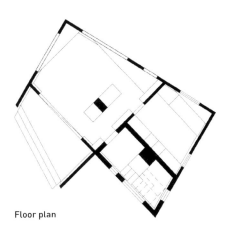

Floor plan

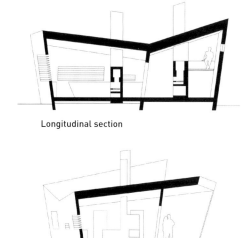

Longitudinal section

Cross section

ECOLOGICAL ENGINEERING CENTRE

The competition proposal for the reuse of the Packard automobile plant converts the former industrial buildings, once a symbol of the country's industrial heyday, now sadly representing the decline of Detroit, into an ecological engineering centre and a new suburban hub, which has a positive impact on both the environment and the community.

The idea of promoting a usage based on biological circular economy with closed water, energy and nutrient cycle flows, with vertical farming, fish breeding, waste to energy concept and water recycle system, arose from an environmental analysis of the Midewest region. These activities are open to the local community and integrated into public spaces, thus encouraging participation. New construction complements the scheme with other urban functions, creating together an active, dynamic and safe centre for the local community.

Die Ausschreibung bezog sich auf den Umbau des ehemaligen Packard-Automobilwerks, das einst als Symbol für die industrielle Blütezeit des Landes galt und jetzt in trauriger Weise den Abschwung Detroits widerspiegelt. Ziel war ein Zentrum für Umwelttechnik mit positiven Auswirkungen auf Umwelt und Stadt. Aufgrund der Bedeutung dieses Ortes wurde ein Großteil der Gebäudestruktur erhalten. Das Nutzungskonzept der vertikalen Landwirtschaft mit effizientem Energie-, Abfall-, Wasser- und Nahrungsmittelmanagement für Fischzucht und Pflanzenanbau entstand aus einer Umweltanalyse für den Mittleren Westen. Das Projekt möchte die Bürger mit seinen Gärten und öffentlich zugänglichen Orten dazu anregen, sich an den Veranstaltungen des Zentrums, sowie an wirtschaftlichen und umweltbewussten Programmen zu beteiligen.

Dans une proposition pour ce concours d'architecture, l'ancienne usine automobile Packard, ancien symbole de l'âge d'or de l'industrie du pays, représentant maintenant, tristement, le déclin de Detroit, est convertie en centre d'ingénierie écologique qui a un impact positif à la fois sur l'environnement et sur la communauté locale. La conservation de la majorité de la structure du bâtiment est un hommage à l'importance du lieu. L'idée de promouvoir un usage basé sur le concept de l'agriculture verticale, soutenu par un système de gestion efficace de l'énergie, des déchets, de l'eau et des nutriments utilisés dans la pisciculture et la pousse des plantes, est née d'une analyse environnementale de la région du Midwest. Cette proposition vise à encourager la participation des citoyens aux événements du centre et aux programmes économiques et environnementaux en incorporant les jardins et les espaces publics dans le design.

La propuesta para este concurso convierte la antigua planta automovilística Packard, antiguo símbolo del apogeo industrial del país y ahora símbolo de la decadencia de Detroit, en un Centro de Ingeniería Ecológica que genere un efecto positivo sobre el medio ambiente y sobre en la comunidad. La preservación de la mayor parte de la estructura de los edificios rinde homenaje a la importancia del lugar. Del análisis ambiental de la zona del medio Oeste surge la idea de promover un uso basado en el concepto de agricultura vertical, apoyado en una eficiente gestión de la energía y los residuos y también del agua y los nutrientes utilizados en la producción de plantas y peces. La propuesta pretende fomentar la participación ciudadana en los eventos y programas económicos y ambientales del centro, para lo cual se sirve de jardines y espacios públicos integrados en el diseño.

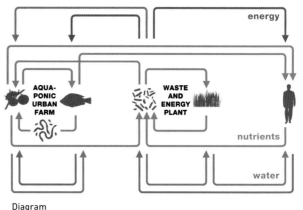

Diagram

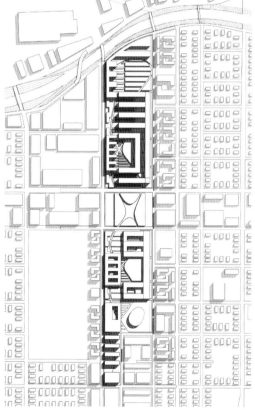

Site plan

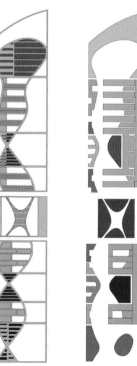

Ground level
Public spaces

Ground level
Outdoor public spaces
and circulation

Ground level
Indoor activities

Upper level
activities

VEELAERT ARCHITECTEN

WWW.VEELAERTARCHITECTEN.BE

Veelaert Architecten is an ambitious, experienced collective in Antwerp. An enthusiastic, close-knit team of architects, specialists and office staff, connected by one thing: their intense interest in high-quality contemporary architecture. In 2018, this architectural agency will celebrate its 33rd birthday. Founder and CEO Jan Veelaert's achievements are extensive and varied. Veelaert Architecten has completed residential projects, as well as care centers, offices and shopping centers. The common theme between all of these projects is a well-calculated play of mass and material, of dynamic layering, of sculptural strictness that, in all its simplicity and minimalism, manages to evoke emotion. As part of this, particular attention is paid to the perfectly executed detail.
Veelaert Architecten's "Sisters Annonciaden" received the 2017 Special Prize for a Sustainable Mixed-Use Project at the European Architecture Awards.

Veelaert Architecten est un collectif ambitieux et expérimenté d'Anvers. Une équipe d'architectes, de spécialistes et de personnel de bureau enthousiastes, soudés, reliés par un point commun : leur intérêt majeur pour une architecture contemporaine de qualité supérieure. En 2018, ce cabinet d'architecture fêtera son 33ème anniversaire. Les accomplissements du fondateur et directeur Jan Veelaert sont nombreux et variés. Veelaert Architecten a des projets résidentiels ainsi que des centres de soins, des bureaux et des centres commerciaux à son actif. Le thème commun à tous ces projets est un jeu très calculé des volumes et de matériaux, de superpositions dynamiques, de rigueur sculpturale qui, dans toute sa simplicité et son minimalisme, parvient à évoquer l'émotion. Pour compléter cet effet, une attention particulière est prêtée au détail parfaitement exécuté.
« Sisters Annonciaden » de Veelaert Architecten a reçu le Special Prize for a Sustainable Mixed-Use Project récompensant un projet d'aménagement mixte durable aux European Architecture Awards.

Veelaert Architecten ist ein ehrgeiziges und erfahrenes Gemeinschaftsunternehmen in Antwerpen. Ein enthusiastisches und zusammengewachsenes Team aus Architekten, Experten und Angestellten, vereint durch einen gemeinsamen Wert: das enorme Interesse an hochwertiger zeitgenössischer Architektur. 2018 feiert das Architekturbüro sein 30-jähriges Gründungsjubiläum. Die Errungenschaften des Gründungs- und Vorstandsmitglieds Jan Veelaert sind umfangreich und vielfältig. Veelaert Architecten realisierte sowohl Wohngebäude als auch Bürogebäude, Pflege- und Einkaufszentren. Allen Projekten gemeinsam ist das wohlkalkulierte Zusammenspiel aus Menge und Material, dynamischer Schichtung und genauer Bauweise, die trotz Schlichtheit und Minimalismus Gefühle hervorruft. Ein besonderer Fokus liegt dabei auf perfekt ausgeführten Details.
Das Veelaert Architecten-Projekt "Sisters Annoncieren" erhielt bei den European Architecture Awards 2017 den Sonderpreis für ein nachhaltiges Mehrzweckprojekt (Special Prize for a Sustainable Mixed-Use Project).

Veelaert Architecten es un experimentado y ambicioso colectivo en Antwerp. Un entusiasta y cohesionado grupo de arquitectos, especialistas y personal de oficina, con un punto en común: su gran interés por la arquitectura contemporánea de calidad. En 2018, esta agencia celebrará su 33° aniversario. Los logros de Jan Veelaert, fundador y gerente, son vastos y variados. Veelaert Architecten ha completado proyectos residenciales así como centros de día, oficinas y centros comerciales. El tema común entre todos estos proyectos es un calculado juego de volumetría y materiales, de capas dinámicas, de rigidez escultural que, en toda su simplicidad y minimalismo, consigue provocar emoción. Además, se presta especial atención al detalle perfectamente ejecutado.
«Sisters Annonciaden» de Veelaert Architecten recibió en 2017 el premio especial para proyectos de uso mixto sostenible de los premios de arquitectura europeos.

[ANNONCIADEN]

ANNONCIADEN

Situated in a location with a strong historical context, the project involved developing a mixed-use complex including 89 subsidised flats, offices, shops, and service areas within a park. Analysis of the site led to the inclusion of three historic buildings within the project and the construction of a new building in harmony with the urban environment whose diagonal lines energise and visually unite the different parts of the overall development. The architects took into account the age mix and population levels and their specific requirements, in order to address social issues such as isolation, mobility, inclusion or poverty. The outcome is a logical combination of design, architecture, sustainability, and urban design with a refreshing perspective of what life in the future might be like.

Bei diesem Projekt ging es um den Bau eines Gebäudekomplexes mit 89 einzelnen Wohnungen, Büros, Geschäften und Serviceeinrichtungen in einem Park an einem Ort mit reichem historischem Erbe. Nach einer Analyse des Ortes entschieden sich die Architekten, drei der historischen Gebäude zu belassen und ein neues zum städtischen Umfeld passendes Gebäude hinzuzufügen, durch dessen diagonale Linien die einzelnen Elemente visuell verbunden wirken. Dabei berücksichtigten sie die unterschiedlichen Arten von Bewohnern mit einer breiten Altersspanne und deren unterschiedliche Bedürfnisse. Zu berücksichtigen waren hier gesellschaftliche Probleme wie Isolation, Mobilität, Inklusion oder Armut. Das Ergebnis ist eine logische Kombination aus Design, Architektur, Nachhaltigkeit und Städteplanung mit einem erfrischenden Vorgeschmack auf die Lebensweise der Zukunft.

Situé dans un site à fort contexte historique, ce projet impliquait le développement d'un complexe multi-usages comprenant 89 appartements subventionnés, des bureaux, des magasins, et des zones de services à l'intérieur d'un parc. L'analyse du site a conduit à l'inclusion dans le projet de trois bâtiments historiques en harmonie avec l'environnement urbain dont les lignes diagonales énergisent et réunissent visuellement les différentes parties du développement global. Les architectes ont pris en compte la mixité générationnelle et les niveaux de population et leurs besoins spécifiques, pour répondre aux questions sociales comme l'isolement, la mobilité, l'inclusion et la pauvreté. Il en résulte une combinaison logique de design, d'architecture, de durabilité, et de design urbain avec une perspective rafraîchissante sur ce à quoi pourra ressembler la vie dans l'avenir.

Situado en un emplazamiento con un fuerte contexto histórico, el proyecto desarrolla un complejo inmobiliario de uso mixto que incluye 89 apartamentos asistidos, oficinas, comercios y zonas de servicio dentro de un parque. El análisis del lugar impulsó la integración de tres edificios históricos en el proyecto y la construcción de un nuevo edificio que armoniza con el entorno urbano y cuyas líneas diagonales dinamizan y unen visualmente las diferentes partes del conjunto. Los arquitectos tuvieron en cuenta la mezcla de diferentes edades y capas de la población y sus necesidades específicas, para poder responder a problemas sociales como el aislamiento, la movilidad, la integración o el empobrecimiento. El resultado es una combinación lógica de diseño, arquitectura, sostenibilidad y diseño urbano con una refrescante perspectiva de cómo podría ser la vida en el futuro.

Site plan

Building elevations

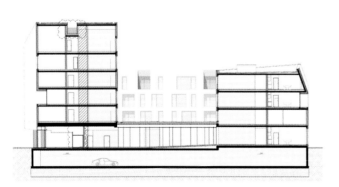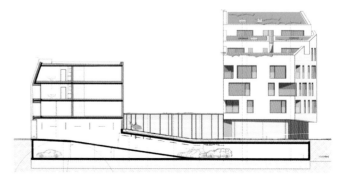

Building sections

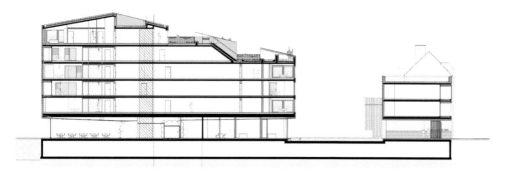

Building sections

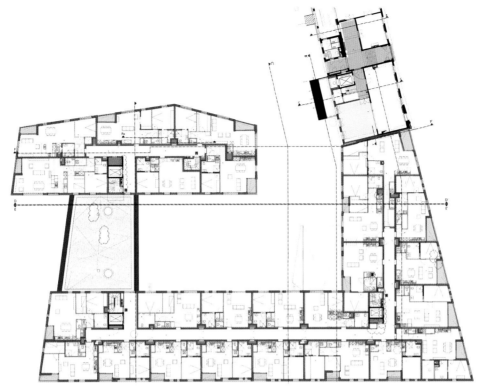

Typical floor plan

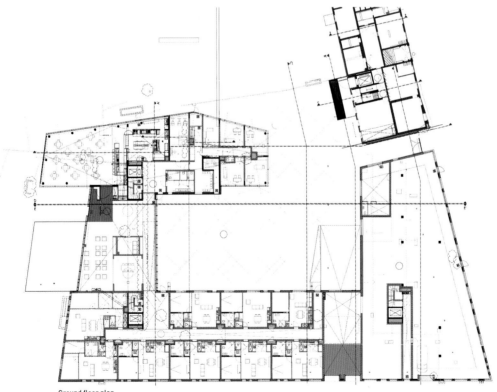

Ground floor plan

WOHA
ARQUITECTURA

ANTONIOMACIA.COM

WOHA architecture is a studio working in several different fields, even in those located within the boundaries of the same. This occasionally peripheral status means that it can partake of contributions from other schools of knowledge or professional sectors: architecture, product design, landscaping, R & D, retail design and organising exhibitions.

Three fields mark WOHA architecture's productions: people, teaching and research and learning through nature. Throughout our history, we have always taken these three aspects into account, in such a way that each project, regardless of its size, is treated with equal intensity and ends up being a work with its own unique identity distinct from passing fads or styles.

WOHA architecture est un studio qui opère dans plusieurs domaines d'architecture, jusqu'aux confins de leurs limites. Ce statut occasionnellement périphérique signifie qu'il peut prendre part aux contributions d'autres écoles de savoir ou secteurs professionnels : l'architecture, le design de produit, l'architecture de paysage, la recherche et le développement, le design de vente et l'organisation d'expositions.

Trois domaines différents marquent les productions de WOHA architecture : les personnes, l'enseignement et la recherche, ainsi que l'apprentissage par la nature. Au cours de notre histoire, nous avons toujours pris ces trois aspects en compte, de telle façon que chaque projet, quelle que soit sa taille, est traité avec une intensité égale et, finalement, devient un travail avec sa propre identité hors des tendances passagères et des styles.

Das Architekturstudio WOHA architecture arbeitet in den vielfältigsten Bereichen und Marktnischen. Somit beteiligt es sich auch an Projekten in anderen Wissensbereichen und Branchen wie Architektur, Produktdesign, Landschauftsbau, Forschung und Entwicklung, Einzelhandelsdesign und Organisation von Ausstellungen.

Die Projekte von WOHA architecture konzentrieren sich vor allem auf die drei Komponenten Menschen, Lehren und Forschen und Lernen durch die Natur. Diese drei Kernkomponenten prägten unsere gesamte Unternehmensgeschichte. Wir gehen all unsere Projekte – unabhängig von deren Größe – mit gleicher Anstrengung an und möchten ihnen eine eigene Identität jenseits von Stilrichtungen oder Trends einhauchen.

WOHA arquitectura es un estudio que trabaja en diversos ámbitos de la disciplina, incluso, en los situados en los límites de la misma. Esta condición a veces periférica hace que se nutra de aportaciones de otros segmentos del conocimiento o sectores profesionales: arquitectura, diseño de producto, paisajismo, I+D+I, *retail design* y organización de exposiciones.

Tres líneas marcan la producción de WOHA arquitectura: las personas, la docencia e investigación y el aprendizaje a través de la naturaleza. A lo largo de nuestra trayectoria, siempre hemos tenido muy presentes estos tres aspectos, de tal manera que cada proyecto es tratado con igual intensidad, independientemente de su tamaño, y acaba siendo una obra con identidad propia alejada de modas y estilos.

[OTONIEL OFFICES]

[CAFETERÍA CALAHORRA]

OTONIEL OFFICES

The refurbishment of this two-storey hanger converting it into offices had a double aim: decorate the main façade with a unique material that would highlight the vertical garden, proposed as the building's centrepiece and redistribute the inner spaces. The material chosen to clad the façade was a corrugated perforated sheet of metal acting as a natural filter for the light penetrating the interior. During the daytime, the sheet metal gives the building the appearance of an opaque, flat defined volume; at night, the cladding fades progressively, exposing the light and the inner space. In addition to its inherent environmental and social qualities, the explosion of vegetation and of colour represented by the vertical garden, highlighted within the neutral plane formed by the perforated sheets of metal, acts as a powerful visual attraction for the company.

Der Umbau dieses zweistöckigen Anbaus in ein Bürogebäude hatte gleich zwei Ziele. Einerseits sollte die Hauptfassade mit einem einzigartigen Material gestaltet werden, um den vertikalen Garten als Gebäudemittelpunkt besonders in Szene zu setzen. Die zweite Aufgabe war die Neuaufteilung der Innenräume. Bei der Fassade entschied man sich für ein perforiertes und gewelltes Metallblech, das auf natürliche Weise das eindringende Licht filtert. Tagsüber lässt das Metallblech das Gebäude undurchlässig und flach erscheinen. Nachts wirkt die Fassade deutlich dunkler und bringt Licht und Innenraum zur Geltung. Das Gebäude überzeugt durch seine umweltbewussten und sozialen Vorzüge; der vertikale Garten mit seiner Vielfalt an Pflanzen und Farben, der inmitten des neutralen perforierten Metallblechs besonders zur Geltung kommt, wirkt als ganz besonderes Aushängeschild für das Unternehmen.

La rénovation de ce hangar à deux étages pour le convertir en bureaux avait un double objectif : décorer la façade principale avec un matériau unique qui ferait ressortir le jardin vertical, proposé comme pièce maîtresse, et redistribuer les espaces intérieurs. Le matériau choisi pour barder la façade était une plaque de métal ondulé perforée servant de filtre naturel pour la lumière pénétrant à l'intérieur. Pendant la journée, cette tôle donne au bâtiment l'apparence d'un volume opaque, plat ; la nuit le bardage s'estompe progressivement, laissant voir la lumière et les espaces intérieurs. En plus de ses qualités environnementales et sociales intrinsèques, l'explosion de végétation et de couleurs représentée par ce jardin vertical, souligné par la neutralité du plan formé par les tôles perforées, agit comme une signature visuelle puissante pour la compagnie.

La reforma de esta nave de dos plantas destinada a oficinas tuvo un doble objetivo: vestir la fachada principal con un único material que hiciera resaltar el jardín vertical propuesto en el centro de la composición y la redistribución de los espacios interiores. El material escogido para revestir la fachada fue una chapa perforada grecada que actúa como tamiz de la luz natural que penetra en el interior. De día, la chapa presenta el edificio como un volumen opaco de planos definidos; de noche, la envolvente se desvanece de manera progresiva, dejando al descubierto la luz y el espacio interior. Además de sus inherentes cualidades medioambientales y sociales, la explosión de vegetación y de color que representa el jardín vertical, destacando dentro del plano neutro que conforma la chapa perforada, actúa como potente reclamo visual para la empresa.

First floor plan

Ground floor plan

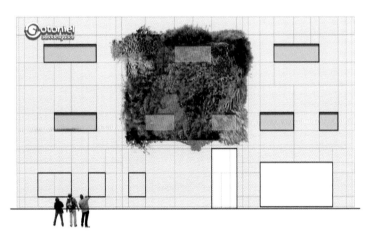

Elevation

1. Entry	7. Online sales	15. Events room /
2. Interpretation	8. Private office	conference room
centre	9. Archive	16. Break room
3. Cashier	10. Storage	17. Changing room
4. Shopping / sales	11. Toilet room	18. Showers
5. Management	12. Lift	19. Relaxation room
offices	13. Staircase	20. Mechanical room
6. List removal	14. Meeting room	21. Cleaning room

CAFETERÍA CALAHORRA

The project, promoted by the city council of Elche, transformed a 140 m^2 urban space delimited by a party wall and located in an area with a rich historical heritage. This intervention opts for an invisible construction, integrated into a vertical garden covering the flanking wall and containing a cafeteria, toilets, and a warehouse. The remaining space is occupied by a multi-functional terrace linked to the cafe. A lattice structure of steel scaffolding attached to the party wall, covered by a 10 mm layer of PVC and a double layer of felt, provides a garden with the necessary mass to contain the inner spaces. The vertical garden is a 105 m^2 mosaic formed by more than 3000 Mediterranean plants, some with high botanical value, such as myrtle, St. John's wort, lavender, sedge, or fountain grass, providing the area with enhanced environmental benefits.

Bei diesem vom Stadtrat Elche beauftragten Projekt ging es um die Umgestaltung eines 140 m^2 großen städtischen Raumes mit Grenzmauer innerhalb eines Gebiets mit reichem historischen Erbe. Hier entschied man sich für eine unsichtbare Konstruktion als Teil eines vertikalen Gartens mit Cafeteria, Toiletten und Lagerhaus, hinter der die Grenzwand verschwindet. Der restliche Platz wird von der Mehrzweckterrasse der Cafeteria eingenommen. Das gitterartige Stahlgerüst an der Grenzmauer ist mit einem 10 mm dicken PVC-Belag und einer doppelten Filzbeschichtung überzogen und beinhaltet einen Garten, der groß genug für die Innenräume ist. Der vertikale Garten ist ein 105 m^2 großes Mosaik aus mehr als 3.000 teilweise aus botanischer Sicht sehr wertvollen mediterranen Pflanzen wie Myrthe, Johanniskraut, Lavendel, Riedgras oder Springbrunnengras, die sich vorteilhaft auf die Umwelt auswirken.

Ce projet, porté par le Conseil municipal de Elche, a transformé un espace urbain de 140 m² délimité par un mur de séparation et situé dans une zone ayant un riche patrimoine historique. Cette intervention a opté pour une construction invisible, intégrée dans un jardin vertical recouvrant le mur latéral et contenant une cafétéria, des toilettes, et un entrepôt. L'espace subsistant est occupé par une terrasse multi-fonctions reliée au café. Un treillage sur structure en acier rattachée au mur latéral, recouverte d'une couche de PVC de 10 mm et d'une double couche de feutre, procure un jardin ayant la masse nécessaire pour contenir les espaces intérieurs. Cet oasis vertical est une mosaïque de 105 m² composée de plus de 3000 plantes méditerranéennes, certaines ayant une grande valeur botanique, comme la myrte, le millepertuis, la lavande, le carex, ou le pennisetum, procurant des bienfaits environnementaux supplémentaires.

El proyecto, promovido por el Ayuntamiento de Elche, transforma un espacio urbano de 140 m^2 delimitado por una medianera y situado en una zona con un gran patrimonio histórico. La intervención opta por una construcción invisible, integrada en un jardín vertical que cubre la medianera y cuyo volumen aloja en su interior una cafetería, aseos y un almacén. El resto del espacio se destina a terraza multifuncional vinculada a la cafetería. Una estructura triangulada de perfiles de acero sujeta a la medianera, cubierta por una capa de PVC de 10 mm y una doble capa de fieltro, da el volumen necesario al jardín para albergar los espacios interiores. El jardín vertical es un mosaico de 105 m^2 formado por más de 3.000 plantas mediterráneas, algunas de alto valor botánico, como el Mirto, Hipérico, Lavanda, Cárex o Pennisetum, que aporta grandes beneficios medioambientales a la zona.

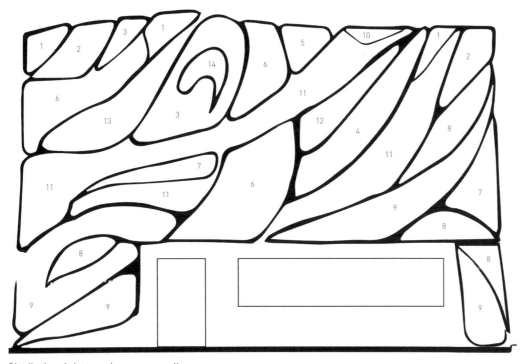

Distribution of plant species on green wall

1. Myrtle
2. *Buddleja d.*
3. Perforated St
   John's-wort
4. *Pennisetum s.*
5. Rosemary
6. Lavender
7. Daisy (*Erigeron r.*)
8. Sage
9. Carex
10. Yuca
11. *Tulbaghia v.*
12. White Lampranthus
13. Red Lampranthus
14. *Pennisetum r.*

Vertical garden system: Vertical landscaping system intended for the planting of species on vertical surfaces

Components: Total thickness 20 mm

Substructure: Galvanized steel batten system anchored to support Dimensions according to load requirements and to the state of the support

Spacing: 40 cm

Amnioplastic panel: P-URB panel (commercial brand), 10 mm thick, screwed to support

Substrate subjection: Phyto-generator Polifelt ph, type P-URB (commercial brand), 3 mm thick, stapled to panel

Organic coverage: Species selected according to the façade's characteristics

Watering system: Automated-controlled system and remote security type NPKSYSTEM-5000 (commercial system). Irrigation with 5 cm elbow drip lines

Conservation and maintenance: The fertigation control is completely automatic, so that the maintenance consists of the periodic inspection of the installations, as well as the filling of the fertilizer tanks

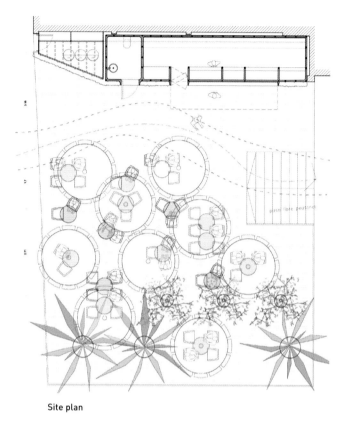

Site plan

Galvanized substructure

Horizontal crossbeams

Horizontal battens

Waterproof aminoplastic panel

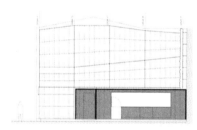

Longitudinal section

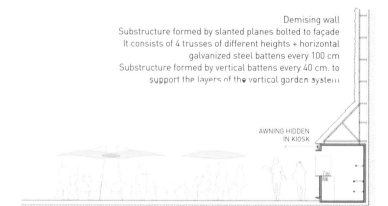

Demising wall
Substructure formed by slanted planes bolted to façade
It consists of 4 trusses of different heights + horizontal galvanized steel battens every 100 cm
Substructure formed by vertical battens every 40 cm. to support the layers of the vertical garden system

AWNING HIDDEN IN KIOSK

Cross section

Kiosk. Cross section

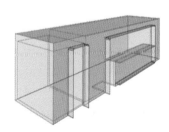

Kiosk. Axonometry

Kiosk box: self-supporting fibreglass item
Supported on concrete base 246 x 50 x 60 cm
Levelling shims

YYA-YUJI YAMAZAKI ARCHITECTURE

WWW.YYANY.COM

Yuji Yamazaki, AIA is a Japanese architect from Tokyo, he is a licensed architect in New York State and principal of YYA based in New York City. His extensive design practice covers a wide range of disciplines and projects. Prior to establishing YYA, Yuji served as a senior associate at Janson Goldstein and created projects for Giorgio Armani, W Hotel, The Breakers Hotel, Calvin Klein and Saks Fifth Avenue. At Vignelli Associates, his projects included Harbor Circus in Kobe, Japan, auditorium seating design for Walt Disney Concert Hall in Los Angeles, Millennium Message art installation for Smithsonian Institution, train car interior design for Fiat, and streetscape design for New York City. Yuji attended School of Visual Arts and Fashion Institute of Technology, State University of New York and holds Bachelor of Fine Arts degree in Interior Design, and a Master of Science degree in Landscape Design from Columbia University.

Yuji Yamazaki, AIA (Institut des architectes des États-Unis), est un architecte japonais originaire de Tokyo, agréé par l'État de New York et directeur de YYA, implanté dans la ville de New York. Sa vaste expérience du design couvre un vaste éventail de disciplines et de projets. Avant de créer YYA, Yuji a été associé principal chez Janson Goldstein et a créé des projets pour Giorgio Armani, W Hotel, The Breakers Hotel, Calvin Klein et Saks Fifth Avenue. Parmi ses projets chez Vignelli Associates, on trouve le Harbor Circus de Kobe, au Japon, le design de sièges pour l'auditorium de la salle de concert Walt Disney, à Los Angeles, l'installation artistique Millenium Message pour la Smithsonian Institution, la conception de l'intérieur de wagons ferroviaires pour Fiat et celle d'aménagements urbains pour la ville de New York. Yuji a suivi les cours de la School of Visual Arts and Fashion Institute of Technology à l'Université d'État de New York et détient un diplôme des Beaux Arts en décoration d'intérieur et un Master en architecture du paysage de l'Université Columbia.

Yuji Yamazaki, AIA ist ein japanischer Architekt aus Tokio. Er verfügt über die Zulassung als Architekt im US-Bundesstaat New York; die YYA-Hauptniederlassung befindet sich in New York City. Seine enorme Design-Erfahrung deckt eine Vielzahl von Bereichen und Projekten ab. Vor der Gründung von YYA war Yuji Vorstandsmitglied bei Janson Goldstein und realisierte Projekte für Giorgio Armani, W Hotel, The Breakers Hotel, Calvin Klein und Saks Fifth Avenue. Zu seinen Projekten bei Vignelli Associates gehörten der Harbor Circus in Kobe, Japan, die Gestaltung des Zuschauerraums für die Walt Disney Concert Hall in Los Angeles, die Kunstinstallation Millennium Message für die Smithsonian Institution, das Innendesign des Autozugs von Fiat und die Gestaltung des Straßenbilds von New York City. Er besuchte die School of Visual Arts (Schule für bildende Künste) und das Fashion Institute of Technology (technische Universität für Mode) der State University of New York und verfügt über einen Bachelor of Fine Arts der Innenarchitektur und einen Master of Science der Landschaftsarchitektur der Columbia University.

Yuji Yamazaki, AIA, es un arquitecto japonés natural de Tokio. Es director de la oficina YYA afincada en la ciudad de Nueva York y tiene licencia como arquitecto para todo el estado. Su vasta experiencia en diseño abarca una amplia gama de disciplinas y proyectos. Antes de establecerse en YYA, Yuji fue socio senior en Jan Goldstein, donde creó proyectos para Giorgio Armani, Calvin Klein y Saks Fifth Avenue, así como los hoteles W Hotel y The Breakers Hotel. Durante su etapa en Vignelli Associates, sus proyectos incluyeron el Harbor Circus de Kobe, Japón, el diseño de la platea de un auditorio para el Walt Disney Concert Hall en Los Ángeles, la obra de arte *Millennium Message* para Smithsonian Institution, el diseño interior de un vagón para Fiat y el trazado de calles para la ciudad de Nueva York. Yuji estudió en la School of Visual Arts y el Fashion Institute of Technology, en el estado de Nueva York y se graduó en diseño interior. Además, posee un máster en paisajismo de la Universidad de Columbia.

[FINOLHU VILLAS]

FINOLHU VILLAS

An extreme sensitivity towards climate change and rising sea levels turned the Maldive Islands into the ideal place to promote a model for a sustainable resort. The complex balances recreation with ecology, combining enjoyment of the beautiful beaches with the capture of solar energy generated by 6200 m² of solar panels supplying the entire island. The panels are built into all aspects of the resort's design and are strategically located to generate shade when walking around. The design of the villas favours the natural cross-ventilation and regulates the entry of sunlight through a system of vertical wooden slats. The complex's outdoor areas use a palette based on native vegetation, whose positioning between the buildings and the ocean constitutes a natural barrier against the threat of tsunamis.

Ein besonderes Bewusstsein für den Klimawandel und den Anstieg des Meeresspiegels machte die Malediven zum idealen Ort, um ein Model für ein nachhaltiges Resort zu entwickeln. Der Komplex bietet die perfekte Balance aus Freizeit und Ökologie; Gäste genießen die wundervollen Strände, während 6.200 m² Sonnenkollektoren die gesamte Insel mit Energie versorgen. Die Sonnenkollektoren sind in alle Designelemente des Gebäudes integriert und strategisch so platziert, dass die Gäste entspannt im Schatten spazieren können. Das Design der Villen begünstigt die natürliche Querlüftung und reguliert den Einfall des Sonnenlichts durch ein System aus vertikalen Holzlatten. Im Außenbereich gedeiht eine große Vielfalt an einheimischen Pflanzen, die so zwischen Gebäude und Meer platziert sind, dass sie als natürlicher Schutzwall gegen Tsunamis fungieren.

Une sensibilité extrême au changement climatique et l'élévation du niveau de la mer a fait des Maldives le lieu idéal pour promouvoir un modèle de complexe hôtelier durable. Celui-ci équilibre le loisir et l'écologie, en mêlant l'avantage des superbes plages à l'absorption d'énergie solaire générée par 6200 m² de panneaux solaires qui fournissent toute l'île en électricité. Ceux-ci sont intégrés à tous les aspects de la conception de la station et sont stratégiquement placés pour produire de l'ombre pour les passants. Le design des villas favorise une aération transversale naturelle et régule l'ensoleillement grâce à un système de lattes de bois verticales. Les zones extérieures du complexe, dont le positionnement entre les bâtiments et l'Océan constitue une barrière naturelle à la menace des tsunamis, arborent une palette basée sur la végétation indigène.

Una extremada sensibilidad hacia el cambio climático y hacia la subida del nivel de los océanos convertían a las Islas Maldivas en el lugar ideal para promover un modelo de resort sostenible. El complejo equilibra recreo con ecología, combinando el disfrute de playas paradisíacas con la captación de energía solar generada por 6.200 m² de paneles fotovoltaicos que abastecen a toda la isla. Los paneles se integran en todos los aspectos del diseño del resort y se ubican estratégicamente para generar sombra sobre los recorridos a pie. El diseño de las villas favorece la ventilación natural cruzada y regula la entrada de la luz del sol mediante un sistema de lamas verticales de madera. Las zonas exteriores del complejo presentan una paleta basada en vegetación autóctona, cuya posición entre los edificios y el océano constituye una barrera natural frente al riesgo de tsunamis.

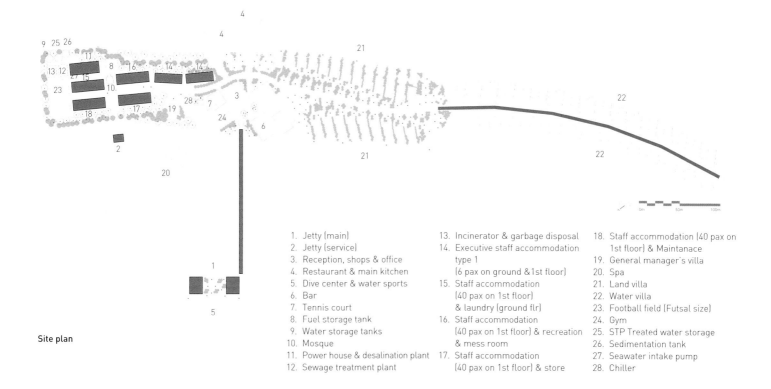

Site plan

1. Jetty (main)
2. Jetty (service)
3. Reception, shops & office
4. Restaurant & main kitchen
5. Dive center & water sports
6. Bar
7. Tennis court
8. Fuel storage tank
9. Water storage tanks
10. Mosque
11. Power house & desalination plant
12. Sewage treatment plant

13. Incinerator & garbage disposal
14. Executive staff accommodation type 1 (6 pax on ground &1st floor)
15. Staff accommodation (40 pax on 1st floor) & laundry (ground flr)
16. Staff accommodation (40 pax on 1st floor) & recreation & mess room
17. Staff accommodation (40 pax on 1st floor) & store

18. Staff accommodation (40 pax on 1st floor) & Maintanace
19. General manager's villa
20. Spa
21. Land villa
22. Water villa
23. Football field (Futsal size)
24. Gym
25. STP Treated water storage
26. Sedimentation tank
27. Seawater intake pump
28. Chiller

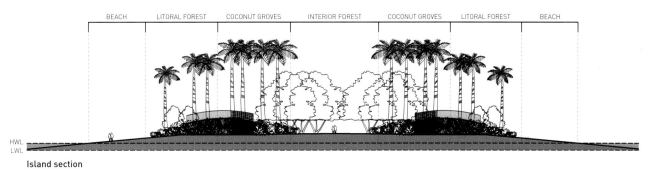

BEACH   LITORAL FOREST   COCONUT GROVES   INTERIOR FOREST   COCONUT GROVES   LITORAL FOREST   BEACH

HWL
LWL

Island section

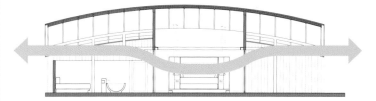

Cooling system diagrams

DIRECTORY

ACTUAL / OFFICE

SLEEVE HOUSE

LOCATION: Taghkanic, NY, USA

TOTAL AREA: w250 m² / 2,500 sq ft single family residence

DESIGN: 2013-2015

CONSTRUCTION: 2015-2017

ARCHITECT: Actual / Office

PRINCIPALE: Adam Dayem

PROJECT MANAGER: Farzam Yazdanseta

STRUCTURAL ENGINEER: Taconic Engineering

GENERAL CONTRACTOR: Lorne Dawes Construction

MECHANICAL SYSTEMS: Dell's Plumbing and Heating

SOLAR SYSTEM: Lotus Energy

SUPPLIERS:
Windows: Zola
Wood Facade: Delta Millworks
HVAC system: Mitsubishi
Heat Recovery Ventilator: Zehnder
Oven, range, refrigerator, dishwasher: Miele
Microwave: Wolf
Toilets, sinks, bathtub: Duravit
Light fixtures: Lightolier
Plumbing fixtures: Grohe
Door hardware: Emtek
Countertops: Corian
Fireplace: FireOrb

PHOTO CREDITS: © Michael Moran

AWARDS:

- Gold A' Design Award - Architecture, Building and Structure Design Category, 2017–2018
- Second place in the 2017 American Architects Building of the Year Competition

ALAIN CARLE

LA HÉRONNIÈRE

LOCATION: Wentworth, Quebec, Canada

AREA: 465 m² / 5,005 sq ft

YEAR OF COMPLETION: December 2014

LEED: Gold Certification

ARCHITECT: Alain Carle

CONCEPTION TEAM:
Project manager: Jean-François Marceau
Assistant: Isaniel Lévesque

Contractor: EcoHabitations Boréales

TYPE OF CONSTRUCTION: wood and steel

CLADDING: white cedar (natural and stained)

LIGHTENING: Lambert & Fils

MILLWORK: BWA Ebenisterie

PHOTO CREDITS: © Adrien Williams

AWARDS: Grand Prix du Design 2015 - Espace résidentiel de plus 3 200 pi²

ARCHITECTEN EN BOUWMEESTERS

ENERGY PLUS OFFICE GEELEN COUNTERFLOW

ARCHITECT & BREEAM EXPERT: Architecten en Bouwmeesters www.architectenbouwmeesters.nl

PROJECT MANAGEMENT: Wagemans Bouwadviezen & Bouwmanagement BV www.wagemansbouwadvies.nl

INSTALLATION CONSULTANT: Dubourgraaf - www.dubourgraaf.nl

CLIENT: Geelen Counterflow www.geelencounterflow.com

AWARDS: BREEAM - Award 2017

PHOTO CREDITS: © John Sondeyker, Adam Mørk

ZERO ENERGY HOME

ARCHITECT: Architecten en Bouwmeesters www.architectenbouwmeesters.nl

PROJECT MANAGEMENT: Wagemans Bouwadviezen & Bouwmanagement BV www.wagemansbouwadvies.nl

CLIENT: private

PHOTO CREDITS: © John Sondeyker

ARKIS

HOLMEN AQUATICS CENTER

LOCATION: Asker, Norway

SITE AREA: 15,300 m² / 164,688 sq ft

GROSS FLOOR AREA: 5,319 m²

PROJECT: 2016

COMPLETION: June 2017

FUNCTION: indoor swimming pool, therapy pool, gym and multifunction hall

ARCHITECTS: ARKÍS arkitektar

ENGINEERS: Verkís

OWNER/CLIENT: Asker Commune

AWARDS:
- Building of the Year in Norway 2017
- Selected one of Futurebuild's Model Project, 2016

PHOTO CREDITS: © Lasse Leonhardsen, Tove Lauluten, Geir Andres Rybakken Orslien

SNÆFELLSSTOFA VISITOR CENTER

LOCATION: Skriduklaustur í Fljótsdal

AREA: 750 m² / 8,073 sq ft

CONSTRUCTION DATE: June 2010

FUNCTION: visitor center, visitor information center, tourist information center

ARCHITECT: ARKÍS arkitektar ehf Birgir Teitsson architect faí, Arnar Þór Jónsson architect faí, Lárus Guðmundsson faí

OWNER/CUSTOMER: Vatnajökulþjóðgarður - Vatnajökull galcier

AWARDS:
- Icelandic Concrete Prize, 2016
- Nomination to the Mies van der Rohe award in architecture, 2010

PHOTO CREDITS: © Karl Vilhjálmsson, Sigurgeir Sigurjónsson

HOLMSHEIDI PRISON

LOCATION: Reykjavik Iceland

SITE AREA: 37,400 m² / 402,570 sq ft

GROSS FLOOR AREA: 3,595 m² / 38,696 sq ft

COMPLETION: 2016

FUNCTION: Prison including womens ward, custodial ward and reception- and short sentence ward

ARCHITECTS: ARKÍS arkitektar Bjorn Gudbrandsson architect

ENGINEERS: Mannvit, Verkís, VSI

OWNER/CLIENT: The Ministry of the Interior

AWARDS:
- 1st place in architectural design competition
- Nomination to the Mies van der Rohe award in architecture, 2016

PHOTO CREDITS: © Hreinn Magnusson

BAOSOL

MARTAK PASSIVE HOUSE

LOCATION: Masonville, Colorado, USA

AREA: 116 m² / 1,248 sq ft TFA

COMPLETION: 2016

TEAM: Andrew Michler designer/ builder John Parr builder

SUPPLIERS:
475 High Performance Supply
Intus Windows
Rockwool Mineral Wool
Applegate Cellulose

CLIENT: Andrew Michler

AWARDS: 2017 Green Home of the Year Grand Overall Winner, Green Builder Magazine

PHOTO CREDITS: © Andrew Michler

SOL COFFEE

LOCATION: Longmont Colorado

SIZE: 10 m² / 107 sq ft

COMPLETION: 2017

TEAM:
Concept: Darren Wurtzburg
Fabrication: Frank Stanley
Design: Andrew Michler

SUPPLIER: Astoria Espresso Magnasine Inverter

CLIENT: Sol Coffee

PHOTO CREDITS: © Andrew Michler

ASGK DESIGN

ENERGY EFFICIENT WOODEN HOUSE ZILVAR

LOCATION: Lodin, Czech Republic

TOTAL AREA: 109 m² / 1,173 sq ft

CONSTRUCTION: 2014

PRINCIPAL ARCHITECT: Gabriela Kapralova, ASGK Design s.r.o.

COLLABORATORS: Vitek Donat, Peter Hricovec

CLIENT: Withheld at owner´s request

GENERAL CONTRACTOR: Tesari Osik

MATERIALS: wood, glass

PHOTO CREDITS: © Petra Hajska, Veronika Nehasilova, Gabriela Kapralova

BCHO

JEDONG RANCH_MEDITATION SPACE

LOCATION: 16, Gyorae-ri, Jocheon-eup, Jeju-si, Jeju-do, Korea

GROSS FLOOR AREA: 60 m² / 646 sq ft

USE: meditation space

PROJECT TEAM: Choi, Hye-eun / Ann, Jun-ho / Kim, Jeon-am

STRUCTURE: reinforced concrete

PHOTO CREDITS: © Wooseop Kwang

TILT ROOF HOUSE

LOCATION: Jipyeong-myeon, Yangpyeong-gun, Gyeonggi-do, South Korea

SITE AREA: 658 m² / 7,083 sq ft

GROSS FLOOR AREA: 162 m² / 1,744 sq ft

YEAR OF DESIGN/COMPLETION: 2012-2014 / 2014

BUILDING TYPE: residence

STRUCTURE: reinforced concrete

PHOTO CREDITS: © Sergio Pirrone

C.F. MØLLER ARCHITECTS

COPENHAGEN INTERNATIONAL SCHOOL NORDHAVN

LOCATION: Levantkaj, Nordhavnen, Copenhagen, Denmark

AREA: 25,000 m² / 269, 098 sq ft (1,200 students)

YEAR: 2013-2017

ARCHITECT: C.F. Møller Architects

LANDSCAPE ARCHITECT: C.F. Møller Landscape

ENGINEER: Niras

CLIENT: Property Foundation Copenhagen International School (ECIS)

PHOTO CREDITS: © Adam Moerk

MAERSK TOWER

LOCATION: Nørre Campus, Blegdamsvej, Copenhagen, Denmark

AREA: 42,700 m² / 459,619 sq ft (24,700m² / 265,868 sq ft laboratories, offices and shared facilities and 18.000 m² / 193,750 sq ft foyer, canteen, auditoria, classrooms, plant)

YEAR: 2010-2017

ARCHITECT: C.F. Møller Architects

LANDSCAPE ARCHITECT: SLA

ENGINEER: Rambøll

CLIENT CONSULTANT: P & Partners

COLLABORATORS: Aggebo & Henriksen, Cenergia, Gordon Farquharson, Innovation Lab

SUPPLIERS: Per Aarsleff A/S, Skælskør Anlægsgartnere A/S, Mogens V. Zeltner A/S, Zurface A/S, Elementmontøren ApS, Hansen & Andersen A/S, Zublin A/S, N. H. Hansen & Søn A/S, Bladt Industries A/S, Waagner-Biro Stahlbau AG, Juul & Nielsen A/S, Tæppeland Erhverv A/S, Malermester Willi Becke ApS, A & C tagdækning ApS, Elindco Byggefirma A/S, L&H Rørbyg A/S, Airteam A/S, Lindpro A/S, Otis A/S, Wicotec Kirkebjerg A/S, Drivhuseffekten ApS, Labflex A/S og, Bent Brandt A/S.

CLIENT: The Danish Property Agency for the University of Copenhagen; supported by the A.P. Møller Foundation

Donation: A.P. Møller og Hustru Chastine Mc-Kinney Møllers Fond til Almene formål

PHOTO CREDITS: © Adam Moerk

CONG SINH ARCHITECTS

VEGETABLE TRELLIS

LOCATION: District 9, Ho Chi Minh City, Vietnam

PROJECT YEAR: 2016

ARCHITECTS: Cong Sinh Architects

PRINCIPAL ARCHITECT: Vo Quang Thi

PROJECT ARCHITECTS: Vo Quang Thi, Nguyen Thi Nha Van, Phung Kim Phuoc, Tran Ngoc Hung, Tran Tan Phat, Nguyen Phuc Bao Thang, Nguyen Nhat Anh, Vu Hoang Phi Long, Le Thien Trieu.

CONTRACTOR: Thanh An Interior & Construction Co.,Ltd

AWARDS: Winner of World Architecture Festival Awards (WAF) 2017

PHOTO CREDITS: © Hiroyuki Oki

THE GILLS

LOCATION: District 7, Ho Chi Minh City, Vietnam

PROJECT YEAR: 2014

PRINCIPAL ARCHITECT: Vo Quang Thi

PROJECT ARCHITECTS: Vo Quang Thi, Nguyen Thi Nha Van, Nguyen Phuc Bao Thang. Nguyen Nhat Anh

CONTRACTOR: Thanh An Interior & Construction Co.,Ltd

PHOTO CREDITS: © Hiroyuki Oki

EDRA ARQUITECTURA KM0

CASA TIERRA

LOCATION: Ayerbe, Huesca, Spain

AREA:
Building area: 276 m² / 2,971 sq ft
Total useful: 215 m² / 2,314 sq ft

STARTING DATE: June 2011

COMPLETION DATE: February 2016

CLIENT:
Alejandro Ascaso Sarasa
Àngels Castellarnau Visús

AWARDS:
- Terra Award 2016, Premio Internacional de Arquitectura Contemporánea en Tierra Cruda
- Premio de Construcción Sostenible de Castilla y León 2015-2016.

PHOTO CREDITS: © Doblestudio - Xavier d'Arquer

GISTAÍN

LOCATION: Gistaín, Huesca, Spain

AREA:
Building area: 281.70 m²
Total useful: 161.55 m²

STARTING DATE: May 2016

COMPLETION DATE: December 2017

CLIENT:
Elena Barea Villaroya
Francisco Jurado Sánchez

PHOTO CREDITS: © Doblestudio - Xavier d'Arquer

ES ARQUITETURA

CASA 01

LOCATION: Criciúma, Brazil

AREA: 1,421 m² / 15,295 sq ft

PROJECT YEAR: 2017

ARCHITECT IN CHARGE:
Diego Justo do Espírito Santo

TEAM: Diego Justo do Espírito Santo, Maicon Fedrigo Padilha, Valério Doca and Rodrigo Estrella

LIGHTING DESIGN:
Amanda Pamato de Souza

LANDSCAPE DESIGN: Benedito Abbud

ENGINEER: Mauro César Sônego

INTERIOR DESIGN: Vânia Marroni Búrigo

AWARDS:
- Saint Gobain Sustainability Award, Residential Modality, 2017 | Saint-Gobain Group. Winner
- Building of The Year 2018, Archdaily. Final Classification Jury

PHOTO CREDITS: © Mariana Boro, SLA PHOTOSTUDIO

H&P ARCHITECTS

TERRACES HOME

LOCATION: Ha Tinh city, Vietnam

COMPLETION DATE: December 2015

ARCHITECT: H&P Architects

ARCHITECT IN CHARGE:
Doan Thanh Ha & Tran Ngoc Phuong

TEAM: Chu Kim Thinh, Nguyen Hai Hue, Ho Manh Cuong, Trinh Thi Thanh Huyen, Nguyen Van Thinh

AWARDS:
- The American Architecture Prize 2017, Winner (USA)
- Green Architectural Prize 2017-2018 (Vietnam)

PHOTO CREDITS: © Nguyen Tien Thanh

BES PAVILION

LOCATION: Ha Tinh, Vietnam

TOTAL FLOOR AREA: 123 m² / 1,324 sq ft

AREA: 18 m x 13 m / 59 ft x 43 ft

COMPLETION DATE: August 2013

ARCHITECTS: H&P Architects

ARCHITECT IN CHARGE: Doan Thanh Ha & Tran Ngoc Phuong

TEAM: Chu Kim Thinh

CONTRACTOR: HPA Vietnam jsc

AWARDS
- ARCASIA Awards for Architecture 2015, Gold medal
- National Green Architectural Awards 2014-2013, Vietnam

PHOTO CREDITS: © Tran Tuan Trung, Tran Ngoc Phuong

AD-BB HOME

LOCATION: Cau Dien Town, Tu Liem District, Ha Noi, Vietnam

TOTAL FLOOR AREA: 44 m² / 144 sq ft

COMPLETION DATE: September 2013

ARCHITECTS: H&P Architects

ARCHITECT IN CHARGE: Doan Thanh Ha & Tran Ngoc Phuong

TEAM: Chu Kim Thinh, Erimescu Patricia, Nguyen Van Manh, Nguyen Khanh Hoa, Nguyen Quynh Trang, Tran Quoc Thang, Pham Hong Son, Hoang Dinh Toan, Pham Quang Thang, Nguyen Hai Hue, Nguyen Khac Phuoc

AWARDS:
- The American Architecture Prize 2017, Winner (USA)
- WAN Small Space Awards 2014, Winner (UK)

PHOTO CREDITS: © Doan Thanh Ha

HIROSHI NAKAMURA & NAP

BIRD'S NEST ATAMI

LOCATION: Shizuoka, Japan (RISONARE Atami 2-13-1 Minaguchi, Atami, Shizuoka, 413-0016)

SITE AREA: 65,000 m² / 688,654 sq ft

TOTAL FLOOR AREA: 10 m² / 108 sq ft

COMPLETION: March 2014

ARCHITECT: Hiroshi Nakamura & NAP Treehouse Creations

STRUCTURAL DESIGN: Arup

CONTRACTOR: Takashi Kobayashi & Treehouse Creations

PRINCIPAL USE: Teahouse

STRUCTURE:
Main Structure: Steel Three-Dimensional Truss
Upper Structure: Timber Framework
Foundation: Diamond Pier

AWARDS:
- AR Emerging Architecture Awards 2015 highly recommended prize
- Architizer A+Awards 2017, Finalist in Architecture+Sustainability

PHOTO CREDITS: © Koji Fujii / Nacasa and Partners Inc.

KAMIKATZ PUBLIC HOUSE

LOCATION: Kamikatsu, Tokushima

TOTAL FLOOR AREA: 115 m² / 1,238 sq ft

COMPLETION: May 2015

ARCHITECT: Hiroshi Nakamura & NAP

PRINCIPAL USE: Micro brewery

STRUCTURE: Timber structure

STRUCTURE DESIGN: Yamada Noriaki Structural Design Office

CONTRACTOR: Daiso Co.,Ltd

PRODUCE: TRANSIT GENERAL OFFICE

FURNITURE DESIGN: Wrap

AWARDS:
- WAN Sustainable Buildings Award 2016 Winner
- Architizer A+Awards 2017, Finalist in Architecture + Sustainability

PHOTO CREDITS: © Koji Fujii / Nacasa and Partners Inc.

JURI TROY ARCHITECTS

SUNLIGHTHOUSE

LOCATION: Pressbaum, Lower Austria

YEAR OF COMPLETION: 2010

ARCHITECTURE: Juri Troy Architects

BUILDING PHYSICS: IBO, Danube University Krems

BUILDER, DAYLIGHT PLANNING: VELUX Austria GmbH

CLAIM/DESIGNATION: CO_2 neutral*, energy-plus**

TYPE OF OBJECT: Single-family dwelling, 193 m NFL

AWARDS:
- 2010 State Environment and Energy Technology Prize
- 2010 Active Architecture Award
- 2011 Vorarlberg Wooden Construction Prize
- Green Good Design Award

PHOTO CREDITS: © Adam Mork, Kopenhagen

HOUSE 3B

LOCATION: Bottenwil, Switzerland

BUILDING VOLUME: 818 m³ / 28,887 cu ft

TOTAL FLOOR AREA: 286 m² / 3,078 sq ft

YEAR OF COMPLETION: 2017

CONSTRUCTION PERIOD: 2.5 years

PHOTO CREDITS: © Juri Troy

HOUSE UNDER THE OAKS

LOCATION: Hutten, Austria

TOTAL AREA: 100 m² / 1,076 sq ft (9 kWh/m²a heat amount)

CONSTRUCTION:
Start of Planning: May 2012
Start of Construction: November 2012
Completed: June 2013

PHOTO CREDITS: © Juri Troy

K20 ARCHITECTURE

BALLARAT REGIONAL SOCCER FACILITY

LOCATION: Morshead Park Stadium, Redan,Ballarat, VIC, Australia

AREA:
Indoor building: 800 m² / 8,611 sq ft
Site total: 5,400 m² / 58,125 sq ft
Outdoor space: 4,600 m² / 49,513 sq ft

COMPLETION: February 2015

BUILDER NAME: Contract Control Services

STRUCTURAL ENGINEER: AGB Engineering Group

BUILDER NAME (STAGE 2): Searle Bros

SERVICES ENGINEER: Intrax Consulting

STRUCTURAL ENGINEER: Calibre Consulting

CLIENT TEAM: Constructed for City of Ballarat

SUPPLIERS:
Thermal chimneys:
- Type: Fiberglass Board
- Surface Finish: Matt Duct Liner

Low VOC paint:
Haymes Ultra-Premium Acrylic Sealer Undercoat
Haymes Ultra-Premium High Gloss Enamel
Haymes-Premium High Gloss Enamel

Grandstand seating:
- Company: Cossett
- Type: Recycled plastic with double dipped zinc steel frame with colour powder coat finish.

Under floor air-plenum:
- Company: Ecocanopy
- Type: ecoaircurtain

AWARDS:
Finalist – BPN Sustainability Awards, Public Building, 2016

PHOTO CREDITS: © Peter Bennets Photography

HINDMARSH SHIRE COUNCIL OFFICES

LOCATION: Nhill, Victoria, Australia

SIZE: 1,295 m² / 13,939 sq ft

COMPLETION: 2014

ARCHITECT: k20 Architecture

BUILDER: Behmer & Wright Pty Ltd

PROJECT MANAGER: Hindmarsh Shire Council

BUILDING SURVEYOR: Hindmarsh Shire Council

STRUCTURAL ENGINEER: Intrax

HYDRAULICS, MECHANICAL AND ELECTRICAL ENGINEER: Elms & George

CLIENT TEAM: Hindmarsh Shire Council

MAIN MANUFACTURERS/SUPPLIERS:
Glulam beams: Vicbeam – 'Vic Ash'
Glass: Viridian
Metal suspended ceiling canopies: Armstrong – 'Axiom Canopy Knife Edge'
Perforated metal ceilings: Lysaght – 'Perforated Mini Orb'
Furniture: UCI
Carpets: Interface
Building Management System: Eaton Corporation

AWARDS:
- Winner – Australian Timber Design Awards, People's Choice Award, 2014
- Finalist – BPN Sustainability Awards, Large Commercial, 2014

PHOTO CREDITS: © Peter Bennets Photography

PORT MELBOURNE FOOTBALL CLUB

LOCATION: Port Melbourne, Victoria, Australia

SIZE: 900 m² / 9,687 sq ft

COMPLETION: 2015

CLIENT TEAM: City of Port Phillip

ARCHITECT: k20 Architecture

IMAGES: Peter Bennets

BUILDER: 2Construct

ENGINEER: Macleod Consulting

FABRICATOR: 2Construct

AWARDS
- Silver Winner - Melbourne Design Awards, Architecture - Public & Institutional, 2017
- Finalist – BPN Sustainability Awards, Public Building, 2016
- Winner – Australian Timber Design Awards, Sustainability Category, 2015

PHOTO CREDITS: © Peter Bennets
Photography

KJELLGREN KAMINSKY

KOLLASTADEN SCHOOL

LOCATION: Kolla, Kungsbacka, Sweden

AREA:
School: 6,500 m² / 69,965 sq ft
Athletic hall: 4,500 m² / 48,438 sq ft

YEAR OF COMPLETION: 2014

TYPE: Primary and high school + Athletic
hall

LEAD ARCHITECT: Joakim Kaminsky
& Fredrik Kjellgren

PROJECT ARCHITECT: Joakim Kaminsky

DESIGN TEAM: Joti Weijers-Coghlan,
Michael Björeling, Mélia Parizel, Maria
Syrén, Michael Tuuling, Michele Pascucci,
Kay Fang Chang, Maëlis Grenouillet,
Sanna Johnels, Johan Brandström,
Pamela Paredes, Gaby Andersson,
Paulina Kaluzna, Paco Pomares

PARTNERS: Ramböll, 02 landskap, Anna
Törnqvist

COMISSION: Competition 1st prize

CLIENT: Eksta Bostads AB

AWARDS: 2015 World Architecture
Festival, Nominated

PHOTO CREDITS: © Mikael Olsson

ÖIJARED HOTEL

LOCATION: Öijared, Sweden

SIZE: 2,300 m² / 24,757 sq ft

YEAR OF COMPLETION: 2014

TYPE: Hotel

LEAD ARCHITECT: Joakim Kaminsky &
Fredrik Kjellgren

PROJECT ARCHITECT: Johan Brandström

DESIGN TEAM: Sanna Johnels, Mélia
Parizel, Sofia Wendel, Michael Björeling,
Maria Syrén, Paco Pomares

CLIENT: Öijared Country Club

AWARDS: 2015 World Architecture
Festival, Nominated

PHOTO CREDITS: Åke Eson Lindman

KWK PROMES

LIVING GARDEN HOUSE

LOCATION: Katowice, Poland

SITE AREA: 3,872 m² / 41,677 sq ft

FLOOR AREA: 411 m² / 4,424 sq ft

DESIGN: 2009

CONSTRUCTION: 2012-2014

ARCHITECT: Robert Konieczny

COLLABORATION: Magdalena
Adamczak, Katarzyna Furgalińska,
Aleksandra Stolecka, Adam Radzimski

CONSTRUCTION: Jan Głuszyinski, Kornel
Szyndler

INSTALLATIONS: CEGROUP

CLIENT: private

AWARDS:
- Nomination to European Union Prize for
Contemporary Architecture
- Mies van der Rohe Award 2015
- Honourable mention of Living-Garden
House in Katowice in Architecture of the
Year 2014 in Silesian Region Competition

PHOTO CREDITS: © Jakub Certowicz

STANDARD HOUSE

LOCATION: Poland

USABLE FLOOR AREA: 224 m² / 2,411 sq ft

COMPLETION: 2011

ARCHITECT: Robert Konieczny

COLLABORATION: Katarzyna Furgalińska

STRUCTURAL ENGINEERING: Grzegorz
Komraus

SUPPLIERS: Soprema, Rockwool, Rehau,
Viessmann, Invado door (indoors), Libet,
Barlinek, MOCO wood, Marazzi, BLACK
RED WHITE, Magnat paints, Amica,
Cekol construction products, Dupont
Corian, Glasspol glass on the floor, Nap
furnitures, Rigips, Koło

CLIENT: private

PHOTO CREDITS: © Mariusz
Czechowicz / Murator

LI XIAODONG

THE LIYUAN LIBRARY

LOCATION: Wisdom Valley, Jiaojiehe
Vellage, Huairou District, Beijing

FLOOR AREA: 175 m² / 1,004 sq ft

CONSTRUCTION PERIOD:
March 2011 - October 2011

PRINCIPAL ARCHITECT: Li Xiaodong

PROJECT TEAM: Liu Yayun, Huang
Chengwen, Pan Xi

COMMISSIONING DONORS: Luke Him
Sau Charitable Trust And Pan Xi

CONSTRUCTION COST: RMB 1050,000

CLIENT: Jiaojiehe Village

AWARDS:
- 2012, WAF (World Architecture Festival)
winner (cultural category) (Singapore)
- 2013, Architecture of Necessity, winner
(Sweden)
- 2014, Moriyama RIAC Prize, winner
(Canada)

PHOTO CREDITS: © Li Xiaodong

THE SCREEN

LOCATION: Ningbo, China

PROJECT AREA: about 600 m² / 6,458 sq ft

PROJECT YEAR: 2013

FIRM: Li Xiaodong Atelier

ARCHITECT: Li Xiaodong

TEAM: Martijn de Geus, Jerry Hau, Ying
Xin, Renske van Dam

PROJECT COST: 8 million RMB

PHOTO CREDITS: © Li Xiaodong

OHLAB

MM HOUSE

LOCATION: Palma de Mallorca, Spain

BUILDING AREA: 196 m² / 2,110 sq ft

PROJECT COMPLETION DATE: 2015

ARCHITECTURE AND INTERIOR DESIGN:
OHLAB / Oliver Hernaiz Architecture Lab

OHLAB TEAM: Paloma Hernaiz, Jaime
Oliver (directors), Rebeca Lavín, Walter
Brandt, Sergio Rivero de Cáceres

BUILDING ENGINEER: Jorge Ramón

SITE SUPERVISION: Paloma Hernaiz,
Jaime Oliver (architects) Jorge Ramón
(quantity surveyor)

STRUCTURAL ENGINEER: Jesús Alonso

ENERGY EFFICIENCY ADVISOR: Anne Vogt

CLIENT: Private

AWARDS
- 2017. Winners as the best eco-design
project by IED awards (Istituto Europeo
di Design)
- 2017. Winners as one of the Record Houses
of the year by Architectural Record
- 2016. Winner at WAF (The World
Architecture Festival)

- 2016. Best energy efficiency project in
X NAN architecture and construction
awards

PHOTO CREDITS: © José Hevia

PASEO MALLORCA 15

LOCATION: Paseo Mallorca, 15. Palma de
Mallorca, Spain

BUILDING AREA: 4,300 m² / 46,285 sq ft

ESTIMATED STARTING DATE: June 2018

ARCHITECTURE AND INTERIOR DESIGN:
OHLAB / Oliver Hernaiz Architecture Lab

OHLAB TEAM: Paloma Hernaiz, Jaime
Oliver (directors) con Robin Harloff, Pedro
Gómez-Limón, Rebeca Lavín, Silvia Morais,
José Allona, Tomo Konjevod, Mercé Solar,
Loreto Angulo, Maria Bruna Pisciotta, Laura
Colomer, Agustín Verdejo, Luis Quiles

BUILDING ENGINEER: Tomeu Tous

STRUCTURAL ENGINEER: HIMA
Consultores de Estructura

MEP ENGINEER: AMM technical group

LANDSCAPE DESIGNER: Jonathan Bell
Studio

CLIENT: Ramis Promociones

PHOTO CREDITS: © OHLAB

PDP LONDON

ONE CHURCH SQUARE STREET

LOCATION: One Church Square,
2-6 - Moreton Street, Pimlico
City of Westminster

AREA: GIA 2,400 m² / 25,833 sq ft (excl.
communal circulation)

COMPLETION DATE: October 2013

PROJECT VALUE: £7.2 M

ARCHITECT: PDP London

ENGINEER: Clancy Consulting

M&E: KUT

SUSTAINABILITY ENGINEER: Energist,
CEN, Eight Associates

CONTRACTOR: Wates Living Space

PLANNING CONSULTANT: Rolfe Judd

COST CONSULTANT: DBKProject

CLIENT/DEVELOPER: Dolphin Living

PHOTO CREDITS: © Adam Parker

PKDM

ÁRBORG HOUSE

LOCATION: Selfoss, Iceland

BUILT AREA: 256 m² / 2,755 sq ft

COMPLETION YEAR: 2009

ARCHITECT: PKdM Arkitektar

TEAM: Pálmar Kristmundsson, Fernando de Mendonça, Dagni Wiest, María Stefánsdóttir and Sóley Brynjarsdóttir

CONSULTANTS: Conis Verkfræðiráðgjöf, Verkhönnun

PHOTO CREDITS: © Rafael Pinho, Helge Garke

BHM
VACATION RENTAL COTTAGES

LOCATION: Brekkuskógur, Iceland

FLOOR AREA: 103 m² / 1,109 sq ft

PROJECT: 2012 Competition 1st Prize

COMPLETION YEAR: 2015

CONSULTANTS: Verkhönnun, Landark

DESIGN TEAM: Pálmar Kristmundsson, Andrew Burges, Fernando de Mendonca, Erna Vestmann, Sunna Dóra Sigurjónsdóttir, Liidia Grinko

CLIENT: Association Of Academics Vacation Cottages

PHOTO CREDITS: © Rafael Pinho, Bjarni Kristinson

BRÆÐARHÚS

LOCATION: Miðhúsaskógur, Iceland

BUILT AREA:
bræðrahús 1: 175 m² / 1,884 sq ft
bræðrahús 2: 220m² / 2,368 sq ft

COMPLETION YEAR:
-bræðrahús 1: 2014
-bræðrahús 2: 2016

TEAM: Pálmar Kristmundsson, Fernando de Mendonça, Sunna Dóra Sigurjónsdóttir, Andrew Burgess and Matheus Diniz.

CLIENT: Private

PHOTO CREDITS: © Rafael Pinho, Bjarni Kristinsson

PROARH

HIZA

LOCATION: Kumrovec, Croatia

BUILT AREA: 230 m² / 2,475 sq ft

SITE AREA: 3,865 m² / 41,602 sq ft

COMPLETION DATE: 2012

ARCHITECT: Davor Matekovic / PROARH

DESIGN TEAM: Oskar Rajko

BUILDING ENERGY CONCEPT, BUILDING PHYSICS AND BUILDING DETAILS DESIGN: Assist. Prof. Mateo Bilus, MEAU Faculty of Architecture, University of Zagreb mateo.bilus@arhitekt.hr

CLIENT: private

AWARDS
- 2015. World Architecture Festival, Small Project Category-finalist
- 2015. World Architecture Festival, House- Completed Buildings Category-finalist
- 2014. Iconic Awards, Architecture– Best Of The Best-winner
- 2013. Mies Van Der Rohe Prize –nominee

PHOTO CREDITS: © Miljenko Bernfest, Damir Fabijanić

ISSA MEGARON

LOCATION: Vis Island, Croatia

BUILT AREA: 420 m² / 4,521 sq ft

SITE AREA: 70,135 m² / 754,927 sq ft

COMPLETION DATE: 2016

ARCHITECT: Davor Matekovic / PROARH

DESIGN TEAM: Vedrana Jancic, Bojana Benic

STRUCTURAL DESIGNER:
Branko Galić, MSc, branko.galic@statika.hr
Radionica statike Ltd., www.statika.hr

BUILDING ENERGY CONCEPT, BUILDING PHYSICS AND BUILDING DETAILS DESIGN
Assist. Prof. Mateo Bilus, MEAU Faculty of Architecture, University of Zagreb
mateo.bilus@arhitekt.hr

MAIN CONTRACTOR: GRIŽA graðevinski obrt marin-griza.petkovic@du.t-com.hr

CLIENT: private

AWARDS
- 2018. National Architectural Award "Drago Galić" – House/Housing Category – Nominee
- 2017. International Piranesi Award – Nominee
- 2015. A'design Award – Gold
- 2015. World Architecture Festival - House – Future Projects Category-1. Prize

PHOTO CREDITS: © Miljenko Bernfest berni@bxl-studio.com, Damir Fabijani´c fabijanic@fab.hr

RICHARD + SCHOELLER

JEAN MOULIN SCHOOL

LOCATION: Montargis (Loiret), France

AREA: 2,800 m² / 30,139 sq ft

YEAR: 2015

ARCHITECTS: Isabelle Richard, Frederic Schoeller

COST: EUR 6,000,000 TTC

QUANTITIES SURVEYOR: DAL, Paris

ENGINEER: Alpes Structures

CONSTRUCTION COMPANY: TPBAT

BUDGET: EUR 6,000,000 TTC

CLIENT: Mairie de Montargis (28) France

PHOTO CREDITS: © Luc Boegly

CULTURAL CENTRE GARENNE-COLOMBES

LOCATION: Rue Herold, La-Garenne-Colombes 92 France

AREA: 2,876 m² / 30,957 sq ft

CONSTRUCTION: 2013-2015

TEAM: Isabelle Richard + Frederic Schoeller

BET STRUCTURES : Batiserf

BET HVAC : ALTO

ECONOMIST: DAL

ACOUSTIC : CIAL

TEAM: Cultural center

PROGRAMME: auditorium 150 seats; exhibition; public library

COST BUILDING: HT 5,8 M euros HT Furniture 0,4 M euros HT

CONTRACTORS:
Structure: CBM
Façades: MIC
Partitions: Décor Isolation
Woodwork: Barthelemy and PRM
Light-current engineering: STEPC
Heavy-current engineering: STEPC
Floors: Boulenger
Paint: Socape
Stones: EDMC
Plumbing: ERCC
Waterproof system: SETRIM
Hvac: CELSIO

Furniture: R + S Architecture, Atout Bois, Transformeurs et Partenaires: (Morlaix), USM.

PRODUCTS
White concrete: LAFARGE
Steel columns façade: Timber curtain Wall, RAICO, Germany
Rubber floor: Boulenger (Paris)
Waterproof: Soprema
Wood: Wisabirch
Sanitaries: Allia
Shading glasses with silkscreened+ stainless steel: MIC (France)

CLIENT: Mairie

PHOTO CREDITS: Sergio Grazia & Emmanuelle Blanc(bl)

SIGURD LARSEN
Photo Sigurd Larsen: © Michael Brus

THE ROOF HOUSE

LOCATION: Copenhagen, Denmark

AREA: 150 m² / 1,614 sq ft

COMPLETION: 2016

TEAM: Sigurd Larsen with Simon Jendreizik, Timm Lindstedt and Martina Camarri

CONSULTANTS: Groenbo Huse

SUPPLIERS:
Wooden elements: Froeslec Trae.
Windows: Velfac. Roof Windows: Vitral.

CLIENT: Debois Baandrup

AWARDS: 2017 World Architecture Festival Price, Shortlisted

PHOTO CREDITS:
Stylist: Mette Helena Rasmussen, Photographer: © Tia Borgsmidt

THE GREEN HOUSE

LOCATION: Lejre, Denmark

AREA: 82 m² + 32 m² / 883 sq ft + 344 sq ft Winter Garden

COMPLETION: 2017

PHOTO CREDITS:
Stylist: Mette Helena Rasmussen
Photographer: © Tia Borgsmidt

THE LIGHT HOUSE

LOCATION: Lejre, Denmark

AREA: 135 m² / 1,453 sq ft

COMPLETION: 2017

PHOTO CREDITS:
Stylist: Mette Helena Rasmussen
Photographer: © Tia Borgsmidt

STUDIO DELBOCA & PARTNERS
CASA SUL PARCO

LOCATION: via Gramsci, 82 – 43036
Fidenza (Parma) - Italy
Latitude: 44.51482 Longitude:10.03389

AREA: 1,400 m² / 15,069 sq ft

WHEN: 2015 / 2017

CONTRACTOR: Montanari Costruzioni SrL
Fidenza (Parma)

BUDGET: 3,800 euros/m²

PROJECT LEADER: Studio delboca+
PARTNERS, Arch. Giovanni del Boca –
Arch. Alessandra Amoretti with Carlotta
Dardanello, Marta Moccia, Simona
Pittaluga, Giulia Ghidini, Francesca
Giannini, Fabio Bozzetti

LOCAL ARCHITECTS: Arch. Giovanni e
Simona Rossi, Fidenza (Parma)

LIGHT DESIGN: Rada Markovic

LANDSCAPE DESIGN: Anja Werner

CLIENT: Montanari Costruzioni SrL
Fidenza (Parma)

PHOTO CREDITS: © Matteo Piazza,
Marco Campanini

TERRITORI 24
BARÓ DE VIVER CIVIC CENTER

LOCATION: Beato Domènec Savio, nº1,
Barcelona, Spain

BUILT AREA: 1,652 m² / 17,782 sq ft

BUDGET: (VAT included) EUR 2,175,678.83

DEVELOPER: Districte de Sant Andreu –
Barcelona City Council

BUILDER: UTE Serom-Sogesa

ARCHITECTS: Territori 24: Adrià Calvo
L'Orange, Ivan Pérez Barés, Bet Alabern
Cortina, Alvaro Casanovas Leal

ENGINEERS: Caba Sostenibilitat: Xavier
Saltó Batista

AWARDS:
- +Sostenible Award from the Barcelona
  City Council 2017
- Selected for the FAD Awards 2016
- PREMIS NAN'15 - wining project -
  energy efficiency category

PHOTO CREDITS: © Adrià Goula
www.adriagoula.com

TONI YLI-SUVANTO ARCHITECTS
WOODEN SAUNA PAVILION

LOCATION: Lapland, Finland

GROSS FLOOR AREA: 30 m² / 323 sq ft

TYPE AND YEAR: to be completed in 2018

ARCHITECTURE: Toni Yli-Suvanto
Architects

CLIENT: Private

PHOTO CREDITS: © Toni Yli-Suvanto
Architects

BAMIYAN CULTURAL CENTRE

LOCATION: Bamiyan Province,
Afghanistan

GROSS FLOOR AREA: 2,300 m² / 24,757 sq ft

TYPE AND YEAR: Open international
competition 2015

ARCHITECTURE: Toni Yli-Suvanto
Architects

VISUALISATION: Toni Yli-Suvanto
Architects

CLIENT: UNESCO and the Ministry of
Information and Culture of Afghanistan

PHOTO CREDITS: © UNESCO and the
Ministry of Information and Culture of
Afghanistan

PACKARD AUTOMOTIVE PLANT -
ECOLOGICAL ENGINEERING CENTRE

LOCATION: Packard Automotive Plant,
Detroit, Michigan, USA

GROSS FLOOR AREA: 240 000 m²

TYPE AND YEAR: Open international
competition, third prize 2014

ARCHITECTURE: Toni Yli-Suvanto Architects

VISUALISATION: Toni Yli-Suvanto
Architects

CLIENT: Parallel Projections

PHOTO CREDITS: © Clayton Studio

VEELAERT ARCHITECTEN
ANNONCIADEN

LOCATION: Turnhoutsebaan 400,
Wijnegem, Antwerp, Belgium

BUILDING AREA: 17,000 m² / 18,299 sq ft
89 assist appartements + 1 office, a bakery,
a barber, 1 restaurant and a medical practice

TEAM: Veelaert Architectenteam

CONSULTANT EPB, TECHNIQUES AND
STABILITY: Studie 10 ingenieursbureau

CLIENT AND PROMOTOR: Costermans
projects

SUPPLIERS: Xella, Gypsum, Reynaers
aluminium

AWARDS
Special Prize for a Sustainable Mixed-Use
Project at the European Architecture
Awards 2107

PHOTO CREDITS: © Bart Gosselin

W-O-H-A ARQUITECTURA
World Of Holistic Architecture
CAFETERÍA CALAHORRA

LOCATION: Elche, Spain

AREA OF SCOPE OF WORK: 20 m² +
120 m² / 215 sq ft + 1,292 sq ft terrace

PROJECT AUTHOR: Antonio Maciá Mateu

COLLABORATORS: Ana Mora Vitoria,
architect; Laura Brotons Martinez,
architect; Veronica Leuzzi Betosini,
architect

PROJECT MANAGEMENT: Rebeca
Cebrián, architect

MATERIALS MANAGEMENT: Elena Rogel

LIGHTING: Tecnoluz Iluminación

LANDSCAPING: Ignacio Solano.
Paisajismo urbano, SL

BUDGET FOR MATERIAL EXECUTION:
EUR 75,000

Developer: MUSEUM

PHOTO CREDITS: © David Frutos,
Paisajismo Urbano, Elche Diario

OTONIEL

LOCATION: Alicante, Spain

AREA OF SCOPE OF WORK: 700 m² /
7,534 sq ft

PROJECT AUTHOR: Antonio Maciá Mateu

COLLABORATORS: Ana Mora, architect

LIGHTING: Tecnoluz Iluminación

DEVELOPER: Desguaces Otoniel

LANDSCAPING: Ignacio Solano.
Paisajismo urbano, SL

BUDGET FOR MATERIAL EXECUTION:
EUR 225,000

PHOTO CREDITS: © Rafael Zarza

YYA - YUJI YAMAZAKI
ARCHITECTURE
FINOLHU VILLAS

LOCATION: North Male Atoll,
The Maldives

ARCHITECT: YYA (Yuji Yamazaki
Architecture PLLC)
Contact: Yuji Yamazaki

AOR: Design 2000 Pte. Ltd.
H Mundooge, Violet Magu, Male' 20017,
Maldives
Contact: Ahmed Saleem

CLIENT:

OWNER: Crown Company Pte. Ltd.
Fasmeeru Building, Boduthakurufaanu
Magu,ÑMale' Rep. of Maldives
Contact: Hussain Afeef

OPERATOR: Club Med Finolhu Villas
491B River Valley Rd, Singapore 248373
Contact: Heidi Kunkel

PM: Crown Company Pte. Ltd.
Fasmeeru Building, Boduthakurufaanu
Magu,
Male' Rep. of Maldives
Contact: Ibrahim Noordeen, Walter
Kaufmann

SOLAR PANEL: T&D Water Technology
Via Fermi, 6, 35020 Polverara
Padova – Italy
Contact: Aldo Talamali

MEP: T&D Water Technology
Via Fermi, 6, 35020 Polverara
Padova – Italy
Contact: Aldo Talamali

CONTRACTOR: Flight Timbers
Contact: Gary Walker

FURNISHING: Warisan
Contact: Paul Campbell

AWARDS:
- 2015 Interior Design Magazine's Best of
  Year Award - Best Resort Hotel
- 2015 International Hotel and Property
  Award - Best Beach Hotel

PHOTO CREDITS: © YYA (Yuji Yamazaki
Architecture PLLC)